IRON EYES

IRON EYES

The Life and Teachings

of the Ōbaku Zen Master Tetsugen Dōkō

HELEN J. BARONI

STATE UNIVERSITY OF NEW YORK PRESS

Cover photo courtesy of Rodman Low

Published by
STATE UNIVERSITY OF NEW YORK PRESS,
ALBANY

© 2006 State University of New York

All rights reserved

Printed in the United States of America

For information, address
State University of New York Press
194 Washington Avenue, Suite 305, Albany, NY 12210-2384

Production by Michael Haggett
Marketing by Anne M. Valentine

Library of Congress Cataloging-in-Publication Data

Baroni, Helen Josephine.
  Iron eyes : the life and teachings of Obaku Zen master Tetsugen Doko / Helen J. Baroni.
    p. cm.
  Includes bibliographical references and index.
  ISBN-13: 978-0-7914-6891-3 (hardcover : alk. paper)
  ISBN-10: 0-7914-6891-7 (hardcover : alk. paper)
  ISBN-13: 978-0-7914-6892-0 (pbk. : alk. paper)
  ISBN-10: 0-7914-6892-5 (pbk. : alk. paper)   1. Tetsugen Doko, 1630–1682.
2. Priests, Zen--Japan--Biography.   3. Obaku (Sect)--History.   I. Title.
BQ990.E88B37 2006
294.3´927092--dc22

                                                            2005036301

10   9   8   7   6   5   4   3   2   1

For my mother,

Lena C. Baroni

Contents

Acknowledgments   ix

Introduction   1

HISTORICAL BIOGRAPHY AND ANALYSIS   9

    Chapter One   The Life of Tetsugen   11

    Chapter Two   Carving the Scriptures   39

    Chapter Three   The Teachings of Tetsugen   55

    Chapter Four   The Myth of Tetsugen   79

TRANSLATIONS   89

PART I   TEACHING TEXTS   91

    The Dharma Lesson in Japanese of Zen Master Tetsugen of
      Zuiryūji   93

    Instructing the Community   119

    Dharma Words   125

    Response to the Lay Buddhist Noritomi Tessen   131

    Letter to Acting Head Monk Hōshū   135

PART II   TEXTS RELATED TO THE BUDDHIST SCRIPTURE
PROJECT   139

    An Opportunity for Instruction   141

    A Brief Account of the History of Carving the Buddhist
      Scriptures   147

    A Report on Progress Made on the New Edition of the
      Buddhist Scriptures   151

    An Account of Completing the Buddhist Scriptures   155

Part III   Poetry   159

Part IV   Other Letters and Historical Documents   171

An Affidavit Concerning the Dharma Debate in Mori   173
Letter to Lord Kurushima Requesting that He Spare Lives   183
Letter to Yamazaki Hanzaemon Regarding the Famine   189

Appendix: Biographies   195

The Deeds of Master Tetsugen, Founder of Zuiryūji Temple   197
The Monk Tetsugen, from *Biographies of Unusual People of the*
   Early Modern Period   209
Tetsugen's Edition of the Complete Buddhist Scriptures,
   (From *The Elementary School Japanese Reader*)   213
Notes   217
Bibliography   251
Index   255

Acknowledgments

I began the research that eventually developed into this book many years ago. Paul Watt, then my adviser at Columbia University, recommended that I look at the writings of Tetsugen and consider him as a dissertation topic. I began reading his *Dharma Lesson* on my daily commute into and out of Manhattan, and was deeply effected by the clarity of Tetsugen's message. When I read his description of human suffering during the famine of 1682 and his appeal for help in responding to the crisis, I wanted to understand the man and his teachings. Although the Ōbaku sect rather than Tetsugen became the central focus of my earlier work, Tetsugen remained a compelling figure to me over the years. I wish to thank Paul Watt for introducing him to me.

I took up the present project while on a sabbatical leave from the Department of Religion at the University of Hawaii, during which I completed the translations presented here and the bulk of the analytical chapters. I drew upon earlier research related to Tetsugen completed as part of my dissertation work. Funding from the Japan Foundation and a Whitehead fellowship supported that initial stage.

Several colleagues and friends assisted me in the project over the years. Gay Sibley, Julia Sopalski, and Sarah Thal read and commented on parts of the manuscript in its various stages. Many of my students at the University of Hawaii have read and commented on the translations, in a few cases checking my work with the Japanese originals. I especially wish to thank Leighton Ito, who made a special effort to provide me with a student's perspective. Robert Aitken made helpful suggestions to improve the translations of some of the more difficult passages in the teaching materials. Poul Andersen kindly provided assistance with a few of the more obscure passages in Chinese.

I am forever grateful for the loving support of Rod Low, my husband, and our children Lena and Philip.

Introduction

Tetsugen Dōkō (1630–1682) is perhaps the best known Ōbaku Zen monk in Japan and the West. He is credited with producing the first complete wood block edition of the Chinese Buddhist scriptures in Japan. Many older Japanese still remember reading about Tetsugen in school textbooks used in the first half of the twentieth century. Those textbooks included a lesson about Tetsugen that recounted a traditional legend: Tetsugen twice used the funds he had arduously raised for printing the scriptures to feed the victims of various natural disasters, and only with his third effort did he succeed in completing his original goal of printing the scriptures. In recent years, Tetsugen has been the subject of a television movie as well as several books geared toward a popular reading audience. Even among Western followers of Zen, his story has become well known and his name appears on numerous Buddhist websites. As is often the case, popular stories related to an historical figure are partly historical and partly legendary. The following chapters will explore both aspects of Tetsugen's story, and serve as an introduction to the translations of Tetsugen's writings that follow. Before turning attention to Tetsugen himself, however, an overview of the broader religious context in which he lived and worked may be helpful.

BUDDHISM DURING THE TOKUGAWA PERIOD

Tetsugen was born early in the Tokugawa period (1600–1867), what is commonly known in the West as Japan's early modern period. By that time, Buddhism had been a part of Japanese culture for more than ten centuries, having been first introduced in the sixth century. For many centuries during the medieval period, Buddhist thought dominated the intellectual and religious life of Japan, particularly among the elite classes. During the Tokugawa period, however, Buddhist institutions came under government constraint, and the tradition faced intellectual competition from movements within both the Confucian and Shintō communities. Nevertheless, important changes occurred within the realm of Japanese Buddhism during the Tokugawa period that both broadened Buddhism's audience and circumscribed its role in society.

In order to eliminate certain officially banned religious movements, especially Christianity, the Tokugawa government established policies that effectively ensured that all Japanese individuals and families were affiliated with a Buddhist temple. At the same time, the government established policies constraining the growth of Buddhist temples and the behavior of Buddhist monks and nuns. The Tokugawa government developed a policy, known as the parishioner system (*danka seidō*), which enlisted the assistance of Buddhist institutions and clergy to control the religious affiliation of ordinary Japanese as well as to monitor certain religious behavior. This system, at first targeting areas heavily influenced by Christianity, eventually required every Japanese family throughout the country be officially affiliated with a local Buddhist temple. Families initially registered with a local Buddhist monk as members of a particular congregation. Subsequently, the family reported all demographic changes within the family, including marriages, births, and deaths. Eventually, the government extended the parishioner system to require that each individual be registered as a member of a recognized temple, and that the clergy continually monitor them for active affiliation as a prerequisite for ongoing certification. In this way, the government sought to ensure that individuals were not affiliated with any officially banned religious groups. In areas where Christianity had once been popular, for example, individuals were required to swear oaths rejecting any affiliation with the Christian faith. In this manner, at least outward behavior if not always internal belief could be brought under official scrutiny.[1]

The parishioner system thus garnered for Buddhist temples a captive audience of members, which tended to enrich temple coffers even when the affiliation was not necessarily wholehearted. Throughout the seventeenth century, more and more ordinary Japanese villagers and townspeople became affiliated with Buddhist temples, until the country reached nearly universal Buddhist membership. For most commoners, this represented the first time that they actually joined a parish. Previously, it was only common for wealthier and more prominent families and individuals to establish such a relationship, because membership amounted to patronage. Parishioners were obligated to make monetary donations or to offer manual labor in support of the temple. In most cases, with the exception of Pure Land and Nichiren devotees, families chose a temple based on geographic proximity rather than personal devotion to a particular school or sect of Buddhism.[2]

The legacy of required Buddhist membership survives even today, with the majority of Japanese families retaining some Buddhist affiliation. One sees this especially in the nearly universal use of Buddhist funeral and ancestral memorial rituals for the deceased. Indeed, the association of Buddhism with funerals represents another related legacy resulting from Tokugawa government policy. The government required that a member of the Buddhist clergy write up the certificate of death for all Japanese. This helped to popularize the already existing practice of offering Buddhist funerals and memorial services for lay Buddhists. By the eighteenth century, Buddhist temples were requiring their members to make use of their services for funerals and ancestral memorial services as a prerequisite for temple certification of membership.

The vast majority of Buddhist monks served as parish priests at small local temples in villages and city neighborhoods. They provided for the ritual needs of their community, primarily by offering funeral and memorial services for the deceased and observing Buddhist holidays. In addition, many monks held services in times of special need, for example, to make rain or to heal an individual from spirit possession. It was not uncommon for monks to run small schools for local children. The Buddhist clergy enjoyed prestige in many communities both because of their spiritual authority and their education. As today, clergy sometimes misused their position, leading to scandals. As a result, the degenerate or debauched monk became a standard character in literature during the period.

While government policy expanded Buddhist affiliation to all Japanese, it also sought to bring Buddhist institutions and leaders under stricter control. Various government regulations and policies related to temples and clergy (*jiin hatto*) were enacted throughout the seventeenth century. For example, the government severely limited the right of Buddhist monks to publicly engage in intersectarian debates. Debates were regarded as potential threats to the peace. In addition, monks and nuns were constrained in their travel, and were encouraged to remain at home in their temples and monasteries, engaged in appropriate monastic activities such as ritual services, meditation, sutra chanting, and scholarship.

Buddhist clergy actively engaged in scholarship in the early Tokugawa period that had a lasting impact on Japanese Buddhist studies down to the present. Many of today's Buddhist universities had their origin in sectarian institutes established in the seventeenth century. In addition, some of the work done by various scholar monks of the seventeenth and eighteenth centuries continues to influence research done today by religious and secular scholars alike. In particular, Buddhist scholars began to study and publish basic texts from within their own sects. Within the Sōtō Zen sect, for example, scholars such as Manzan and Menzan studied the writings of Dōgen and other founding figures of the sect. They published not only commentaries of their own, but the first wood block editions of Dōgen's writings, thus establishing what now serves as the canonical basis of their sect.

On a more popular level, many Buddhist monks made efforts to deepen ordinary people's commitment to Buddhism. A number of Buddhist monks, including Tetsugen, became well known as popular preachers, giving lectures on the basic teachings of Buddhism.[3] In some cases, Buddhist monks held ceremonies inviting laypeople to express their commitment to Buddhism by taking the so-called Bodhisattva Vows. Within the Zen world, monks such as Suzuki Shōsan and Bankei Yōtaku taught laypeople Zen practices that they regarded as accessible to ordinary people living busy lives as householders.[4]

As the period progressed, and more people became literate, monks and lay practitioners published Buddhist works designed for a lay audience, including picture books and religious tracts written in vernacular Japanese. Tetsugen's *Dharma Lesson in Japanese*, a translation of which is included in this volume, was one such text.

ZEN IN THE EARLY TOGUGAWA PERIOD

At the beginning of the seventeenth century, the Zen community included monks and nuns affiliated with the Rinzai and Sōtō traditions. The Ōbaku lineage, which became the third major sect of Zen in Japan, was established only later in the century. Like their colleagues from other schools of Buddhism, the majority of Zen monks served local parishes. They spent most of their time on ritual services, and only a small minority of monks concentrated their efforts on practicing meditation. In the Sōtō school, for example, it is estimated that only about 1 percent of monks regularly practiced meditation.[5] Meditation was the primary focus only at certain of the major training monasteries and at a few smaller monasteries, depending on the talent and proclivity of the abbot.

We know relatively little about the practice of Zen at the training monasteries of the day.[6] The early years of the Tokugawa period are overshadowed by the major reform movements of the eighteenth century, identified most closely with the work of Hakuin Ekaku (1685–1768) in the Rinzai sect and Menzan Zuihō (1683–1769) in the Sōtō sect. Until very recently, scholars in Japan and the West generally ignored seventeenth century Zen, regarding it as ossified and degenerate, lacking in strong leadership, and not at all edifying for those seeking to understand the teachings of Zen Buddhism. Scholars are now reconsidering the truth of these assumptions, and current research paints quite a different picture. There were indeed strong, and in some cases quite popular, leaders both within the mainstream of the Zen establishment and at its fringes. In addition, there is growing interest in the more popular manifestations of Zen religiosity.[7]

Many of the Zen voices of the seventeenth century called for the reform of Zen, seeking a restoration of an idealized past. In this regard, Zen monks were in step with the mood of the times. Intellectuals throughout the fields of Confucian thought, Shinto studies and Buddhism actively carried out research into the great texts and the founding teachers of their respective traditions. Within a Zen context, this "back to the original sources" movement could take as its focus any of three basic possibilities: first, the writings of early Japanese founding figures such as Dōgen; second, the recorded saying of Chinese masters from the Tang and Sung dynasties; and finally, the older canonical scriptures of the Mahayana Buddhist tradition. Tetsugen's production of a complete wood block edition of the Buddhist scriptures served the latter purpose.

The early voices for reform in the Zen world included Sōtō masters such as Gesshū Sōko (1618–1696), Manzan Dōhaku (1636–1715), Baihō Jikushin

(1633–1707), and Tenkei Senson (d. 1735), the Rinzai teachers Takuan Sōhō (1573–1645), Gudō Tōshoku (1579–1661), and Mujaku Dōchū (1653–1744), as well as supporters of the new Ōbaku movement including Ryōkei Shōsen (1602–1670) and Chōon Dōkai (1628–1695). They considered such issues as the proper method for Dharma transmission, how to interpret and uphold monastic disciple, and the role of kōan in Zen practice. While everyone seems to have favored reform, much discussion and disagreement arose as to the best methods to employ toward that end.

Monks within the Rinzai and Sōtō communities generally enjoyed close and mutually beneficial relationships. It seems likely that during the seventeenth century, sectarian consciousness was much lower than it became later in the period, after the reform movements of Hakuin and Menzan promoted purging the respective sectarian traditions of "foreign" influences.[8] Early in the period, Zen scholar monks exchanged ideas both through their writings and in direct interchange in a manner that suggests that they regarded their community of scholarly discourse in broad terms to include all Zen practitioners. They formed alliances on common issues regardless of lineage, and sometimes collaborated in a common cause.

Exchange of ideas was not limited to the scholarly level, but extended to the realm of Zen practice. It was not at all uncommon for monks to travel outside the confines of their home monastery to practice for a season or two with masters from other lineages, crossing sectarian lines with apparent freedom. Zen masters at the larger training monasteries and in some cases at smaller local temples held intensive practice periods twice annually. Commonly known as the summer and winter retreats, these sessions lasted for three months each, and afforded monks a chance to practice under the direction of different teachers without necessarily altering their original affiliation.

The Chinese and Japanese monks who eventually founded the Ōbaku sect in the latter half of the seventeenth century participated in the interchange of the day. They contributed significantly to the transformation of Zen that continued into the eighteenth century. The Ōbaku sect emerged as a result of an influx of a small number of Chinese Buddhist masters to Japan and their interactions with their own Japanese disciples and with other members of the Rinzai and Sōtō communities. In time, Ōbaku became the third major sect of Zen in Japan.[9]

INTRODUCTION OF ŌBAKU ZEN

The Ōbaku sect of Zen was established in Japan in the latter half of the seventeenth century by a small group of Chinese Zen teachers and their Japanese disciples.[10] Tradition recognizes Yinyuan Longqi (1592–1673), the oldest and most prominent of the Chinese masters, as the founder of the new sect. Ōbaku never existed as an independent or distinct sect in China, although all of its Chinese teachers were affiliated with the same monastery in Fujian province,

Huangboshan Wanfusi. Yinyuan and the first group of his Chinese disciples arrived in Nagasaki Japan in 1654 with the intention of serving the needs of the Chinese expatriate community residing there. Many Japanese Zen practitioners visited Yinyuan in Nagasaki, and some of them joined his assembly and practiced as his disciples.

Yinyuan seems to have originally planned to stay in Japan for a few years and then to return to China. A small group of his Japanese disciples and other supporters, however, hoped that the master would remain permanently in Japan and provide guidance as abbot of a major training monastery within the Rinzai sect. They arranged for government permission for Yinyuan to relocate in the Kyoto area. Friction within the Rinzai establishment precluded Yinyuan from assuming the position as abbot at Myōshinji as his supporters had hoped, thus eventually leading to the establishment of a new monastery. In 1661, Yinyuan took up residence as the founding abbot of Ōbakusan Mampukuji, which would become the main monastery of the fledgling Ōbaku sect.

Yinyuan and his Chinese disciples practiced Zen in a somewhat different style than that seen at Japanese Rinzai or Sōtō monasteries, preserving the customs that they brought with them from China. This made Ōbaku monasteries unique within the world of Japanese Zen. Chinese and Japanese monks alike donned Chinese-style robes and shoes, chanted the sutras in the Fujian dialect of Chinese, accompanied by musical instruments previously unknown in Japan. Ōbaku monasteries were governed according to a monastic code, the *Ōbaku shingi,* which reflected the Chinese practices of the day, and which sought to preserve the Chinese character of the group. In addition, Ōbaku monastic services incorporated practices such as chanting the name of Amida Buddha (known in Japanese as *nembutsu*), which struck many Japanese observers as inappropriate within a Zen context.

Later generations of Japanese Zen teachers would argue that the primary difference between Ōbaku and its close relative Rinzai Zen is the matter of combined practice, that is, the use of both Zen and Pure Land techniques. As I have argued elsewhere, the differences were at once more subtle and more diverse.[11] As the decades passed, Ōbaku became less obviously Chinese in style, and more like its Japanese counterparts. At the same time, elements of practice unfamiliar to the Japanese before the arrival of the Chinese Ōbaku monks became commonplace at Rinzai and Sōtō temples. In the late seventeenth and early eighteenth centuries, Japanese described the experience of entering Mampukuji as if they had been transported to China, so foreign did it appear to them. This is not the case today. With a few notable exceptions, such as the style of sutra chanting (which continues to be done in an approximation of Fujian dialect), Ōbaku temples and monasteries appear very like their Rinzai neighbors.

Within the context of Zen Buddhism during the Tokugawa period, Tetsugen stands out as a fine example of several trends that gained in significance as the period progressed. Among these, the following chapters will stress his contribution to the back to the sources movement within the Buddhist world and his emphasis on keeping the precepts both for monastic and lay practitioners. Tetsugen supported the trend to read and study the original sources of the Buddhist tradition in a concrete fashion through his project to produce a woodblock edition of the Buddhist scriptures. His efforts greatly increased the availability of Buddhist scriptures for scholar monks within all sect of Buddhism. In his own teachings, Tetsugen preached from the scriptures, rendering them into Japanese in order to make them accessible to lay audiences.

Tetsugen did not actively seek to reform the Buddhism of his day on an institutional level. Many such reformers were active during his lifetime and in the generations that followed. Indeed, the founding of the Ōbaku sect can be seen as one part of a reform movement current in the Rinzai Zen community during the seventeenth century. That particular current within the reform movement placed great stress on keeping the precepts and restoring monastic discipline as a vehicle for reinvigorating the Zen sect. Tetsugen clearly felt a great affinity for this approach to Buddhist practice. Within his own life and in his dealing with his disciples, Tetsugen stressed the importance of keeping the precepts as the only possible basis for genuine Buddhist meditation. In his lectures and in his writings, he enjoined his audience to establish Buddhist moral principles as the first step in their practice of Zen Buddhism.

༈༇༆༈

What follows are four analytical chapters presenting the life, work, and teachings of Tetsugen, followed by a series of annotated translations of Tetsugen's writings. The appendix includes translations of three biographies of Tetsugen, two from the Tokugawa period as well as the above mentioned textbook lesson. Chapter 1 provides a biographical sketch of Tetsugen. Chapter 2 describes the project to produce a complete woodblock edition of the Buddhist scriptures. Chapter 3 presents the major themes found in Tetsugen's teachings, as well as a discussion of the techniques and pedagogical styles that Tetsugen employed. Chapter 4 explores the hagiography related to Tetsugen and the early modern and modern uses of his story.

Tetsugen wrote in both classical Chinese and in Japanese, depending on the purpose of the text and its intended audience. Each of the documents that follows includes a brief introduction providing the purpose of the piece, the language and style of the original, and the source used as the basis for the translation; whenever possible, I have also included the date and intended audience. I have divided the writings into four categories: teaching materials, texts related to the scripture project, poetry, and miscellaneous writings. The selections represent the bulk of Tetsugen's writings that have been preserved. I made an effort to include all the material of interest from a pedagogical perspective, that is, with significant teaching content, as well as items of interest from a social historical perspective. I included approximately one-third of the poetry preserved in the *Yuiroku*, since Zen teachers commonly composed poetry as a part of their interaction with disciples. I chose not to include any examples of certain genre, such as bell inscriptions and eulogies, which I did not think would be of great interest to a contemporary audience. There is one major work attributed to Tetsugen, the *Kōmori bōdanki* (*The Forgotten Written Account about Bats*), which I chose not to include among the translations. The problems related to attributing this text with any certainty to Tetsugen are included in chapter 3, along with selected passages.

Historical Biography and Analysis

CHAPTER ONE

The Life of Tetsugen

Tetsugen was born to the Saeki family, who lived in the Mashiki region of Higo province (now Kumamoto prefecture), on New Year's Day of Kan'ei 7 (1630). We know little of his family or his childhood, not even the names by which Tetsugen was known as a youth. The Saeki family was devoted to Pure Land Buddhism, and Tetsugen's father Jōshin served in some capacity as a member of the Buddhist clergy. Most likely he was a shrine monk (*shasō*) who served at the Buddhist temple within the compound of the nearby Hachimangū shrine.[1] Other traditions suggest that he was the resident monk at a True Pure Land[2] temple, Kōnenji.[3] Virtually nothing is known of Tetsugen's mother; the *Deeds of Tetsugen,* the biography written by his leading disciple, merely states that she was a virtuous woman. A memorial stone indicates that Tetsugen had at least one sibling, a brother.

It seems likely that Tetsugen married as a young man, as was the norm for True Pure Land priests. Until the modern period in Japan, only True Pure Land priests married, while all other Buddhist clergy were required to maintain the traditional Buddhist rule of monastic celibacy. None of the Ōbaku biographies, such as the *Deeds of Tetsugen,* make any mention of a wife, although nonsectarian sources from the period do so. The nonsectarian sources suggest that Tetsugen married a woman from his home region and that he left her permanently when he converted to Zen at age twenty-six. The biographical sketch of Tetsugen that appears in *Biographies of Unusual People of the Early Modern Period,*[4] for example, states

> Although [Tetsugen] was already married, he was dissatisfied that in the [True Pure Land] sect, people without talent or merit held high rank in the temple hierarchy. Therefore, he went up to Mount Ōbaku and followed [the instruction] of Muan.

> His wife came to [Mount Ōbaku Mampukuji] to find him, but he did not wish to meet her. So she camped outside the temple gate and watched for him to emerge. Finally, one day when he had no choice but to go out, she asked

him to accompany her to their home province and return to their village. He
escaped up the street and returned to the temple.

Several versions of the same basic story exist; some of them lean toward pious
interpretations of events rather than the more ribald accounts in which Tetsugen hides from his wife as long as possible and then escapes up the street once
she has cornered him. In the more sedate and instructional versions, Tetsugen
accompanies his wife back to their home village and there converts both his
former wife and mother-in-law to Zen. The two women then became Zen
nuns and, as Tetsugen's disciples, aided him in his scripture project.[5] There is
no external historical evidence to confirm any of these stories.

TETSUGEN'S EARLY BUDDHIST EDUCATION

Tetsugen began his Buddhist education at the age of seven, when his father
taught him to read the Meditation Sutra (*Kanmuryōjukyō*),[6] one of the three
sutras that form the basic canon for the Pure Land schools of Buddhism. At the
age of twelve, Tetsugen took the tonsure and continued his education under the
guidance of a local monk called Kaiun. Nothing is known for certain about this
monk except that he was a True Pure Land priest, and probably the resident
monk at Shōsen-bō, a small branch temple of the Nishi Honganji in the village
of Notsu.[7] Tetsugen studied with Kaiun for at least the next four years.

In 1646, when Tetsugen was sixteen years old, he became the disciple of
a well-known True Pure Land priest named Saigin (1605–1663). Saigin was
an unusual True Pure Land teacher, with a broad background in the Chinese
classics and Zen Buddhist thought. As a young monk, Saigin practiced for a
time under the Zen master Sessō (d. 1649)[8] in Bungo province, and then went
to Kyoto, where he practiced for a period of three years at the Zen temple
Tōfukuji.[9] Only later, when he returned to Kyushu, did he dedicate himself to
the exclusive study and practice of True Pure Land Buddhism.

Tetsugen first encountered Saigin when he attended a lecture on *The
Awakening of Faith*[10] that Saigin gave in the nearby town of Kokura in Buzen
province. Saigin served as abbot at Eishōji, a large Honganji branch temple in
Kokura. According to the *Deeds of Tetsugen,* the young man was deeply affected
by the lecture. Tetsugen may have accompanied Saigin to Kyoto the following
year, when Saigin took up the post as the headmaster of the new True Pure
Land academy (now Ryūkoku University).

The exact chronology of Tetsugen's time at the True Pure Land academy
in Kyoto is not clear. He may well have left Kyūshū as early as 1647, departing
for Kyoto when Saigin did, although the *Deeds of Tetsugen* makes no mention
of this. Whether Tetsugen move to Kyoto in 1647 or 1650, his education was
interrupted in 1650 by word of his mother's death. At that time, he traveled
back to his home village to perform the appropriate memorial services and
thus fulfill his filial obligations. According to the inscription on his mother's

memorial stone, which Tetsugen erected in 1662 on the thirteenth anniversary of her death, she died on the twenty-first day of the sixth lunar month of Keian 3 (1650).[11] The *Deeds of Tetsugen* indicates that he subsequently traveled to Kyoto to resume his education, but dates his departure to the spring of the same year.

In Kyoto, Tetsugen rejoined Saigin and studied with him at the True Pure Land academy. It is very difficult to assess the lasting influence Saigin had on Tetsugen, especially given the paucity of primary materials connecting the two men. Tetsugen seems to have been deeply impressed by Saigin's lectures, and both men shared a similar passion for teaching and lecturing based on Buddhist texts. The traditional pattern of instruction under a master such as Saigin would have included a great deal of memorization on the students' part. Tetsugen and the others would have listened to Saigin's lectures and repeated them in whole or in part to the best of their abilities, ultimately committing large portions to memory for their own use later.[12] Tetsugen was known for his skill in this technique. In this way, the master's teachings naturally became a part of the disciple's unless some kind of break occurred between them. Tetsugen's change to Zen practice would have constituted such a break.

Tetsugen heard Saigin explicate many Buddhist scriptures, and yet, as far as we know, he only included one of these, *The Awakening of Faith*, in his own repertoire. Nonetheless, Saigin's overall approach may well have had a more extensive impact than this alone suggests. Certainly, as a Zen monk Tetsugen would not have lectured on the Pure Land texts that comprised the majority of topics for Saigin's lectures. It is perhaps more reasonable to posit that Saigin's lasting influence on Tetsugen can be found in his openness to other Buddhist traditions, especially Zen. As Saigin's early monastic training demonstrates, Saigin may have shared with Tetsugen some inclination toward the Zen understanding of Buddhism. Indeed, Saigin's detractors specifically accused him of contaminating True Pure Land doctrine with Zen ideas and interpretations. Tetsugen's case may be an indication that these accusations had some basis in reality. Saigin's "contamination" of Tetsugen's training, his refusal to exclusively teach True Pure Land ideas, may have actually helped precipitate Tetsugen's break from True Pure Land Buddhism.

LEAVING TRUE PURE LAND BUDDHISM

When considering the possible reasons why Tetsugen broke off his True Pure Land affiliation in favor of Zen, one enters into the realm of speculation. Tetsugen never mentioned his decision to leave True Pure Land in any of his extant writings,[13] and his disciples did not address the issue in their biographical pieces. In fact, there is a significant gap in the *Deeds of Tetsugen* for a five-year period immediately preceding Tetsugen first entering the Ōbaku Zen monastic community in Nagasaki. The biography jumps from a brief entry for the year 1650, when Tetsugen returned to Kyoto to take up his studies, to 1655, when

Tetsugen traveled from Kyoto to Nagasaki to meet with Yinyuan. We know from other sources that, during the intervening years, conditions in Kyoto changed significantly, and that these changes would have had considerable impact on Tetsugen.

There are three factors that theoretically may have propelled Tetsugen to leave the sect of his birth and to convert to Zen. First, the Jōō incident, described briefly below, seems to have been the immediate impetus for Tetsugen to leave Kyoto and to reconsider his affiliation with True Pure Land Buddhism. Second, Saigin's intellectual influence may have steered Tetsugen toward a Zen understanding of Buddhism. Third, Tetsugen's own feelings of dissatisfaction with the True Pure Land sect may have motivated him to seek out a form of Buddhist thought and practice more consistent with his growing understanding of the scriptures.

Beginning in 1653, Saigin came under serious attack from colleagues within the True Pure Land sect who accused him of using Zen concepts in his teachings at the academy. The incident is known within the True Pure Land sect as the Jōō incident because it spanned the Jōō era, 1652–1654. Saigin seems to have had the full support of his superiors within the True Pure Land hierarchy, who rejected charges that his teaching was heretical. Unfortunately, they were unable to successfully settle the dispute on their own. When sect officials asked the government to intervene in 1654, the government exiled Saigin's primary detractor, and decided that the academy that lay at the heart of the problem should be closed. Saigin thus lost his position, and eventually returned to Kyushu later the same year. Although we have no reason to believe that Tetsugen was personally involved in the internal struggles of the sect, he and other students would have been directly affected by them. Tetsugen was left without a master to guide his studies, and the school was closed indefinitely. Whatever course Tetsugen would set for himself, as a result of sectarian disputes, he faced a serious decision about his future.

Although the *Deeds of Tetsugen* is silent on the matter, other Edo period biographies suggest that Tetsugen became increasingly dissatisfied with certain aspects of True Pure Land belief and practice, and that this dissatisfaction may have motivated him to look outside the sect for guidance. The passage from the *Biographies of Unusual People of the Early Modern Period* cited above states that Tetsugen felt discouraged about the low caliber of the True Pure Land clergy, especially those in positions of authority.[14] The *Kōko ruisan shūi* contains a similar observation, in somewhat stronger language: "[Tetsugen] despised the fact that individuals were placed in positions of high rank according to temple custom even though they were lacking in learning and merit in the [True Pure Land] sect's teachings."[15]

Major themes from Tetsugen's later writings suggest another area of True Pure Land practice that may have troubled him in his youth, the custom that monks and lay people alike married and ate meat. As an Ōbaku monk, Tetsugen wrote and preached most often on the theme of keeping the Buddhist

Disagree

precepts, especially those against sexual misconduct and killing. For example, in his *Dharma Lesson in Japanese,* he promoted the benefits of celibacy and non-killing even for lay believers by explaining in graphic terms the suffering that the married life and meat eating actually entail from a Buddhist perspective. When explicating the *Śūramgama sutra* in *An Affidavit Concerning the Dharma Debate in Mori,* Tetsugen argued in more direct terms against monks marrying and eating meat. Although it is not known for certain whether or not he intentionally directed his arguments against the practices of the True Pure Land sect, his repeated teaching on this theme and his life-long dedication to the *Śūramgama sutra* suggest at the very least that his personal rejection of these customs was a basic reason for breaking with the sect.

TETSUGEN'S INITIAL ENCOUNTERS WITH ŌBAKU ZEN

When the Chinese Zen master Yinyuan decided to visit Japan, it set off a wave of excitement in the Japanese Zen community throughout the country, especially in Kyoto, where Tetsugen heard the news. Yinyuan arrived in Nagasaki in the seventh lunar month of 1654, the very same month that the government closed the True Pure Land academy. As foreign nationals, Yinyuan and his Chinese disciples were confined to the city of Nagasaki. At this early stage, before the government granted Yinyuan and a few of his disciples freedom of movement, any Japanese person who wished to meet with them had to travel to Kyushu to do so. Tetsugen determined to pay his respects to the famous Chinese master, and set out for Nagasaki in the Autumn of 1655.

Tetsugen made his way first to Osaka, where he awaited a vessel heading for Kyushu. In Osaka, he was fortunate enough to meet the Tokugawa government's administrator (*bugyō*) of Nagasaki, Kurokawa Masanao (1602–1680), who was then returning to Nagasaki from Edo (now Tokyo). It was Kurokawa who granted official permission for Yinyuan to travel to Nagasaki in the first place. Shortly after his return to Nagasaki, Kurokawa himself paid his respects and became a lay disciple of Yinyuan. Kurokawa generously permitted Tetsugen to sail aboard his ship, and in that way, Tetsugen arrived in Nagasaki and made his way to Kōfukuji, the Chinese Buddhist monastery where Yinyuan had taken up residence as abbot.

Tetsugen was admitted to see Yinyuan, and the two men conversed both through an interpreter and in written Chinese. The *Deeds of Tetsugen* briefly describes that first encounter in the following terms:

> [Tetsugen] changed his robes and entered Tōmyōzan [Kōfukuji]. He explained at some length that he was eager to seek the teachings. Master [Yinyuan] knew at a glance that he was a vessel of the Dharma (*hōki*).[16] He allowed him to follow the other monks and enter the monks' hall to begin practicing *zazen.* Tetsugen immediately cast aside what he had previously learned, and took up the matter of his Original Nature untiringly noon and night.

At that time, the assembly was in the midst of the summer retreat, held from the fourth through the seventh months, and Tetsugen thus had the opportunity to participate in its final weeks. The exact date of Tetsugen's admission to the assembly was not recorded, but based on the timing of Kurokawa's audience with Yinyuan, one can assume that it occurred sometime early in the sixth month of 1655.[17]

Tetsugen entered Yinyuan's assembly just as efforts to invite the Chinese master to Kyoto were coming to fruition. After months of planning and work, a group of Rinzai monks gained permission from the government in Edo for Yinyuan to travel to the Kyoto area. Within a month of Tetsugen's arrival, Yinyuan accepted their invitation to take up residence at Fumonji in Settsu province. Yinyuan left Nagasaki early in the eighth month, soon after the close of the summer retreat. After only two months at Kōfukuji, Tetsugen found himself once again without a teacher.

The government would not allow Yinyuan's Japanese disciples to accompany him to Settsu, so Yinyuan made arrangements for Muan, his leading disciple and Dharma heir, to take on responsibility for their guidance.[18] Muan himself had only recently arrived in Nagasaki from China and he was still under the travel restrictions applied to all Chinese nationals. He assumed the position as head monk at another Chinese monastery Fukusaiji, where he remained until receiving permission to join Yinyuan in Kyoto several years later. Tetsugen went to Fukusaiji to meet with Muan, but the first encounter did not go well. The scene from the *Deeds of Tetsugen* suggests that Tetsugen behaved brashly with his new master. First, he went straight up to the master's gate and knocked. When he entered the master's room, he stated his mind forcefully, without deferring to Muan's authority or trying to come to an accord. In typical Zen fashion, Muan slapped his face and dismissed him, refusing him permission to enter the assembly. Zen masters often initially refuse admission to test the disciple's resolve. In this case, Tetsugen did not remain in Nagasaki to seek another meeting with Muan immediately.

At this stage, the *Deeds of Tetsugen* says that Tetsugen wandered about "like a wild crane or a wisp of cloud," and eventually made his way to Fumonji in Settsu where he was allowed to visit Yinyuan once again. It is possible that Tetsugen practiced with Yinyuan for a time, but the sources are unclear. Sometime later, he returned to Nagasaki and once again approached Muan. The second time, Muan admitted him to the assembly, and he remained there until 1661, or so we are lead to believe by the biography's silence.

With the exception of the events outlined above, the *Deeds of Tetsugen* leaves the years from 1655 until 1661 largely a blank. Many scholars have tried to fill in those years, presenting a range of chronologies that indicate that Tetsugen suffered a period of serious doubt during these "dark years," traveling back and forth between Nagasaki, Settsu, and Kyoto. For example, Yoshinaga Utarō pieced together an expanded chronology with information gleaned from various documents that supplement the *Deeds of Tetsugen*. According to his findings, Tetsugen returned to Fukusaiji in 1657 and practiced under Muan for a short time before returning to Kyoto once more in 1658. He contends that for a period of four to five years, Tetsugen experienced terrible doubts and seems to have even left Zen for a period of time.[19] Yoshinaga's chronology stands out among the other scholarly reconstructions because he documented each entry with the textual citation used as its basis. Other scholars present their chronologies as if there were no textual problems in explicating this period in Tetsugen's life.[20] Unfortunately, it is impossible to verify much of the additional information included in these accounts, since they do not document their sources methodically.

Based on historical documents, one can make a few amendments to the account in the *Deeds of Tetsugen* with a reasonable degree of certainty for the years 1655 to 1661. First, based on Hōshū's introduction to the *Tetsugen yuiroku*, it is possible to date Tetsugen's return to Nagasaki and initial admission to Muan's assembly to the year 1657.[21] As for his visits with Yinyuan in Settsu, Yinyuan was living under strict house arrest until the eleventh month of 1655, when a few Japanese visitors were allowed to enter. Therefore, Tetsugen could not have visited Fumonji before the end of 1655. If Tetsugen did actually practice under Yinyuan at Fumonji for an extended period of time, it would have been after the government lightened the restrictions in the seventh month of 1656. After that time, Yinyuan was permitted up to two hundred Japanese disciples in his assembly at Fumonji, and Tetsugen may have been among those who took advantage of the opportunity. Tetsugen probably did make multiple visits to Fumonji during these years and he probably stayed for an extended period of time in order to complete his first venture into publishing Buddhist texts. Tetsugen's name appears on the original woodblock plates as the publisher of Yinyuan's *Gukai hōgi*, dated 1658.[22] In the *Gukai hōgi*, Yinyuan provided a detailed description of the Triple Ordination Platform Precept Ceremony (*Sandan kaie*) used within the Ōbaku community.

TETSUGEN'S ZEN PRACTICE

The year 1661 seems to have been a turning point for Tetsugen, then age thirty. Although he had been struggling with Zen practice for some years, after 1661, he dedicated himself to the practice of Zen with renewed confidence and even began accepting his first disciples. Following a common Zen pattern, Tetsugen placed himself under the guidance of several Zen masters in addition to periodically visiting his primary master, Muan.[23] Muan had by this time left Kyushu for the Kyoto area, where he rejoined Yinyuan and spent the next several years engrossed in the project of establishing Mampukuji. Tetsugen spent more extended lengths of time practicing under the Rinzai monk Kengan Zen'etsu (1618–1690)[24] at Tafukuji in Bungo and the Chinese Ōbaku master Zhifei at Fukujuji in Kokura, but also made brief visits with other masters, including Duzhan, over the years.

As the *Deeds of Tetsugen* notes, Tetsugen attended lectures on the *Śūram-gama sutra*[25] given by Kengan Zen'etsu at Tafukuji during the autumn of 1661. Tetsugen may well have met Kengan at some earlier point in his life, since they shared mutual connections. Kengan had been a disciple of Sessō during the period that Tetsugen was studying with Saigin, and the two men might have met on one of the occasions when their masters visited one another. It is also possible that Tetsugen met Kengan when he visited Yinyuan in Nagasaki. In any case, Kengan introduced Tetsugen to what would become his favorite scripture for lecturing and teaching. Tetsugen lectured on the *Śūramgama sutra* at least eight times in his life, and he used extensive quotations from it in his writings. In fact, he chose that sutra as the topic of his very first public lectures, given in his home village in the spring of 1663 at the Sōtō temple Zenjōji.

More will be said about Tetsugen's lectures on the *Śūramgama sutra* in the context of evaluating Tetsugen's teachings, but a few observations are appropriate here. If, as some have theorized, Tetsugen emerged in 1661 from a period of doubt in which he weighed the relative balance between Zen and True Pure Land practice for his own life, then hearing Kengan explicate the *Śūramgama sutra* may have constituted a decisive factor in his final decision to commit himself once and for all to Zen. Tetsugen once wrote of his own understanding of the sutra,

> Those who practice without keeping the precepts set out by the Buddha all represent the False Dharma. The reason for this [is as follows:] Although practices such as chanting the *nembutsu,* seated meditation, and reciting the sutras are each practiced differently depending on the abilities of the believer, the precepts against taking life, stealing, sexual misconduct, lying and the like are absolute, regardless of the sect. Not to keep them is unacceptable. Therefore these precepts are called "absolutes." (An Affidavit Concerning the Dharma Debate in Mori)

Clearly Tetsugen understood this sutra as a rejection of the True Pure Land assertion that, in the Final Age, keeping the precepts against marrying and meat eating was a hindrance to salvation, implying a reliance on the self. If this was the issue causing his doubts, then perhaps Kengan's lecture helped him put that doubt to rest and move ahead in his practice.

Attending Kengan's lectures was important to Tetsugen for another reason; it was at those lectures that he met Hōshū and Nyosetsu, the two men who would become his leading disciples. Hōshū was a native of Bungo province and was then just eighteen years of age. During the course of the lectures, Hōshū decided to leave his home and take the tonsure. He became Tetsugen's first disciple and followed him thereafter. Hōshū would later become the head monk at all of Tetsugen's temples after the master's death. Less is known about Nyosetsu, since he never received *inka* nor achieved a position of high rank in the Ōbaku sect. Nyosetsu was a native of Tetsugen's home province of Higo, and was one of his most reliable assistants when they were later working on the scripture printing project. Minamoto suggests that Nyokū did not have the right disposition to act as Tetsugen's leading disciple, and so that role fell to the much younger Hōshū.[26]

Based on descriptions of Nyosetsu and certain key dates, Nyosetsu may be an alternative name for the monk later known as Mue Nyokū (1610–1694). Unfortunately, materials are too sparse to be certain. Much more can be said with confidence about Nyokū than of Nyosetsu. Nyokū was born in Higo and had previously served under the *daimyō* of that province, Lord Hosokawa. He participated in the military action to suppress the Shimabara rebellion, and thereafter determined to leave the secular life and take the tonsure. He became a disciple of Tetsugen in 1661 and moved to Osaka with him in 1667 to work on the scripture project. Nyokū acted as steward of Zuiryūji when Tetsugen was away, and took on a great deal of responsibility in managing the scripture project.

Tetsugen had already practiced under Yinyuan and Muan, two of the three great Chinese Ōbaku masters. The third, Zhifei Ruyi had a reputation as the most skilled among the Chinese masters at guiding monks in their meditation and kōan practice. When the opportunity presented itself to practice with Zhifei, Tetsugen responded quickly. In 1665, Zhifei had already decided that he wished to return to China.[27] He nonetheless accepted Lord Ogasawara Tadazane's invitation to found a new Ōbaku temple before continuing on his journey home.[28] Zhifei opened the temple, which he named Kōjusan Fukujuji, in the city of Kokura in Kyushu. He performed the opening ceremony on the anniversary of the Buddha's birth (8th day 4th month 1665), just in time to hold the summer retreat. Around that time, Tetsugen was traveling through the region, giving lectures on the *Lotus Sutra*. When he heard that Zhifei would be opening Fukujuji in nearby Kokura, he took advantage of the opportunity to join his assembly and pass the summer retreat there.

Zhifei selected Tetsugen from among his other disciples to serve as "high seat" *(jōza)*, the monk who directs activities in the meditation hall. The monk appointed as "high seat" ranks second only to the abbot during the retreat season, the title referring specifically to his position beside the abbot on the meditation platform. The "high seat" is entrusted with significant responsibility for the spiritual direction of the other monks, and the position is therefore generally given to a monk who has extensive experience in meditation practice, usually someone who has practiced for more than ten years. The summer retreat of 1665 marked Tetsugen's tenth anniversary as an Ōbaku monk, and Zhifei apparently deemed him worthy of the trust.

The *Deeds of Tetsugen* includes a description of only one encounter between Zhifei and Tetsugen from the summer retreat, but the story suggests that Tetsugen made progress under the master's guidance.

> One day, Master [Zhifei] instructed the monks, asking, "How does one re-
> move something like oil absorbed by noodles?" He had the monks express

their own understanding. Testugen replied, "Stop mixing noodles!" The master praised him highly.

Despite their apparent compatibility, Tetsugen did not stay on at Fukujuji when the retreat came to an end, and he did not practice again under Zhifei. He left Zhifei's assembly at the end of the summer and returned home to Kumamoto. In the end, the summer session may have been the last full retreat in which Tetsugen dedicated himself completely to Zen meditation. Soon after leaving Kokura, he began making plans to import a woodblock edition of the scriptures from China, and from that time on seems to have worked full time on his scripture project.

BEGINNING THE BUDDHIST SCRIPTURE PROJECT

When Tetsugen returned to Kumamoto from Kokura in the Fall of 1665, he was already aware of the practical difficulties facing Buddhist scholars due to the scarcity of many sutras in Japan and he was contemplating the best means to ameliorate the situation. Once Tetsugen came to the conclusion that the best solution would be to produce a woodblock edition in Japan, he and his disciples undertook steps to initiate the project. Since the next chapter describes the scripture project in great detail, only a brief outline will be provided here.

Tetsugen's first step was to move his base of operations to Osaka, closer to the center of Ōbaku monastic support and to the heart of the Japanese publishing world. Tetsugen and his disciples made the move in 1667, eventually establishing the temple Jiunsan Zuiryūji (Mount Cloud of Compassion, Lucky Dragon Temple) in the Naniwa section of the city. Tetsugen continued to use Zuiryūji as his primary residence and the project headquarters until his death. He and his disciples later built two other sites, a storehouse called Hōzōin within the confines of Mampukuji, the main Ōbaku monastery, and a print house in the city of Kyoto.

Tetsugen publicly announced his undertaking to produce a complete woodblock edition of the Chinese Buddhist scriptures at a lecture given in Osaka in 1668. With some initial financial backing from his local supporters and the approval of his superiors Yinyuan and Muan, Tetsugen launched the next stage of scripture project that would continue for twelve years. Tetsugen spent most of the years 1669 to 1680 traveling throughout the country to raise funds for the project. He did this by visiting Zen temples and offering public lectures on various sutras. At these lectures he would describe his project to the monks, nuns and laypeople who attended, and invite them to participate through their donations. While Tetsugen traveled, his disciples managed other aspects of the project in Kyoto and Osaka. It was during his lecture tours that Tetsugen came into conflict with members of the True Pure Land sect.

CONFLICT WITH THE TRUE PURE LAND SECT

Tetsugen engaged in open disputes with True Pure Land followers on at least two occasions, in both cases while giving public lectures on the *Śūramgama Sutra*.[29] As a former True Pure Land priest, it seems likely that Tetsugen drew special attention from his former colleagues when he spoke about the necessity of keeping the precepts. True Pure Land believers who heard Tetsugen speak understood his vehement rejection of monks marrying and eating meat, one of the major themes in his *Śūramgama* lectures, as direct attacks against True Pure Land practice.

Tetsugen selected the *Śūramgama Sutra* as his primary teaching text throughout his career as a Zen monk, lecturing on it more often than any other sutra. Since he did not allow his disciples to take notes during his sermons, no written records of the sermons exist. Information related to his lecture style can be gleaned from two texts written by Tetsugen in response to the second, more serious dispute with True Pure Land members in Mori. Complete translations of "An Affidavit Concerning the Dharma Debate in Mori" and the "Letter to Lord Kurushima to Spare Lives" are included in part II of this volume.

In the autumn of 1669, after building his new headquarters in Osaka and setting the carving and printing operations in motion to produce the first ten volumes of the Buddhist canon, Tetsugen set off for the city of Edo on the first of many fund-raising trips. During his time in Edo, Tetsugen spoke on the *Śūramgama sutra* at Kaiunji in Asakusa. The *Deeds of Tetsugen* observes that his lecture series was an overwhelming success and that donations were generous. What the biography excludes from its account is that Tetsugen debated, at least informally, with a True Pure Land believer in the audience sometime during the lecture series. Tetsugen's choice of text as well as the themes he chose to emphasize from it caused some True Pure Land believers in the audience to conclude that Tetsugen was targeting their sect for ridicule. In particular, True Pure Land believers felt that Tetsugen sought to discredit their sect by stressing the necessity for maintaining the monastic precepts against clerical marriage and meat eating. This confrontation sowed the seeds of a long-lasting controversy between Tetsugen and the True Pure Land sect.

Based on True Pure Land accounts of Tetsugen's lectures at Kaiunji, Kūsei, the head monk at Myōenji, a True Pure land temple in Edo, challenged Tetsugen's interpretation of the *Śūramgama Sutra*, but he proved no match for Tetsugen in debate. "Kūsei exhausted his powers repudiating [Tetsugen's words] and arguing with him, but it was like a praying mantis taking on a chariot of war."[30] True Pure Land believers sent word to Kyoto, requesting that someone better able to defend the sect come to Edo and confront Tetsugen. Sectarian leaders at the head temple sent Chikū, the second director of the reopened True Pure Land academy, who had a reputation as a master debater.[31] Like Tetsugen, Chikū had studied under Saigin, and it is possible that the two men knew each other from their youth. Chikū became Saigin's disciple in 1655, the same year that Tetsugen departed from Kyoto to join Yinyuan's assembly in Nagasaki. There is no primary source material indicated whether or not they became acquainted at that time.[32] Chikū arrived in the post town of Shinagawa on the outskirts of Edo just as Tetsugen was finishing up his lectures. Tetsugen departed immediately to return to Osaka, perhaps unaware that Chikū was on his way.

In this way, the confrontation in Edo concluded without any immediate problems for Tetsugen, but also without any sense of resolution for the True Pure Land believers. What followed is unclear, but it seems that some True Pure Land Believers were so dissatisfied that no live debate took place that their anger continued to fester for some time. According to a True Pure Land text, the *San'yo zuihitsu* by Erin, Chikū initially began to study the *Śūramgama sutra* to prepare for his debate with Tetsugen, and then later lectured on the text himself. He refuted Tetsugen's interpretation of the scripture both in his public lectures and in his writings. The *San'yo zuihitsu* mentions a number of texts that seem to represent an ongoing written debate between Tetsugen and Chikū. While the texts attributed to Chikū are genuine, those attributed to Tetsugen are problematic. The first text attributed to Tetsugen, called *Hashaku hyōhan*, seems never to have existed at all; Ōbaku scholars have found no copies of the text, and I have not identified any external confirmation of its existence. The second text, entitled *Kōmori bōdanki*, did indeed circulate under Tetsugen's name, but its authorship remains controversial. The *Kōmori bōdanki* will be discussed at greater length in chapter 3.

Tetsugen clashed a second time with True Pure Land believers in Kyushu several years later. In 1674, Tetsugen returned to his native Kyushu to nurse his father through his final illness. Tetsugen then remained in Kyushu for several years, probably to fulfill the filial obligations related to his father's death. During that period, he traveled in the region, teaching at various temples and instructing government officials who extended invitations to him. In the winter of 1674, Kurushima Michikiyo (1629–1700), the *daimyō* of Bungo province, who had known and supported Ōbaku masters for many years, invited Tetsugen to lecture in the castle town of Mori. Tetsugen repeated his sermons on the *Śūramgama sutra* at the Kurushima family temple at Anrakuji,[33] starting at the beginning of the eleventh month.

Within a few days of the lecture series opening, a group of True Pure Land believers from neighboring villages gathered to plan a response to Tetsugen's lectures. They approached the administrator of temples and shrines, Ōbayashi Sebei, and demanded permission to debate with Tetsugen at Anrakuji. They claimed that both Tetsugen and Kengan Zen'etsu were evil monks who regularly slandered their sect when reading the *Śūramgama sutra*.[34] No doubt they were likewise familiar with the previous events in Edo, perhaps through Chikū's writings. The administrator confirmed that Tetsugen was indeed reading the scripture, but denied their request for debate on the grounds that Tetsugen was not attacking the True Pure Land sect. All information regarding the incident in Mori is based on Tetsugen's official affidavit and subsequent correspondence addressed to Lord Kurushima, which are included in the translation section.

Tensions did not abate within the True Pure Land community after the initial request for a public debate was refused. The protest spread and several True Pure Land temples in the area became involved, including Senkōji, Kōrinji, and Kōtokuji in the city of Mori, and Shōrenji in the nearby town of Hita. The believers in Kyushu were in contact with the main temple in Kyoto, and a subsequent request for permission to debate came directly from the sectarian headquarters at Nishi Honganji. Tetsugen quoted the administrator's reply in his affadavit,

> Since Dharma debates are prohibited by law, you cannot have one. Furthermore, I myself have had the opportunity to listen to Tetsugen's sermons each day, and to the very end have not heard him disparage any sect at all. Even if you have your doubts about Tetsugen, there does exist in the sutra, as he said, such a thing as the Three Absolutes for all ears to hear. If you would like to question him about the contents of the *Śūramgama Sutra*, then you may go and ask him one by one. This is the etiquette for *mondō* in the Zen sect. If you question him in this manner, then even one thousand of you may ask questions.

The protestors were not satisfied with this option; they preferred to challenge Tetsugen en masse. By this time, a large number of believers had assembled at Kōtokuji, and they continued to press the administrator to concede to their demands. Finally, the protestors threatened that they would take matters into their own hands, charge Anrakuji and seize Tetsugen by force.

When the True Land protestors threatened to use force, the administrator consulted with Tetsugen and the other monks at Anrakuji. The provincial authorities took the threat of violence seriously, perhaps because True Pure Land believers had a history of violent uprisings in insurrections known as *Ikkō ikki*.[35] The provincial officials suggested to Tetsugen and the other monks that they discontinue the lecture series and disperse the monks who had gathered at Anrakuji to hear it. Although the monks felt that the threat was not serious and the sermons could continue, Tetsugen conceded to the wishes of the authorities and left Mori. He explained in his affidavit that he was concerned that since a crowd had already gathered, there was a genuine risk of something happening inadvertently. He believed that if he left, "things would probably quiet down by themselves, the way a fire goes out when it lacks kindling."

Tetsugen feared that even a small disturbance would necessarily entail the direct involvement by the Tokugawa government and that this would cause Lord Kurushima undue anxiety. Moreover, he believed that an angry exchange of words with the True Pure Land believers would be inappropriate behavior for a Buddhist monk, especially one claiming to preach on the *Śūramgama sutra*. "Now, if I were to firmly set up a distinction between self and other and strongly argue over right and wrong even though I was lecturing on the

Śūramgama sutra, it would be like striking my mother's face with the Book of Filial Piety.... If I did not swiftly withdraw, but set up self-conceit and fought back, then it would have been like confronting a dream with a dream, or fighting bubbles with bubbles."

Tetsugen left Anrakuji before dawn on the 27th day of the 11th month 1674 without completing his lectures. The first portion of the trip out of Mori entailed traversing difficult mountain terrain, and Kurushima's retainers wanted to take no risk of Tetsugen being kidnapped. In order to insure Tetsugen's safety, the provincial officials sent a military escort of ten soldiers to accompany him as far as the coast. From the port of Kashiranashi, Tetsugen traveled on by boat to Tsuruzaki accompanied by only two soldiers. Lord Hosokawa had a villa in Tsuruzaki, and Tetsugen stayed there for a time, probably composing his official statement for Lord Kurushima during this visit. According to a story that later circulated among Tetsugen's disciples, Tetsugen was poisoned by some True Pure Land believers while he was staying in Tsuruzaki. According to the tradition, poison was put in Tetsugen's tea and cake and he never fully recovered from its effects. For this reason, it is said that his descendents never offered tea and bean cakes before his image.[36] There is no historical evidence to confirm the tradition.

Soon after Tetsugen left Mori, the provincial authorities arrested and imprisoned two True Pure Land priests whom they regarded as the ringleaders of the incident. Punishment for disturbing the peace and inciting a riot would normally have been death, but the monks were saved by Tetsugen's intervention on their behalf. Tetsugen and Kurushima had been in contact by post in the weeks following the incident, and Tetsugen learned of the arrest from Kurushima himself. The text of Kurushima's letter does not seem to have been preserved, but Tetsugen makes reference to it in his own letter. (Letter to Kurushima) In this response to Kurushima, dated the sixth day of the first month, Tetsugen asked that the monks be pardoned and their lives spared.

> Since what occurred at that time concerned the Dharma, it is distinct from worldly matters. I would be still more grateful to you if you would pardon their offenses and restore them to their previous positions.... Although nothing happened and no crime was committed, after the event took place, it seemed as if a crime had occurred.... I pray that in your great wisdom you will realize that this error was without root, and restore the two temples to peace. (Letter to Kurushima)

Tetsugen's compassion moved Kurushima, and in his reply of the 16th day of the first month, he agreed to abide by Tetsugen's wishes.[37] The Mori incident was thus resolved without any injury or subsequent penalties. There are no indications of any other direct encounters between Tetsugen and True Pure Land believers.

Scholars do not agree whether or not Tetsugen intentionally or directly attacked True Pure Land practice and belief in his lectures in Edo and Mori.[38]

Whether Tetsugen intentionally provoked the True Pure Land believers is impossible to determine from the sources. Regarding the Edo incident, only True Pure Land descriptions exist, while for the Mori incident only Tetsugen's accounts exist. What is quite clear in all the sources is that True Pure Land believers perceived an intentional attack. Descriptions of Tetsugen's encounter with Kūsei suggest that, when challenged, Tetsugen overwhelmed his opponent with the force of his argument. Tetsugen was known for his rhetorical skills, so it would be no surprise if he had proven himself a formidable opponent in debate. According to Tetsugen's own account of the second incident, the True Pure Land believers misunderstood his intentions because he was lecturing on the *Śūraṃgama sutra*. "When they heard I was reading this sort of thing, they thought I was slandering the Ikkō sect. On the contrary, I was not disparaging them at all. This is just the way the Buddha transmitted his precepts." In this case, Tetsugen maintained that he withdrew precisely in order to avoid any inappropriate fighting within the Buddhist sangha and to prevent even the possibility of violence. As Minamoto observes, regardless of Tetsugen's attitude and intentions, the images and themes in the *Śūraṃgama sutra* alone could have incensed his opponents.[39]

Tetsugen's own description of his sermons on the *Śūraṃgama sutra* included in his affidavit indicates the themes that proved most offensive to the True Pure Land believers. Tetsugen paid close attention to the sutra's discussion of the "three absolutes" (*sanjō*) of Buddhist practice, namely, the precepts, meditation, and wisdom.[40]

> I lectured first of all about the good and evil of the False Dharma and the True Dharma in the Final Age, which are referred to as the Three Absolutes in the *Śūraṃgama Sutra*. Those who practice without keeping the precepts set out by the Buddha all represent the False Dharma. The reason for this [is as follows:] Although practices such as chanting the *Nembutsu*, seated meditation, and reciting the sutras are each practiced differently depending on the abilities of the believer, the precepts against taking life, stealing, sexual misconduct, lying and the like are absolute, regardless of the sect. Not to keep them is unacceptable. Therefore these precepts are called "absolutes."

In the sections that follow, Tetsugen considered the consequences of breaking the precepts enumerated above. In doing so, Tetsugen's words parallel those found in the sutra so closely, that he did little more than render the original text in straightforward Japanese. Tetsugen is no more adamant nor definitive than the sutra itself in stressing the necessity for keeping the precepts as the basis of Buddhist practice.

In keeping with the fundamental approach of the *Śūraṃgama sutra*, Tetsugen stressed the necessity for all Buddhists to keep the Buddhist precepts as the first step in their progress along the path to enlightenment. By doing so, he rejected the common belief prevalent within Pure Land schools of Buddhism that during the final age of the Dharma (*mappō*) keeping the precepts had become impossible and even detrimental to the believer.[41] It was perhaps Tetsugen's identity as a former True Pure Land believer more than anything else that led his opponents to see his sermons as direct attacks on their sect. Tetsugen took the words of the sutra to heart in his own life; he had left the one sect that permitted and encouraged married clergy and turned to Ōbaku Zen, which emphasized strictly maintaining the precepts.

MUAN'S DHARMA HEIR

Tetsugen visited with Zen master Muan whenever he was traveling in the Kyoto area. In this way, despite his activities related to the scripture project, Tetsugen continued to submit his understanding of the Dharma to Muan, seeking to make progress in his own practice of Zen. Shortly after his first lecture trip to Edo in 1670, Tetsugen made one such visit. A detailed account of the visit, reportedly written in Muan's own hand, was preserved.

> Chief Librarian[42] Tetsugen lectured on the *Śūramgama sutra.* When [the lectures] were finished, he climbed Mount [Ōbaku Mampukuji] to pay his respects to the master. The master asked, "You look for the mind in the seven places, and in the eighth you still have discriminating sight. What is this mind? How do you see?" [Tetsugen] then responded, "This seeing and hearing are not seeing and hearing." The master said, "This is still dualistic seeing and dualistic mind." [Tetsugen] responded, "Still [text corrupted] one drop of water and ink together make a dragon." The master said, "Darkness far and wide." Tetsugen just bowed. The master said, "Once again, the way of seeing." Tetsugen replied [with a verse]:
>
> > The wind blows in the blue sky
> > The floating clouds have disappeared
> > The moon rises over the blue mountains
> > A single round jewel.
>
> The master said, "Your vision is blurry. Your eyes are confused by delusionary flowers." Tetsugen gave a shout. The master said, "I am defeated."[43]

In this encounter, Muan challenged Tetsugen to express his understanding by drawing a passage directly from the preface to the *Śūramgama sutra,* "You look for the mind in the seven places, and in the eighth you still have discriminating sight."[44] Muan's mention of blurry vision and delusionary flowers later in the exchange is likewise an allusion to the *Śūramgama sutra.* Throughout the sutra, the Buddha likens mistaken views of reality with visions of flowers caused by either cataracts or exhaustion.[45] The exchange suggests that, although Muan was not yet ready to acknowledge Tetsugen's attainment, he was pleased with Tetsugen's progress.

Sometime after the incident in Mori, probably early in the year 1676, Tetsugen returned to the Kyoto area. At that time, he paid a visit on Muan at

Mampukuji and received Muan's *inka*, or designation as a Dharma heir. The passage from the *Deeds of Tetsugen* says simply, "At the time of [Tetsugen and Muan's] *mondō*, their understanding of the kōan was in perfect agreement, and for the first time [Tetsugen] received the seal of the [Buddha] mind *(shin'in)*."[46] Other texts, including Muan's recorded sayings and Gaochuan's introduction to the Preserved Writings of Tetsugen (*Tetsugen Zenji Yuiroku*), provide additional details about the encounter. Gaochuan wrote, "One day, [Tetsugen] entered Master Muan's room. During their *mondō*, the master joyfully bestowed his seal, saying, "Henceforth I shall call you the monk who lectures on the sutras."[47] By far the most detailed account comes from Muan's recorded sayings which provides the gist of their conversation:

> When Tetsugen, the Chief Librarian, returned from Higo, he paid his respects [to Master Muan] at the main temple and said, "I wish to lecture on the *Lotus Sutra* and so repay my debt of gratitude [to my father]."[48] The master held up his whisk and said, "You wish to lecture on the *Lotus Sutra*. In the sutra there is [the verse], 'Do not depart from the four comfortable actions *(shianrakugyō)*.'[49] Do you understand this?" Tetsugen said, "I understand." The master said, "What do you understand?" Tetsugen replied, "Going, coming, sitting and lying down are not separate from this." The master said, "Try another verse." Tetsugen gave a shout *(katsu)*. The master said, "Henceforth I shall call you the monk who lectures on the sutras." Then he held up his whisk, and presented it to Tetsugen saying, "Here is my whisk." Tetsugen bowed once more.[50]

As is often the case in the Zen sect, the bestowal of the master's whisk during an exchange symbolizes the transmission of the Dharma from master to disciple. From that time forward, Tetsugen was free to transmit the Dharma to any of his disciples whom he deemed fit.

The above *mondō* and the earlier exchange quoted above suggest that Muan drew his teaching devices for Tetsugen from the very same sutras about which Tetsugen lectured in public. This would be in keeping with the general Ōbaku preference to draw kōan from the immediate context of the disciple's life rather than relying predominantly on traditional kōan collections. In the earlier case, Muan indicated that Tetsugen's understanding was still dualistic; although he accepted Tetsugen's subsequent verse, he was not completely satisfied. This was not the case in the later exchange. Based on all three versions of Tetsugen receiving *inka* quoted above, Muan appears to have been pleased with Tetsugen's response. Although Tetsugen did not compose an enlightenment verse at the time, Muan's action clearly indicated confirmation of Tetsugen's understanding. With the possible exception of Muan's comment about "the monk who lectures on the sutras," there is nothing especially unusual about the exchange in relation to other accounts of monks receiving *inka* from Muan.[51]

The official Ōbaku lineage charts indicate that Tetsugen became Muan's Dharma heir in the spring of 1676, and that he never designated a Dharma heir of his own. There has never been any question within the Ōbaku sect about the validity of Tetsugen's inheritance of the Dharma. There would have been no further discussion of the matter had not a former disciple called it into question. Twenty years after Tetsugen's death, Tangen Genshu (b. 1644) authored a text which questioned the depth of Tetsugen's enlightenment experience and the nature of his Dharma reception. Attacks of this kind on the validity of an enlightenment experience are not uncommon within the Zen world, since this is an effective way to undermine the authority of an individual or an entire lineage. The questions raised by Tangen almost certainly influenced Hōshū's portrait of Tetsugen in the *Deeds of Tetsugen* and persist in the modern literature.

In 1702, Tangen wrote in the *Zen'aku jamyōron*[52] (An account of the good and evil of a wicked life) that Tetsugen had resolved before he died that he would not transmit his Dharma to any of his disciples, even though he conceded that some of them were advanced enough to be designated as Zen masters. Tetsugen reportedly based his decision on his own misgivings concerning his inheritance of the Dharma; according to Tangen, Tetsugen expressed deep regret that he had received Muan's *inka*, and he did not wish to contribute to the debasement of a Dharma lineage of worthy masters by continuing the line himself. According to Tangen, Tetsugen had been so preoccupied with lecturing and publishing the Buddhist scriptures throughout his life, that he had not taken the time to diligently practice Zen. For this reason, he never fully attained enlightenment and his understanding remained inadequate. Although he was held in high esteem by others, he knew his own failings and therefore chose to die without an heir.[53] A detailed comparison of Tangen's remarks with the version of Tetsugen's final instructions found in the *Deeds of Tetsugen* will be taken up later in the context of discussing Tetsugen's death. At this juncture, Tangen's remarks are relevant primarily because of the debates they have generated among modern scholars.

The Ōbaku sectarian scholar Akamatsu initiated a dispute among modern scholars over whether or not Tetsugen was truly enlightened when he took issue with Tangen's claims to argue that Tetsugen had indeed attained enlightenment.[54] Minamoto took an opposing stand, arguing that Tetsugen was not truly enlightened. Minamoto accepted Tangen's version of events as reasonably reliable, and then drew on various other source materials, including Tetsugen's poetry, letters, and the account of his *mondō* with Muan, to further bolster the case against enlightenment.[55] Schwaller likewise participated in the debate; based on his reading of the *mondō*, Schwaller concluded that Tetsugen was not an enlightened Zen master.[56]

THE MONK WHO LECTURES ON THE SUTRAS

Setting aside the issue of enlightenment, discussions generated by Tangen's writing have also touched on interpretations of Muan's attitude toward Tetsugen, relying on close readings of the historical texts. Tangen himself did not directly question Muan's motivations for conferring *inka* on Tetsugen, but modern scholars have moved the discussion in that direction. Akamatsu based his argument against Tangen on the validity of Muan's *inka*, which in his view could not be challenged. The underlying theme of Minamoto and Schwaller's argument concerning Tetsugen's enlightenment is precisely to attack Muan's transmission of the Dharma to Tetsugen. Neither scholar believes that Muan could have transmitted his Dharma to Tetsugen solely based on the answers reportedly given in the *mondō*. Minamoto harshly criticizes Muan in his assessment of the situation, maintaining that Muan did not fulfill his obligation toward Tetsugen as his Zen master. He suggests that Muan was feeling pressured to reward Tetsugen for his remarkable success with publishing the scriptures and that Tetsugen, in turn, accepted the whisk only as an expedient means to further the scripture project. Minamoto bases this argument on a quotation that he attributes to Mujaku Dōchu from the *Ōbaku geki* which says that Tetsugen at first refused the whisk and only accepted it for the sake of the project.[57] This quotation does not appear in the version of the *Ōbaku geki* preserved at Myōshinji, which is written in Mujaku's own hand.[58] Minamoto apparently used an alternative copy; the story therefore may have been a later interpolation, perhaps one based on Tangen's *Zen'aku jamyōron*. Minamoto comments that Muan's apparent act of kindness actually robbed Tetsugen of any real chance to attain enlightenment and thereby become a genuine Dharma heir.[59]

Both Minamoto and Dieter Schwaller have argued that Muan's true attitude toward Tetsugen is apparent in the short passage describing their *mondō*. They assert that the title Muan gave Tetsugen, "the monk who lectures on the sutras," was in fact a form of criticism that demonstrated Muan's scorn for Tetsugen's level of understanding.[60] Schwaller suggests that these words lessened the value of the *inka* by indicating that Tetsugen's answers were still too bookish.[61] On the other hand, one can argue that the words were spoken and understood at the time as a form of sincere praise not only for Tetsugen's abilities as a preacher, but for his hard work and success in raising considerable sums of money by means of that preaching.

Muan did not speak his words in a context in which it was assumed that Zen masters held a negative attitude toward the scriptures and to their explication, as is sometimes assumed in Zen circles today. The Ōbaku tradition took a very positive attitude toward the scriptures, as evidenced by the sect's overall support for and participation in Tetsugen's scripture project. Moreover, if the words had suggested an element of scorn at the time, it seems unlikely that Gaochuan would have repeated them in his introduction to the *Yuiroku*, which was meant to praise Tetsugen posthumously. Gaochuan states that Muan spoke the words "joyfully," an attitude in keeping with the bestowal of *inka*.

Lecturing on the sutras did not, in fact, distinguish Tetsugen from other Japanese Zen masters of his time. As observed earlier, Tetsugen had learned some of his lecturing skills from the Rinzai monk Kengan Zen'etsu who held public lecture series on the Śūramgama *sutra* at his home temple. It was not uncommon for the abbots at large Zen temples to commemorate a special event by holding a public lecture series on a particular sutra or to invite a visiting master to do so. Such lectures were intended to promote Buddhism among the populace as well as to educate other Buddhist monks and nuns. The Chinese Ōbaku masters did not, to my knowledge, ever hold such public lectures, but this was probably due to the practical limitations of language rather than any philosophical stance. What was perhaps unusual in Tetsugen's case was that he held lectures long before he had attained the status of master. However, as seen in his meeting with Muan in 1676, Tetsugen sought and received explicit permission to do so from his master at least on some occasions. It is also likely that his methods for raising funds were approved by Yinyuan and Muan at the beginning of the project.

TETSUGEN'S SOCIAL WELFARE ACTIVITIES

Throughout his career, Tetsugen performed a variety of services for lay believers, some of which can only be described as social welfare activities. Buddhism encourages two distinct patterns of service: lay believers should provide compassionately for the physical needs of their neighbors and Buddhist monastics as a natural outgrowth of their own religious practice, while Buddhist monks and nuns should serve the religious needs of other sentient beings. Within Buddhist societies, this typically leads to relationships of mutual aid between lay Buddhists and members of the monastic community, in which the laity supplies monks with food, clothing, and other essentials, and monks reciprocate by teaching the people. By the very act of accepting lay donations, monks offer believers the opportunity to build merit, an important element of lay Buddhist practice. Tetsugen fulfilled the more conventional monastic functions vis-á-vis lay believers by instructing individuals through private meetings and Dharma lessons (*hōgo*), lecturing in public, and providing laypeople with the possibility of participating in the meritorious project of printing the scriptures.

By virtue of their religious merit, Buddhist monks were traditionally believed to have greater spiritual capabilities to serve the lay community. They regularly performed memorial services for the deceased, and were sometimes called on to help the sick or those possessed by spirits through prayers of intercession. In one notable example, described in the *Deeds of Tetsugen*, Tetsugen relieved the suffering of a deceased woman whose vengeful spirit had possessed a relative. Of course, such activities can still be understood as meeting the religious needs of others. However, Buddhists did not necessarily draw the somewhat artificial distinction between physical and religious needs. In extraordinary situations, the monastic community might well have provided other sorts of services based on its members' technical expertise in nonreligious fields, their ability to harness broad social support for a project, or their ties to the secular authorities. Japanese monks participated in projects such as building bridges, reclaiming arable land for farming, and other secular activities.

Tetsugen likewise sought to alleviate physical suffering, when it was within his power to do so. For example, according to the *Deeds of Tetsugen*, Tetsugen held a ceremony in 1655, in which he used a *dharani* from the *Śūramgama sutra* to bring rain during a drought in Kyushu. Specific examples of this type of work mentioned in the biography probably represent numerous events of a similar variety left unmentioned.

In the closing sections of the *Deeds of Tetsugen*, Hōshū wrote a short description of his master's accomplishments, praising his intellectual abilities, his deep understanding of Buddhism, his skill at guiding disciples, and his compassion for laypeople. In this context, Hōshū lists without details a number of social welfare activities that Tetsugen had carried out.

> [Tetsugen] distributed food and clothing to the poor and satisfied each one's desire. He provided medicine for the sick without leaving them alone in their homes. When he saw an abandoned child on the road, he would entrust it into someone's care and have him feed and rear the child. When he encountered prisoners on the road, he would petition the authorities to request their release.

There is no historical data to illustrate how Tetsugen cared for abandoned children, although this task did often fall to Buddhist monks. As for petitioning officials for the pardon of criminals, Hōshū mentioned earlier in the biography that Tetsugen intervened with the authorities and successfully petitioned to have ten death sentences commuted. Hōshū illustrated this with one outstanding example, which also appears in external sources: A servant in Osaka had falsely accused another servant of poisoning their master, and the authorities had jailed the accused. Tetsugen appealed for the servant's release, offering to bear the punishment himself if any concrete evidence of the man's guilt were to surface. As a result of Tetsugen's efforts, the authorities pardoned the servant and freed him. External evidence verifies that Tetsugen became involved in such a case, and that he was not universally applauded for doing so. A passage from the *Wakan taihei kōki* criticizes Tetsugen for his interference in the workings of justice.

> Although Buddhism is widely regarded as philanthropic, pardoning terribly evil people is just second guessing Amida. Recently, a monk made it his business to have just such a wicked person pardoned. By doing so, he injured the [workings] of government. If one's sympathy and pity arise from friendship, then that is fine. But when one wishes to pit one's own law against that of the brilliant government, then that must be regarded as a sickness. Last year in Osaka, Settsu [province], there was a case of a servant poisoning his master. At that time the servant, brazenly thinking that he could take everyone in, had his father consult with the monk Tetsugen. Tetsugen did not inquire about the seriousness of the crime, but devised a clever plan and had the death sentence pardoned. What sort of person is this Tetsugen? He is a follower of

the Ōbaku monk Yinyuan who schemed along with his followers. Doesn't he realize that you can't pardon every criminal? I just heard about this and can't stop thinking about it.[62]

TETSUGEN'S WORK IN THE FAMINE OF 1681–1682

The Ōbaku edition of the Buddhist scriptures came to completion in 1680, and Tetsugen carried a complete copy to Edo, along with a dedication letter addressed to the shōgun. Tetsugen planned to present the copy to the shōgun and apply for permission from the government to commence printing and distribution of the scriptures. While Tetsugen waited in Edo in 1681 for the government to respond, a terrible famine ravaged the entire Osaka and Kyoto region. According to the *Eiran gyōjōki* (An Account of the Conduct for Imperial Inspection),[63] Tetsugen heard of the famine in the first month of 1682, and decided to return immediately to Osaka to undertake the direction of a famine relief project. To that end, Tetsugen approached one of the *daimyō* well known to him and borrowed a large sum of money, one thousand *ryō* of gold, before leaving the capital. The identity of the *daimyō* is not given in the *Eiran gyōjōki*, but it was most likely Lord Hosokawa, the lord of Higo province, who was always very generous with Tetsugen and other Ōbaku monks. Tetsugen then returned to Zuiryūji in great haste, traveling the 500 kilometers between Edo and Osaka in only ten days. He set up a food distribution center at his home temple, and word soon reached the hungry throughout Osaka that they could come there daily for assistance.[64]

Our knowledge of Tetsugen's work during the famine is quite detailed thanks to his own dramatic account of it. Within a month of his return to Osaka, Tetsugen could see that the famine was so extensive that his resources would not suffice for long. He wrote a lengthy letter beseeching a wealthy merchant in Edo, Yamazaki Hanzaemon, to donate additional funds (Letter to Yamazaki). Yamazaki was a lay patron of Tetsugen's scripture project, but little else is known about him. The letter is an invaluable resource of information not only about the famine and Tetsugen's social welfare work, but also as an aid for understanding Tetsugen's attitudes regarding the Buddhist principle of compassion.

Tetsugen's letter is unusual for a number of reasons. First, Tetsugen described the suffering that he witnessed in more graphic detail than one would normally expect to find in a letter. Rather than employing the more typical style of suggestion, Tetsugen paints both the suffering and the filth in gruesome detail.

> It is difficult to describe the situation in words. Some of the people are nearly 70 or 80 years old, leaning on staffs, but they find it difficult to relinquish their lives. Others are children of five or three years, dragged along by the hand by their mothers. Some wear a begging bowl. Some wear straw matting. Some of

the sick or blind have not washed their hands even once in a year's time. Their
hands look as if they had seven or eight coats of lacquer on them. There are
some who haven't eaten anything in ten days, and so [their stomachs] have
become swollen and distended. Others have gotten so thin that they are nothing but skin and bones. Truly, the path of hungry ghosts [appears] before my
eyes and [I see] human beings living in hell. . . . They have more lice on their
bodies that there are sesame seeds in an oil shop. If we thrust into the crowd
even slightly to keep them from pushing, the lice move onto our robes, and
[hang there] like so many suspended sesame seeds. When I tried to distribute
[alms] personally, fifty of those "lacquered" hands grabbed at me and pulled on
my hands. I cannot describe how foul their stench was upon my nostrils.

One may speculate that Tetsugen hoped to translate the horrors that he himself
had experienced so accurately that the images would likewise move his patrons
in Edo and motivate them to donate generously.

Second, stricken by the urgency of the situation, Tetsugen made direct,
even blunt requests for funding. He mentions the specific amount needed no
less than three times, twice directly and once with the indirect reference to the
amount previously donated for the scripture project.

Since this sort of situation is rare in one lifetime, or even in two lifetimes, I
ask you to give rise to a great belief in your own Buddha nature and to send
me funds in the amount of 200 *ryō* as mentioned above. I would like to immediately borrow 100 *ryō* from Konomu Saemon here in Osaka. I ask that
you directly reimburse him later. Although I imagine that raising the funds
will be difficult even for you, the situation here is beyond endurance, and so
I ask this of you.

Although this directness may not sound strange in translation, it is highly ir-
regular in a Japanese context. It would almost seem that Tetsugen wished his
patrons to regard feeding the destitute in such an emergency situation to be
analogous to producing the Ōbaku edition itself.

In the letter, Tetsugen illustrated his own dedication to saving the destitute with graphic expressions of determination. He expressed his intention to
continue even if it meant selling his temple or offering his own flesh and blood
as alms. According to the more popular accounts of Tetsugen's social welfare
work, he placed the immediate needs of people in distress ahead even of his
dedication to printing the scriptures, and used funds intended for the scripture
project to feed the poor. While this may not be historically accurate, it does
convey the intensity of his commitment. In the end, Tetsugen did, in a sense,
offer his life to the cause, dying during the relief efforts before the famine had
begun to ease.

As Tetsugen indicated in his letter, he started distributing alms on the 13th
day of the 2nd month 1682 as soon as he reached Zuiryūji. He began lecturing
on the *Awakening of Faith* a week later, on the 21st day of the 2nd month, in

order to raise additional funds. He followed the general pattern of lecturing and collecting funds in the morning and then distributing food and money after the noon hour. According to his own estimation, he and his disciples were then feeding ten thousand people each day. This continued for only a week before Tetsugen himself fell ill on the 29th day of the 2nd month. He continued to lecture as usual for as long as he was able, but his illness soon made that impossible. Within a week he took to his bed never to recover.

It is not known how long Tetsugen's disciples continued to feed the hungry, or how Yamazaki responded to Tetsugen's letter. Tetsugen died in the midst of the famine, at a time when the common people in the region had come to regard him as a sort of living Bodhisattva, calling him "the bodhisattva who saves the world." They paid tribute to him by attending his funeral in large numbers. If one is to believe the *Deeds of Tetsugen,* more than one hundred thousand people attended the ceremony on the day of his cremation, and "the sound of their wailing shook the forests."

TETSUGEN'S FINAL INSTRUCTIONS AND DEATH

The *Deeds of Tetsugen* provides no information regarding the nature of Tetsugen's final illness. Given that Tetsugen and his disciples were working among the poor and destitute, it seems likely that he contracted a disease associated with the famine. Natural disasters and famines were almost always accompanied by epidemics of communicable diseases of various sorts, and Tetsugen and the others came into close physical contact with hundreds of people each day in the process of distributing alms. It is known from other accounts that approximately thirty of Tetsugen's one hundred disciples resident at Zuiryūji also took ill at about the same time, and that four or five of them died as a result.[65] Tetsugen grew progressively weaker, gradually taking less and less food and drink. As the illness grew more grave, he refused the medicines urged on him by doctors, accepting that the illness would be terminal.

On the 7th day of the 3rd month 1682, Tetsugen summoned his closest disciples to divide his property among them and to give them his final instructions as was customary. According to Hōshū, Tetsugen said to them, "My work is finished. Fortunately, you will prosper through the years. Be careful not to become embroiled in worldly desires. Just continue on the Way, and moment by moment investigate the Great Matter. Such a one is my Dharma heir. Printing the scriptures spreads the wise commands of all the Buddhas. For that purpose, I endured great suffering, and now the [task] is complete. If you pass the scriptures on forever, then there is no need to say anything about my teachings." Tetsugen was more concerned that his disciples continue in the ongoing process of printing, binding and distributing the scriptures throughout Japan than that they preserve his own teachings. He did not name a Dharma heir on his deathbed as many masters taken ill suddenly would. Instead, the Ōbaku edition was the only Dharma that Tetsugen chose to transmit.

On the twenty-second day of the same month, Tetsugen wrote a final verse and passed away peacefully. The verse read,

> Fifty-three years of falling down seven times and being thrown down eight times.
> Mistakenly discussing wisdom,
> My sins piled up to the heavens.
> Peacefully floating on a sea of the lotuses,
> I tread through the water across heaven.

According to Hōshū, Tetsugen fulfilled his own prophecy, made in Edo less than three months previously, that he would die by the end of spring. His body was cremated on the third day, with many high-ranking monks and masses of the common people attending the services. Tetsugen's remains were eventually buried in the Western corner of the grounds at Hōzōin, expressing his disciples' belief that the master would never forget the Buddhist scriptures.

Although Hōshū did not mention Tetsugen's instructions for the continued maintenance of his temples, Tangen, the disciple who later rejected Ōbaku and wrote critically of Tetsugen and Hōshū, explained his understanding of Tetsugen's wishes on that score. Tangen claimed that instead of establishing his lineage by transmitting his Dharma to one or more advanced disciple, thus placing his temples under a Dharma heir's guidance, Tetsugen preferred to set up his eight temples as *heisōji*, that is, temples where no monk has attained the rank of master. According to Tangen's account, Tetsugen decided that he would not transmit his Dharma due to his own sense of unworthiness. Tangen observed,

> Throughout his life, [Tetsugen] was, without pause, constantly preoccupied with lecturing and printing the Buddhist scriptures. Although he did this for the sake of the Dharma, his own careful practice and true understanding were deficient, notwithstanding the high reputation and fame of his teaching style. Therefore in his dying verse, he expressed his true feelings with the line, "Fifty-three years of falling down seven times and stumbling eight times". . . .
> He said that in the end he could have made Hōshū, Jikai and Unshū his Dharma heirs, but he feared that this would diminish the virtue of previous masters, so he did not.[66]

According to Tangen, Tetsugen refrained from naming an heir to preserve Muan's line from any deterioration caused by his own shortcomings as a master.

In assessing the relative value of Tangen's observations, there are a number of factors to bear in mind. First, Tangen was a disciple of Tetsugen for many years, having joined him at the time of Tetsugen's first lecture series in Edo in 1669. He had the opportunity to observe firsthand Tetsugen's work and practice over a period of about twelve years. Tangen was present at Zuiryūji when Tetsugen lay dying, although he was not a part of Tetsugen's inner circle of disciples. Tangen remained a part of the Zuiryūji community for several years after Tetsugen's death. He, therefore, had direct experience on which to base his observations about Tetsugen and his assembly. On the other hand, Tangen wrote the *Zen'aku jamyōron* explicitly for the purpose of discrediting Hōshū, who emerged as the new leader at Zuiryūji. Tangen penned the work sometime after Hōshū had expelled him, and Tangen had permanently broken with the Ōbaku sect. For this reason, one may assume that his account was heavily biased against Hōshū. While this does not necessarily mean that he fabricated the whole episode of Tetsugen's dying instructions, he would certainly have presented whatever he knew of Hōshū in the worst possible light. Discrediting a monk by disparaging his master would not have been an unusual response. Moreover, Tangen did not claim to have been present when Tetsugen gathered his closest disciples to explain his last wishes; he maintained that Tetsugen only revealed his decision to cut off his Dharma line to his three dearest disciples, including Hōshū. Tangen did not hear Tetsugen's explanation himself, and his version is in direct conflict with Hōshū's, the only eyewitness account recorded. We are therefore faced with balancing the merits of one account written to discredit the leading disciple and his master, with another written to praise Tetsugen and preserve the reputation of his disciples.

There is, in fact, one letter from Tetsugen addressed to Hōshū that sheds some light on Tetsugen's attitude toward his disciples and the matter of bestowing *inka* on any one of them. Unfortunately, although the letter is a New Year's greeting sent to Zuiryūji while Tetsugen was away, it is otherwise undated. The content suggests that at the time of its writing the scripture project was either completed or near completion, and that Tetsugen was already contemplating his approaching death. Therefore, it is possible that he composed it in Edo in 1682, a few months before his passing. There is, however, no concrete evidence to definitively establish the date. In the text of the letter, Tetsugen indicated that he was indeed seeking a worthy Dharma heir and, at the same time, expressed some regrets about his own attainments. He lamented in his opening remarks, "My one concern is that my Dharma will decline like a temple in the late autumn. If only I could find one person or even half a person who possesses the eye of Zen practice" (Letter to Hōshū). The sentiment expressed here does not suggest dismay with himself or his own unworthiness to transmit the Dharma, but rather a concern for his disciples' progress or lack thereof. Tetsugen indicated that the basic problem with Zen practitioners in his day was that they lacked the quality of selflessness, they "seek only their own enlightenment and fall into the demon's cave [of ignorance and attachment]" (Letter to Hōshū). In Tetsugen's opinion, just the opposite was true of Hōshū whom he regarded as a truly rare individual. In the body of the letter, Tetsugen wrote what amounts to a *hōgo*, or Dharma lesson, encouraging Hōshū to persevere in his practice and take the final and crucial step toward enlightenment. Then in his closing remarks, Tetsugen became self-reflective.

Although I have not yet attained the land of the ancient [masters], still I have not deteriorated into the rut of today's [masters]. My only regret is that the responsibilities for carving the [wood blocks for] the scriptures was heavy and producing the volumes complex. So I have been pulled by karmic connections and have not attained freedom. Now I am old and for the first time I realize my mistake.

These comments may well have been the basis for Tangen's remarks about Tetsugen's assessment of his own attainments and his regrets about his laxity in Zen practice over the years. However, the letter does not support his contention that Tetsugen had determined not to name a Dharma heir regardless of his disciples' progress.

TETSUGEN'S DISCIPLES

Most of Tetsugen's disciples stayed on at either Zuiryūji or Hōzōin in the years immediately following Tetsugen's death and continued to work on the scripture project as Tetsugen had wished. There is no indication in any of the sources that Tetsugen explicitly encouraged his disciples to seek the guidance of another Zen master such as Muan, but this would have been the normal course of action for them to take. We know that Hōshū turned to Muan, and that he became Muan's Dharma heir a few years later in 1684. This elevated Hōshū in the Ōbaku lineage from Tetsugen's disciple to his Dharma brother, but Hōshū continued to revere Tetsugen throughout his life as his former teacher. Although Tetsugen could not technically be accepted as the founder of the Zuiryū line, a lineage officially traced back to Muan through Hōshū, Hōshū and the others saw to it that Tetsugen was honored nonetheless. Even today, Tetsugen's image is given preeminence over Hōshū's at Hōzōin.

Hōshū took it on himself to complete Tetsugen's final, unfinished task in the scripture project by officially submitting the Ōbaku edition to the government officials in Edo. He also honored his former master by editing the *The Dharma Lesson in Japanese by Zen Master Tetsugen* (*Tetsugen zenji kana hōgo*) and the *The Preserved Writings of Tetsugen* (*Yuiroku*), a short collection of Tetsugen's other writings, in 1691. He later wrote the *Deeds of Tetsugen* in 1714 to mark the thirty-third anniversary of Tetsugen's death.

After Hōshū became a Zen master in his own right, he assumed a position of authority as the master at Tetsugen's temples. Hōshū thus effectively changed the temples' status from that of *heisōji* to temples with a designated head monk, an action that some disciples felt contravened Tetsugen's dying wishes. Several of Tetsugen's former disciples, perhaps as many as half of the original number,[67] accepted Hōshū as their master. Some of the others left the assembly at this time in protest to the change.[68]

Tetsugen's disciples published his writings and kept his story alive with written biographies, but the Ōbaku edition continued to be his true legacy for many generations, as he would have wished. For more than two hundred years after his death, the Ōbaku sect continued to print the Ōbaku edition of the Buddhist scriptures, and it served as the primary edition of the scriptures throughout Japan until the modern period. It was superceded as the standard Japanese edition only in the twentieth century with the modern publication of the Taishō edition. A detailed account of the scripture project is taken up in the next chapter.

CHAPTER TWO

Carving the Scriptures

Tetsugen's most significant contribution to the Buddhist world of his day was the Ōbaku edition of the Buddhist scriptures. By means of that massive undertaking, Tetsugen provided practical support for the "back to the original sources" trend that characterized many of the intellectual movements throughout the Tokugawa period. The scripture project spanned more than twelve years, from 1667 until 1680. Tetsugen enlisted assistance not only from his disciples, but his Dharma brothers and superiors within the Ōbaku monastic community. Tetsugen, who came to the monastic life with minimal personal economic resources, financed the project by appealing to Japanese lay people for donations, rather than seeking official government sponsorship. Although this approach required more time and footwork on his part, it fulfilled another goal that Tetsugen voiced, to provide a means for lay people to build merit and establish a connection with the Buddhist Dharma. In this way, the scriptures could serve as "curative medicine" even for those who were unable or unlikely to read the texts for themselves.

THE BUDDHIST SCRIPTURES IN JAPAN

From the time Buddhism was introduced to Japan in the sixth century, Japanese Buddhists dealt with the sutras somewhat differently than Chinese Buddhists. As a result of these differences, the Japanese faced serious problems related to availability of the sutras by the early Tokugawa period. The scriptures came to Japan piecemeal from China and Korea, just as they had poured gradually into China from India and Central Asia. Unlike the Chinese, however, the Japanese did not begin the long process of translating the scriptures into their native tongue, and so did not produce a Japanese version of the scriptures until the modern period.[1] Instead, having adopted Chinese as the written language of the religious and political realms, they used Chinese translations of the scriptures, sometimes marking the texts for easier reading, and thus accepted the Chinese version as their canon.

Individual sutras that were important to one or more Buddhist sects such as the *Lotus Sutra* were copied on a regular basis and were therefore widely available. On the other hand, sutras in less demand could be very difficult to find, except at a temple that possessed a complete edition of the Chinese Buddhist Scriptures. Since only a limited number of these complete editions existed in Japan, gaining access to one of them was a practical impossibility for many individual monks and scholars. At the beginning of the Tokugawa period, if a monk such as Tetsugen wished to study one of the less common sutras or to have access to a complete Chinese canon for research, he had to travel to a temple possessing a copy and request permission to use it. Generally speaking, that would entail a lengthy journey to Kyoto or Edo without any guarantee of success. Temples guarded their sutras like any other rare treasure, and many monks were turned away disappointed.

In China, woodblock editions of the complete Chinese Buddhist scriptures became increasingly common starting in the tenth century when the first imperially sponsored edition, known as the Szechuan edition, was completed in 983. Successive generations of Chinese leaders sponsored a series of such editions, so that approximately twenty had appeared by the early seventeenth century, with at least three separate editions produced during the Ming dynasty alone.[2] Korean Buddhists had likewise produced two woodblock editions of the scriptures, in the eleventh and the thirteenth centuries, using Sung editions as their basis.[3] By contrast, the Japanese had not produced a single complete printed edition before the seventeenth century and were dependent on imported and handwritten copies alone.[4]

The Japanese naturally accepted the traditional Buddhist concept that transmitting and copying the sutras was a meritorious endeavor. They made handwritten copies of individual sutras, especially such important scriptures as the *Heart sutra* or the *Lotus sutra*, as a part of their religious practice. They treasured editions of the Chinese canon that had been brought to Japan from China or Korea, usually by monks returning from years of study abroad or by émigrés. Plans had periodically arisen to produce a Japanese woodblock edition, but none of these attempts ever came to fruition before the early Tokugawa period. In the seventeenth century, several factors converged to make the time ripe for a Japanese edition, and two editions were successfully completed within a few decades of one another.

First, Japanese Buddhists came to feel the need for ready access to the scriptures more acutely in the early seventeenth century than at any previous time. Under the stable conditions of peace and economic development, and with the steady encouragement of the central and provincial governments, Buddhist monks turned their attention more and more fully to scholarship. In much the same way that scholars in other fields were rediscovering and emphasizing a return to basic sources, Buddhist scholars of all sects came to stress the need for scriptural studies. The bulk of this research took place first in Kyoto and then in Edo, where monks and nuns gathered from all over the country to study and hear lectures. Educational institutes associated with the main monasteries of most sects were established in one or both major cities. The sutras were more readily available in Kyoto than in other regions of the country, but even there the situation was by no means convenient due to the heavy demand for limited resources. Once scholars left Kyoto and returned to their home provinces, they might easily find themselves with access to nothing beyond their own personal library. As one sees in Tetsugen's essays on the subject, monks from the Kyushu area discussed this problem with their colleagues from other temples when they gathered for important lectures. Tetsugen observed in the "An Opportunity for Instruction" (*Keen no so*),

> From the middle of last autumn, I gave a lecture series on the *Lotus Sutra* here at Kōtokusan Ryūchōin in the castle town of Kumamoto. The audience gathered like banks of clouds, and participants lined up like so many stars. High-ranking monks from various temples, and Zen monks from the four directions strengthened their resolve to seek the scriptures from China, and so rain down that sweet nectar upon this nation Japan.

One can easily imagine similar discussions taking place throughout the country.

Second, the Japanese populace was becoming increasingly literate and the general social climate was conducive to supporting a major printing project like the Buddhist scriptures. Publishing rapidly became big business in Tokugawa Japan as literacy increased throughout the general population, and the number of works published each year rose significantly during the period. Scholars estimate that over 700 publishing firms were operating in Kyoto alone during the seventeenth century. By the end of the century, publishers produced close to 200 new titles each year, and Buddhist texts comprised the largest portion. Kyoto publishers, for example, listed some 2,796 Buddhist titles during the second half of the century alone.[5] A pool of skilled engravers who made their living carving woodblocks, paper craftsmen who were producing new types of paper especially suited for the purpose, as well as skilled printers and binders were readily available in the major printing centers, primarily Kyoto and Osaka. Various kinds of materials were published, from popular novels to scholarly treatises by Buddhist and Confucian thinkers. Not surprisingly, Buddhist subjects were the most common early on in the Tokugawa period, since literacy was strongest in the Buddhist world.[6] Even those who could not afford to purchase texts could sometimes rent them from lending libraries that spread in the major cities. Although the scriptures would not have appealed to the general public as reading material, enough people were familiar with published works for the project to be sensible to them.

The first complete Japanese edition of the Buddhist scriptures was printed just a few decades before Tetsugen began his project. This was an official edition, sponsored by government funds. A team commissioned by the Tokugawa government and headed by the Tendai monk Tenkai (1536–1643) completed the work in 1648. The Tenkai edition, as it is known, had a few notable problems that prevented it from becoming a standard edition that solved the scarcity problem. First, the edition was printed using a form of moveable type. Unlike woodblocks that can be preserved, thus allowing for an indefinite number of copies, the movable type was reused from text to text, limiting the number of copies to the initial printing. Only about thirty copies of the Tenkai edition were actually produced. Second, it had been based on one of the inferior Yuan editions and was so riddled with errors that it was never regarded as reliable.[7]

THE BEGINNING OF THE SCRIPTURE PROJECT

The *Deeds of Tetsugen* presents Tetsugen's resolve to produce a woodblock edition of the Buddhist scriptures for Japan as a fully developed plan. It quotes Tetsugen's statement of intention, found in "A Brief Account of the History of Carving the Buddhist Scriptures" (*Daizō o kizamu engi sō*), written in 1669, as if this was Tetsugen's idea all along. In reality, Tetsugen's thinking evolved over a long period of time, beginning at least as early as 1663, when he composed his first essay on the topic, "An Opportunity for Instruction." In that essay, Tetsugen set out his initial plan, which was to raise funds from ordinary people and eventually import an edition of the scriptures from China. Apparently, this particular idea did not prove practical, and he abandoned it a few years later in favor of the more ambitious project of producing the woodblocks in Japan. It is possible that Tetsugen encountered difficulties in making import arrangements with Chinese merchants, or that the cost of acquiring copies in China may have been prohibitively expensive compared to the cost of printing texts in Japan. Certainly, importing individual copies would not have solved the basic problem facing Buddhist scholars throughout the country. In any case, by 1667, Tetsugen had determined that publishing a Japanese edition was the best solution. He made new plans accordingly.

Tetsugen and a small group of close disciples, including Hōshū and Mue Nyokū (1610–1694), left Kyushu and moved to Osaka, which was to be their base point for the duration of the project. Tetsugen left no clues in his writings as to why he chose Osaka, but the city had many advantages for a major publishing venture. First, Osaka was quickly becoming the financial center of Japan with many prospering businesses located there, starting with the rice merchants who handled much of the nation's basic cash crop. The Tokugawa government maintained direct control of the city, but permitted *daimyō* from all over the country to keep households there if they wished. Therefore, both wealthy merchants and members of the samurai class resided there.[8] In financial terms, Osaka was therefore a much likelier location for raising large sums through donations than rural Kyushu. Second, by the middle of the seventeenth century, the publishing trade had spread from Kyoto to Osaka, making it one of the three likely sites with a ready supply of the requisite craftsmen and materials.[9] Third, Osaka was reasonably near Kyoto and Uji, approximately a day's journey from each, so that Tetsugen could be in close contact with his superiors at

Mampukuji as well as enjoy easy access to all of the cultural resources in Kyoto. In fact, as a primary transportation node in Japan's extensive system of river and coastal routes, Osaka provided exceptional access to the entire country. Therefore, Tetsugen could travel conveniently back and forth between Edo, Kyushu, Kyoto, and Osaka on his fund-raising missions from a central base point.

At first, while Tetsugen and his disciples went about the business of establishing a financial base for the scripture project, they made their temporary abode with a merchant family named Okuda, who were already Ōbaku supporters.[10] Up until this point in time, Tetsugen had virtually no financial resources of his own on which to draw. Popular tales speak of him as being so poor that he could not even afford a metal begging bowl, so he covered a woven bowl with black paper to make it resemble the proper utensil. The first stage of his work in Osaka would be to build a temple to house the project and to provide for the daily needs for himself and his disciples. Tetsugen found a sponsor, mentioned in the "History of Carving the Buddhist Scriptures," whose identity remains unknown, and eventually was able to lease a small dilapidated temple called Yakushiji in the Naniwa section of the city. Tetsugen gave a lecture at Yakushiji sometime during 1668, so one may assume that he took up residence there in that year. In 1670, a group of faithful lay supporters provided the resources to restore the temple and invited Tetsugen to become the official restorer and first head monk. Tetsugen then renamed the temple Jiunsan Zuiryūji (Mount Cloud of Compassion, Lucky Dragon Temple), though it later became known by its popular name, Tetsugenji.

In the spring of 1668, Tetsugen gave a lecture on the *Awakening of Faith* at a Sōtō temple in Osaka, Chōshōsan Gekkōin and announced publicly, perhaps for the first time, his vow to print the Buddhist scriptures. In the audience was the nun Myōu Dōnin (d. 1678) from Kannonji, who had already been generous in her donations for other Ōbaku projects. Myōu was so moved when she heard Tetsugen describe his plan, that she donated one thousand *ryō* of gold, an enormous donation for a private individual to make.[11] Tetsugen responded to her generosity saying, "I have heard it said that even a tower one thousand feet tall must begin with a foundation.[12] I now have my foundation. Without a doubt, I shall print the entire Buddhist canon!" (Deeds of Tetsugen). Tradition regards this as Tetsugen's first donation, since it proved to be the impetus he needed to take further concrete steps. With a substantial sum far exceeding his own immediate needs, Tetsugen was ready to move ahead with the second stage of the project.

Before Tetsugen could proceed further, however, he needed to formally ask his superiors' permission to undertake the project. Under normal circumstances, Zen monks would not have orchestrated this kind of endeavor, since it posed an obvious interruption in regular Zen monastic practice for an extended period of time. Sometime in the summer or early fall of 1669, Tetsugen paid a visit to Ōbakusan where he called on both Yinyuan and Muan. At that time, Yinyuan had already retired and was living at Shōdōin, his subtemple on Ōbakusan,

while Muan had succeeded him as the abbot of Mampukuji in 1664. Tetsu-
gen consulted both masters, as is recorded in their respective biographies.[13]
Each approved of his plan and marked the occasion with a verse presented to
Tetsugen.[14]

Yinyuan gave Tetsugen his full and enthusiastic support for the project. "I
came to Japan for the sake of the Dharma," Yinyuan said. "The shogun gave me
land and I was able to build [Mampukuji]. [Our Dharma] style has flourished,
and all has gone as I hoped. The only thing missing was to print an edition of
the Buddhist scriptures. Now I know that it was in order that I might hear this
glorious news that my withered body has not passed away. My wishes have
now been fulfilled" (Deeds of Tetsugen). Yinyuan also expressed his support
in tangible terms that further promoted the project. First, he turned over to
Tetsugen his own complete copy of the Chinese canon that he had brought
over from China. Tetsugen used that version, a copy of the Wanli edition, as
the basis for his own, replicating the Chinese text down to the Ming style of
characters, page layout, and binding.[15] Second, Yinyuan sectioned off a parcel
of land on Ōbakusan that he turned over to Tetsugen. Tetsugen initially used
this land to build a storehouse for the woodblocks that he appropriately named
Hōzōin (Treasure Storehouse Temple).

The sources offer no comparable clue as to Muan's reaction to the project
beyond noting that he granted his permission. Muan's biography includes only
the terse entry, "[The master] instructed Tetsugen Jōza (High Seat) to carve
[woodblocks for] the Buddhist scriptures."[16] Most secondary sources, including the Deeds of Tetsugen, do not even note that the meeting took place.

With a small financial base to build on and his superiors' permission se-
cured, Tetsugen had indeed completed the foundation for his Buddhist canon.
He marked the occasion by composing a short essay, "A Brief Account of the
History of Carving the Buddhist Scriptures," which served to publicly an-
nounce the start of the project. In the essay, Tetsugen set forth his reasons for
undertaking it, progress to date, and his hopes for the future. The text reads
in part,

> Since ancient times, our country [Japan] has been called a Buddha Land.
> Since the teachings were first received in the East during the reign of Emperor
> Kimmei, successive emperors have received them, while taking special care to
> reverence the *kami* (indigenous deities of Japan). [The Buddhist teachings]
> have come to be revered and followed by the whole nation, counselors, retain-
> ers, and all classes of people. Moreover, when we reflect on this, [Japan] is not
> inferior to places such as India and China, except that from the beginning,
> there has never been a printed edition of the scriptures published here, mak-
> ing texts quite scarce. Whenever talented men from the various temples and
> monasteries discuss this, they can only regret it. . . .
>
> I bow down and pray that the counselors, officials, wealthy folk, good men and
> virtuous women in all ten directions would each give rise to the thought of

how difficult it is to meet [a Buddha], and manifest a broad mind to help with [the project]. Fund three to five sutras, or even just a single word or half a verse. Doing so would tie a bond with wisdom and complete this important work, and so turn the wheel of the Dharma and eternally bless our country.

THE PROJECT'S STRUCTURE

After meeting with Yinyuan and Muan, Tetsugen consulted with various colleagues and lay sponsors to determine how best to proceed. They decided to review the contents of the Chinese canon and select the most important sutras for immediate publication. According to the *Deeds of Tetsugen*, this first set amounted to ten volumes. The project was then to proceed as steadily as funds allowed, with Tetsugen taking primary responsibility for raising the money. A certain amount is known about how the project was structured, who participated, in what capacity, and where the work was done, and so on. Tetsugen and his advisers determined many of these practical issues in 1669, just before Tetsugen set off on his first major fund-raising trip. Tetsugen's own disciples and the craftsmen they hired performed the bulk of the work, but other members of the Ōbaku community participated as well, contributing according to their own talents and resources.

First, Tetsugen created a triangle of work sites, connecting Osaka, Uji, and Kyoto, that his followers came to refer to as the "three places" (*sansho*). He designated Zuiryūji in Osaka, Hōzōin on Ōbakusan, and the Inbō, or Print Shop,[17] in Kyoto as the headquarters for different aspects of the project, and he assigned disciples to manage each of them in his absence. The latter two structures were built in the autumn of 1669, and Zuiryūji, formerly Yakushiji, was officially restored the following year. Zuiryūji continued to be Tetsugen's primary temple of residence, where he stayed whenever he was not traveling and where the majority of his disciples remained.[18] When he was away, which was much of the time, Tetsugen assigned either Hōshū or Nyokū to act as his deputy at Zuiryūji. The deputy acted in the place of the head monk to oversee the Zen practice of Tetsugen's other disciples. Apparently, Zuiryūji functioned in much the same manner as other Ōbaku temples, except that the daily work undertaken by the monks was most often related to the scripture project.

Tetsugen built Hōzōin on the land within the temple grounds of Mampukuji that Yinyuan had granted to him. Although the name suggests that it was a subtemple, the first structure was nothing more than a small storehouse, where Tetsugen planned to keep the completed woodblocks. He was later able to move Hōzōin to a better site, and the new structure was spacious enough to house the actual printing work when it went into full production. Eventually, Hōzōin did become a full subtemple with an abbot's hall and other temple buildings, but that probably occurred after Tetsugen passed away and Hōshū became head monk.

Tetsugen set up the print shop in Kyoto, usually called simply Inbō, where the carving of the woodblocks took place.[19] This site, located at Nijō and Kiyamachi streets, in the heart of Kyoto's thriving publishing district, was convenient at that time for gathering the woodcarvers who abounded in Kyoto, and later as a business office for selling copies of the scriptures. As the project progressed and more woodblocks were completed, Tetsugen also used the shop as a bindery and distribution center. Since the shop served primarily secular purposes, in particular as the locus for collecting the profits from sales, Tetsugen never regarded it as a regular temple. Tetsugen included a special section on the Inbō in his rules for Hōzōin which reads,

> The Inbō does not allow guests, neither monk nor lay, to stay overnight. Inbō is not like other temples. Its provisions (lit. rice and vegetables) are all reserved for the sake of the Dharma. If they are misused, then both guest and host will have sinned grievously. Do not do this![20]

The instructions were dated the first day of summer, Empō 5 (1677), and signed with Tetsugen's seal. However, given the religious nature of the project, the Inbō did function in some respects as a religious site, and was eventually given the temple name Baiyō-dō (Tāla Leaf Hall). Baiyō is a short form of Baitarayō, or *pattra* in Sanskrit. The term refers to leaves, especially those of the *tāla* tree, on which the sutras were traditionally written. Later directors of the shop all came from Hōshū's Dharma lineage within Ōbaku Zen, and generally served simultaneously as the head monk at Hōzōin. Later generations enshrined images of Tetsugen and Hōshū in one room, where they held memorial services in their honor.[21]

Although Tetsugen had changed his goal and now intended to publish rather than import the scriptures from China, certain aspects of his plan remained constant over the years. It was always his stated resolve to involve as many ordinary people as possible in the project and thereby provide them with a special opportunity to participate in a meritorious act. Tetsugen did not limit his fund-raising activities to visits with government officials or wealthy merchants, although ultimately a large percentage of the funds collected came from them. He took his idea to the common people and used his project as a means to spread the Dharma among them. The words he wrote in "An Opportunity for Instruction," in 1663, described his work throughout the long years of travel.

> ... I will not shy away from the exalted nor overlook the lowly. I will not regard ten thousand *kan* [of rice] as too much, nor one grain of rice as too little. Whatever people can offer, I will accept. I will accept it as it is given and go on begging. ... If a poor woman offers even a single *sen*, although it may seem a meager sum, with that fine thread she will tie a lasting bond with the Dharma. If an orphan without savings amounting to a scrap of toilet paper should give a single grain of millet, he will have planted the great seed of enlightenment.

The vast majority of the contributions that Tetsugen collected were small offerings made by ordinary people, sometimes donated collectively through their local religious confraternities (*kō*). Tetsugen and his disciples did not keep detailed records of the smaller donations they received, so we do not know the exact numbers. Instead, we have lists of place names representing thousands of smaller donations of precisely the sort Tetsugen described in the passage above. In the case of larger individual donations made by government officials or wealthy merchants, Tetsugen recorded the name of the individual and the number of volumes of the scriptures the donation had financed. Tetsugen had an inscription carved on the final page of each volume of the sutras, indicating the donation(s), either by groups or individuals, that had sponsored it.

Tetsugen's primary role in the operation was to raise funds to keep the project in business. There are numerous popular tales of Tetsugen begging on the streets of Osaka or Kyoto, asking passersby for even half a *sen* to support his work. One story, told in a number of variations, has been used within the sect to illustrate Tetsugen's boundless determination. Tetsugen was out begging in a bitter winter storm on the Sanjō Bridge in Kyoto. A samurai passed by on horseback. Although Tetsugen called out to him, the man proceeded on without responding. Tetsugen followed the man on foot, walking as far as the town of Otsu, approximately ten kilometers away. There he addressed the samurai again, politely asking for a small donation for publishing the scriptures. The samurai tossed him a small coin, more to be rid of the tenacious pest than to support the project. But Tetsugen took up the small offering as if it were a treasure. This moved the samurai and the crowd that had gathered to watch, and the encounter gave Tetsugen an opportunity to explain his work at some length.[22]

Tetsugen maintained the practice of begging in the streets to raise funds in the traditional manner, but that method would neither have attracted the public attention nor garnished the funds necessary for a major undertaking. In order to raise larger sums of money, Tetsugen continued to use his greatest skill, his ability as a public speaker, as the basis for his efforts. Tetsugen had a talent for explicating difficult concepts from the Buddhist scriptures in basic terms that common people could grasp, and he had already developed a reputation in Kyushu for his lecturing style before he moved to Osaka. Buddhist lectures were a common feature in Tokugawa period life, and served as a form of entertainment as well as religious education in urban centers and rural villages alike. Large crowds numbering even in the thousands might gather to hear a popular speaker. During the first years of Tetsugen's residence in Osaka, he arranged or was invited to give lectures at several temples in the area and thus began to build his reputation in the Kansai region. As Tetsugen's name became known, he drew larger crowds, and was able to spread the message of his endeavor to a wider audience.

Tetsugen traveled throughout the Kantō, Kansai, and Kyushu regions, lecturing in cities and small villages. Over thirteen years of actively raising funds

for the scripture project, from 1669 through 1682, Tetsugen made five trips to
Edo, lecturing not only in the capital itself, but in the outlying areas and along
the route between Kantō and Kansai. He spent an extended period of time,
from 1674 through 1676, traveling around Kyushu, lecturing at various temples
and instructing regional officials. According to Akamatsu Shinmyō's estimation, Tetsugen traveled through and collected funds in some forty provinces.[23]
The *Deeds of Tetsugen* lists only six major lecture series that Tetsugen gave at
large, important temples over the thirteen years, but other sources mention at
least three others. There is no way to estimate the less formal appearances that
he made at smaller temples, but the number of donations from various confraternities around the country suggest that these must have been numerous.

Traveling was much safer during the peaceful years of the Tokugawa period than in earlier times, and the well-established routes made the process
more convenient. Nonetheless, the years of traveling took their toll on Tetsugen
and he faced certain hazards. There is one story of him being robbed while
returning home to Osaka after a successful trip to Edo. While making his
way along a route following the Kiso River, Tetsugen was attacked by a robber.
The man took the packet of money that Tetsugen was carrying and pushed
Tetsugen into the raging river. Tetsugen only saved himself from drowning by
grabbing hold of a willow branch hanging down in the water. Tradition has it
that a man named Takehara, one of the believers who sponsored the restoration of Yakushiji and who invited Tetsugen to serve as abbot, later confessed to
Tetsugen that he had been the robber. Takehara then became one of Tetsugen's
most generous sponsors for the scripture project.[24]

SUPPORT FROM THE ŌBAKU MONASTIC COMMUNITY

Hōshū indicated in his *Deeds of Tetsugen* that Tetsugen distributed responsibilities for the project among his many disciples, but we know little of the details.
Nyokū was most often left as Tetsugen's deputy at Zuiryūji, and was given the
title Temple Administrator (*kan'in*).[25] Other senior disciples would have served
similar managerial roles at Hōzōin and at the Inbō to direct the work of the
hired craftsmen. Hōshū probably worked primarily at the latter two sites when
he was not accompanying Tetsugen on a journey. Early on in the project, Nyokū
recommended to Tetsugen that they build a small temple in Fushimi to facili-
tate communications between the three sites. Fushimi was a key transportation
node, where travelers changed boats depending on their destination. Nyokū
believed that a temple there could serve as a relay point for messages and as
a convenient resting house for Ōbaku monks in transit. They assigned the job
of establishing such a temple to one of Nyokū's disciples, a young man named
Kūgan, in the first month of 1671. Unfortunately, the arduous process of finding
sponsors and arranging for government permission to build a new temple took
nearly five years. The temple was not completed until the end of 1675 and never
proved to be an important addition to the workings of the scripture project.

Somewhat more is known of the help provided by other senior Ōbaku monks, including Tetsugyū Dōki (1628–1700), Ryōō Dōkaku (1630–1707), and Damei Xingshan (J. Daibi Shōzen; 1616–1673). Tetsugen first met Tetsugyū in 1655 in Nagasaki, when the two of them were practicing under Yinyuan at Kōfukuji. Both monks subsequently became Muan's disciples, and Tetsugyū received *inka* from the master in 1667, a few years before Tetsugen began the scripture project in earnest. Even before Tetsugen consulted with Yinyuan and Muan, he requested the support of his Dharma brother Tetsugyū, who was then living in Edo.[26] In the autumn of 1668, Tetsugen commissioned one of Tetsugyū's disciples, Chigen Genjō (ordained 1654, d. 1697?), who visited Zuiryūji while passing through Osaka on his way to Edo, to carry his appeal to Tetsugyū. Tetsugyū responded enthusiastically to Tetsugen's request for assistance. According to one biography, Tetsugyū commented that he had always hoped to produce an edition of the sutras himself and would gladly extend a hand in any way possible to a Dharma brother with the same intention.[27]

Tetsugyū's biography spells out a number of ways in which the master fulfilled his promise to support Tetsugen.[28] First, Tetsugyū had extensive contacts among government officials and other leading samurai in Edo, and was well known in the city. He used these connections to promote Tetsugen's plan, setting the stage so that Tetsugen, previously unknown in the capital, would receive a warm welcome when he first visited in 1669. When Tetsugen arrived in Edo, the two men were able to confer in person and Tetsugyū advised Tetsugen how best to proceed. Tetsugyū can be partially credited with the financial success of Tetsugen's first fund-raising expedition, since he vouched for Tetsugen's character among the officials who made substantial donations. Tetsugyū may well have also been responsible for the unusually large turnout that came to hear Tetsugen lecture at Kaiunji in Asakusa in the fall of 1669, his first appearance in the city.[29] Apparently, Tetsugyū played a similar promotional role within the Ōbaku sect itself. He defended Tetsugen's plan when other monks scoffed that it was too large a task for any individual monk to manage. He had faith in Tetsugen's abilities when the others did not yet know his mettle, and he convinced them to support the project. Finally, it is said that Tetsugyū took it on himself to do the proofreading for most of the prepared blocks, although, given Tetsugyū's schedule, this last item stretches credulity.

Like Tetsugyū, Ryōō centered his work in the Kantō area, so he was not directly involved in the scripture project. He practiced under several Ōbaku masters, including Yinyuan, Zhifei, and Gaochuan throughout his life, and became Gaochuan's Dharma heir in 1695. His early years of Zen practice were interrupted several times by sickness. As a result, he studied medicine and eventually set up a successful medical school and pharmacy in Edo.[30] In 1665, Ryōō made a vow to use the funds acquired from selling his medicines to purchase copies of the Buddhist canon and donate them to various temples in order to promote the Dharma. He was especially generous with Tendai and Zen temples, including several Ōbaku temples. At first, he purchased copies of the scriptures, such as the Tenkai and Chinese editions, as they became available to him. Later, he offered financial support to Tetsugen's project, and after the Ōbaku edition was completed, he ordered numerous complete and partial copies that he presented as donations to various temples.

Damei was one of the Chinese monks who accompanied Yinyuan to Japan in 1654. He served as Yinyuan's attendant until the master's death in 1673. Damei received Yinyuan's *inka* in 1665, and recognized a single Dharma heir, Bairei Dōsetsu (1641–1717). Damei assisted Tetsugen in a most unusual manner, by donating his own subtemple at Ōbakusan for use as the new site for Hōzōin. In 1665, Damei built himself a retreat called Tōrinin in a secluded area of the temple grounds. His site was situated to the east of the main temple, on high, dry land, and far from any other structure. His property was therefore relatively safe from the dangers of fire and water damage, making it a perfect location for storing the woodblock plates. In contrast, the land that Yinyuan originally gave to Tetsugen lay to the west of Mampukuji, on low, moist ground, close to the kitchen, which greatly raised the fire risk.

The story of Damei's donation is preserved not only within the Ōbaku sect, but was included in the *Settsu meisho zue*, a Tokugawa period collection of illustrations of famous sites in Settsu province that includes some relevant tales. Damei's Dharma heir Bairei built a temple in Settsu and named Damei as the founder. It was through this connection that a story set in Uji came to be included in a Settsu collection. The story reads

> One day when Tetsugen was first at Ōbakusan, he was so poor that he did not have a metal begging bowl for when he left the temple to beg. He found a rough bamboo basket and covered it with black paper and used that. In that area, there was a man called Master Damei of Tōrinin. He was a wealthy Chinese monk. He had books, Buddhist implements and gold coins. He was a millionaire, but had a close relationship with Tetsugen. One day, Tetsugen was talking to himself and said, "I have completed the first half of the wood blocks for the Buddhist scriptures, but my temple is small so there is no room to store them. Master Damei's lodgings are larger and off to the side of the mountain ..." Damei heard him muttering through the fence, and said to himself, "I was born wealthy but my life has no merit. Though Tetsugen is poor, he has undertaken the great merit of printing the sutras. After today, I will give him my temple in exchange for his. After today, I will trade places with Tetsugen." When Damei's disciples asked him if he were taking his Buddhist images and texts with him, he laughed and said, "No. I said that we would change places. The little bamboo bowl that Tetsugen had is now mine. When we trade places, not one single treasure or implement will be moved." One can see that Damei was also a wise and virtuous man, and so he has been mentioned here.[31]

Shortly after Yinyuan died and Damei was himself sick and dying, he offered to make a trade with Tetsugen: he and his disciples would move to Hōzōin and Tetsugen would have Tōrinin. Damei prepared a deed explaining the trade in order to prevent any trouble or confusion for future descendents. It read in part:

> The most revered thing in the world is the Buddha; the most treasured is the Dharma; and the most respected is the sangha. A person who believes in the Three Treasures is called wise. With only the Buddha and not the Dharma, one cannot save sentient beings. The sangha without the Dharma cannot attain enlightenment. Therefore, bodhisattvas make expounding the Dharma tantamount among all their practices.

> Be that as it may, although this land has long been called a Buddha land, and although the emperor, retainers, and all classes of people revered the Three Treasures and built temples, they had the sutras alone without having the woodblocks. Like a fire without a source or water without an origin, [the Dharma] cannot grow and be transmitted to all [Dharma] lineages.

> Tetsugen, a virtuous Zen monk and skilled at spreading the sutras, travels everywhere to give lectures, clearly explaining the Great Teaching. His fame is extensive. He gave rise to the mind of *bodhi* and practices the bodhisattva way. He has gathered great men from the ten directions to print the Buddha's wise commands. His [work] will allow the Dharma to be transmitted forever. How deep is his merit!

> Now the woodblocks are halfway done, and Tetsugen believes that he will not have sufficient storage space. He has lamented this fact to me. For the sake of the Dharma, I have given up my whole life just to seek understanding of half a verse. How much more readily will I give up an external thing! I think that my land at Tōrin is especially dry and far removed from any fire hazard, and therefore quite suitable. It is the most secluded area of Ōbakusan....

> Written by the hand of the founder of Tōrinin, Damei Xingshan, in agreement with my ten disciples.[32]

The text is dated the twenty-fifth day of the ninth month 1673, less than a month before Damei's death on the eighteenth day of the tenth month. As can be seen in the text, Damei had consulted with his disciples, and they were in agreement as well. Although the sources are not explicit on this point, it seems likely that Damei consulted with them as a part of the deathbed distribution of his property. Tetsugen took possession of Damei's retreat and built a larger storehouse on the property, while Damei's disciples moved to the former site of Hōzōin.

OUTSIDE SOURCES OF SUPPORT

In addition to the help that Tetsugen's disciples and other Ōbaku monks offered in completing the scripture project, Tetsugen received practical assistance from outsiders. For example, according to tradition, the Tokugawa government

official who administrated the Nara region, identified by some scholars as Mizo-
guchi Nobukatsu, was said to have supported Tetsugen's undertaking by en-
abling him to use Yoshino cherry trees for the woodblocks. The cherry trees in
Yoshino, reputed to be the finest cherry wood in all of Japan, were protected by
government order, and cutting them was strictly forbidden. In order to make
them available for use, the official proclaimed a group of the trees dead and
ordered them to be cleared. He then donated the wood to Tetsugen. Although
the woodblocks are indeed cherry, scholars have been unable to confirm this
tradition as to the source of the wood.[33] As Satō Fumitsugu points out, there
are similar stories told about cherry trees being donated from other regions,
so it is possible that Tetsugen received donations of wood from a number of
sources.[34]

Tetsugen also received support from monks affiliated with other Buddhist
sects. There are two examples that stand out in the sources, although a great
number of Buddhist monks and nuns contributed funds and promoted the
project in other ways over the years. A Shingon monk named Kakugen Jōgon
(1639–1704),[35] met Tetsugen in Kyoto sometime in 1674 and was deeply impressed by his work. Tetsugen invited Kakugen to see the printing operation
and gave him a tour of the facilities. Kakugen had long wished to have access
to the sutras and had arranged an extended stay in Kyoto for just that purpose.
When he saw the progress being made by Tetsugen, he wanted to be of some
assistance. Kakugen offered to identify the esoteric sutras so that these could
easily be grouped as a subset that would then be circulated among Tendai and
Shingon temples.[36] Tetsugen agreed, and Kakugen created an index for the
esoteric collection within the Buddhist canon.[37] Kakugen also provided approximately ten additional texts that were not included in the original Wanli
edition, which he requested that Tetsugen include in the Ōbaku edition in
order to complete the esoteric canon.[38]

A second example of outside assistance came from an unlikely source, a
True Pure Land monk named Suiin from Hita. Sometime in 1675, shortly
after Tetsugen had a serious encounter with True Pure Land believers in Mori,
Suiin sent one of his disciples to see Tetsugen to reprimand him for attacking
the True Pure Land sect. At that time, Tetsugen's relations with the True Pure
Land sect had deteriorated so badly that he was generally regarded as the sect's
sworn enemy. Tetsugen cordially received Suiin's disciple and, in order to defuse
a potentially volatile situation, expressed his respect for Suiin's learning. As a
result, despite the inauspicious beginning to their interchange, Suiin eventually
donated one hundred gold coins for the scripture project.[39]

COMPLETION OF THE BUDDHIST SCRIPTURE PROJECT

After twelve years of steady work, Tetsugen's team of assistants finally completed the actual carving of the woodblocks for the Buddhist canon sometime in 1680. In the end, there was a total of 6,956 bound volumes, with over

60,000 individual blocks. Each wood block has four pages of text, two pages carved onto each face. The blocks measure approximately thirty-two inches by ten inches and are three-quarters of an inch thick. According to literature distributed at Hōzōin, it takes a team of five expert printers to print and bind a complete set.

In anticipation of its completion, Tetsugen ordered that an advance copy of the scriptures (approximately the first 6,930 volumes) be prepared for the retired emperor Gomizunoo in the fall of 1678. Tetsugen composed a short dedication for the emperor in ornate Chinese, "A Report on Progress Made on the New Edition of the Buddhist Scriptures" (*Shin shinkoku daizōkyō hyō*), dated the 17th day of the 7th month 1678, and attached it to the prepared volumes. Tetsugen then presented this first wood block copy of the Buddhist canon printed in Japan to the emperor.

According to the *Deeds of Tetsugen,* the emperor received the volumes with great pleasure and praised the quality of the workmanship and the magnitude of Tetsugen's accomplishment. "The volumes of the Buddhist scriptures are as numerous as this, and yet they were well printed. One must regard [Tetsugen's] resolve as firm and sincere. Truly he is a meritorious servant of the Buddhist teachings and will reap good fortune in his future life. Such distinguished service to the court is unprecedented." Gomizunoo eventually dedicated his copy of the Ōbaku edition to Shōmyōji, the temple dearest to him.

By 1681, four more complete copies were ready for presentation. Tetsugen dedicated the second copy to Ishōji in Ise as an offering to the *kami* Amaterasu. The third was intended for the Tokugawa government, although Tetsugen was never able to present it himself. He gave the fourth copy to Lord Hosokawa, *daimyō* of Higo, to repay his kindness over the years. Finally, Tetsugen dedicated the fifth copy to Yinyuan at Ōbakusan Mampukuji. Tetsugen's assistants kept a register, known as the *Daizōkyō shōkyo sōchō* (*Complete Record of Orders for the Buddhist Scriptures*), in which were recorded the destinations by province and temple of the first four hundred complete copies and the partial printings made during the same period. The register basically covers the years when Tetsugen and his disciple Hōshū were alive and managing the operation.[40] Later generations kept similar records, and the officials at Hōzōin today estimate that something over two thousand complete or partial copies were produced during the first 200-year history of the Ōbaku edition.

Tetsugen proceeded to Edo in 1680 in order to officially present his edition of the scriptures to the Tokugawa government. Just as he had done for the emperor, Tetsugen composed a memorial essay in Chinese for the shogun, "An Account of Completing the Buddhist Scriptures," which he planned to attach to the shogun's copy. Because he was awaiting permission to present the volumes, Tetsugen dated the essay only with the year, 1681, leaving the month and date blank. Although Tetsugen remained in Edo throughout the entire year, he received no reply to his petition. Called away by urgent events in Osaka, Tetsugen left Edo for the last time early in 1682 without completing his mission. After his death, his disciple Hōshū took it upon himself to complete his master's task. Hōshū likewise failed on his first attempt. The government finally accepted its copy of the Ōbaku edition in 1690.

THE CONTINUATION OF THE
BUDDHIST SCRIPTURES PROJECT

Tetsugen's disciples fulfilled their master's final wishes, and the scripture project continued to prosper. Hōshū, Kyōdō, and later generations of abbots in the Zuiryū line managed the work at Hōzōin and the Inbō. Under their guidance, a few select titles were appended to the original set of woodblocks. These were primarily Ōbaku sectarian texts including works related to Tetsugen's life and teachings. Printing activities remained in full swing well into the modern era, until the Ōbaku edition was superceded by the Taishō edition of the Chinese Buddhist canon. For two-and-a-half centuries, the Buddhist scriptures were almost inevitably associated with the name Tetsugen in Japan. In the modern period, copies of Tetsugen's edition even made their way to Europe and the United States, and were used by Western scholars in early studies of the Buddhist scriptures.

The original woodblocks of the Ōbaku edition have been carefully preserved at Hōzōin where they are stored in a new structure, specially designed to retard deterioration. Even after generations of steady use, they remain in excellent condition. Printing does continue today on a very limited basis. The temple still employs one craftsman trained in the traditional art of printing and binding who instructs visitors on the history of the woodblocks while demonstrating his craft. He regularly produces a few of the more popular sutras, especially the *Heart sutra*, and fills special orders as they arise. In this way, the temple continues to honor Tetsugen's final command: "Printing the Buddhist scriptures is the way to spread the Buddha's wise commands ... See to it that [the scriptures] are transmitted forever" (*Deeds of Tetsugen*).

CHAPTER THREE

The Teachings of Tetsugen

Today, Tetsugen is known principally as the editor and driving force behind the Ōbaku edition of the Buddhist scriptures, and that work must be regarded as his primary contribution to Japanese Buddhism of the early modern period. In his own day, Tetsugen was already widely acclaimed for his work on the scripture project. By editing the scriptures and making them readily available in Japan, Tetsugen lent concrete support to one of the major scholarly movements of Tokugawa Buddhism, the study of the basic and definitional texts of Buddhism. Tetsugen's life work on the Ōbaku-ban provided generations of Buddhist scholars access to the most important texts of the Buddhist tradition. However, Tetsugen believed that access to the scriptures was necessary not only to serve the purposes of scholarship, but to better serve the needs of lay believers. Tetsugen stressed the responsibility of Buddhist monks, as the educated elite within the Buddhist community, to convey their knowledge to others.

In addition to his renown as publisher of the scriptures, Tetsugen enjoyed a fine reputation as an effective public speaker, who strove to convey the principles of Buddhist thought and practice to the common people. During his lifetime, Tetsugen touched scores of lay believers throughout the country with the lectures he gave on fund-raising tours. Based on what we know of his lectures, Tetsugen stressed the need for laypeople and clergy alike to keep the Buddhist precepts as a basis for their religious practice. In this regard, Tetsugen represents a widespread emphasis among religious leaders and other intellectuals throughout the period who championed ethics and personal moral development as a means to improve individual lives and society as a whole.

After his death, Tetsugen continued to have some influence in the Buddhist community through a small corpus of written works, which were published posthumously by his disciples. Some portions of his teachings were appended to the Ōbaku-ban and circulated as an additional volume, and other writings circulated as independent works. In particular, Tetsugen's largest piece, the *Dharma Lesson in Japanese*, became known throughout the Japanese Zen world. The *Dharma Lesson* can be seen as Tetsugen's most important contribution to the growing corpus of vernacular Buddhist texts written and published during the Tokugawa period. Tetsugen thus participated in both his lecturing and his writings in another major movement that characterized Tokugawa Buddhism, the fostering of Buddhism on the popular level among the lay community.

TETSUGEN'S TEACHINGS

Tetsugen spent a large portion of his career as a Zen monk traveling throughout Japan, preaching the Dharma and raising funds for his Tripitaka project. His lectures were open to all classes of people: monks, nuns, and lay believers alike. We know from outside sources and the donation lists associated with the Ōbaku edition of the scriptures that he drew large crowds and thus reached extensive numbers of people on his tours. Unfortunately, we have no written accounts of Tetsugen's sermons with the exception of the description of his lectures on the *Śūramgama sutra* found in his affidavit concerning the incident at Mori. His remarks in that context are limited to those issues that had aroused True Pure Land believers' ire, and so even that account is partial. Without the benefit of textual sources, there is no basis to judge Tetsugen's style of oration; we cannot know whether he spoke in a formal or colloquial manner, whether he drew examples from the immediate context or relied exclusively on traditional images. Our knowledge of Tetsugen's teachings rests upon the small corpus of his written material gathered and published by his disciples after his death.

Tetsugen showed a willingness to set his teachings on paper, although he subordinated literary pursuits to his primary responsibilities related to the scripture project. He had little opportunity during the years of constant travel to write at any great length. Since he died immediately following the scripture project's completion, just at the stage in his life when he may have had the leisure time to take up the brush, his complete works form only a slender volume. Nonetheless, he left behind a varied collection of writings, the bulk of which can be described as teaching materials. These texts include letters to ordained and lay disciples, short essays, a number of lessons in Chinese (*hōgo*) which were compiled and published by Hōshū in the *Yuiroku,* as well his longest piece, the *Dharma Lesson in Japanese,* a lengthy lesson written in Japanese and published as an independent volume. Tetsugen composed other types of texts including poetry, bell inscriptions, and introductory essays for specific copies of the Ōbaku-ban. Not all of these materials are pedagogical in nature.

When writing for purposes of instruction, Tetsugen typically used a clear, direct style of prose, whether writing in classical Chinese or vernacular Japanese. He set out his arguments in a logical progression that led the reader along to the desired conclusion. Although he made generous use of technical Buddhist terminology and canonical quotations, he generally took care to explain and elucidate the terms and references so that they advanced his argument, especially when his audience included lay people or newcomers to the Zen tradition. When Tetsugen wrote texts specifically intended for his own disciples, however, such as *jishū* (instructions for the community) or *hōgo* (Dharma words) addressed to an advanced practitioner, his writing style shifted significantly.

When writing for advanced practitioners, Tetsugen could assume a more thorough training in Buddhist thought, and he used technical terminology freely without explanation. His choice of quotations frequently shifted to include many more references to the Zen corpus of literature, which he would mention without a gloss, often omitting even the title of the source. In these texts, instruction in the most common sense was not the goal, and Tetsugen abandoned the clear and logical style characteristic of his more popular writing. In the more advanced writings, Tetsugen challenged his readers to strive forward in their meditative practice, and for this purpose he employed quite different tactics.

Tetsugen thus tailored his message to address the needs and abilities of his target audience. In the *Dharma Lesson,* Tetsugen expressed a self-conscious awareness that a Zen master must take care to consider how much of the teachings can appropriately be revealed to any given disciple lest the teacher inadvertently undermine the disciple's continued progress. In the section explaining the final hindrances to enlightenment, specifically the types of confusion that arise in relation to the *alaya* consciousness, Tetsugen maintained that even the Buddha faced this basic pedagogical quandary.

> Since this consciousness resembles the true original mind, but isn't the original mind, even the Buddha couldn't easily teach about it to foolish people. This is because, if he taught that this consciousness itself was the truth, then sentient beings would stop there, and thinking this [level of attainment] was sufficient, not persevere in their practice. [On the other hand,] if he taught that it wasn't true, then sentient beings would think that everything is completely void, doubt the existence of the original mind and fall into nihilism. Then they would indeed be unable to awaken to the original mind. That is what I mean when I say that this is a very great matter, and not even the Buddha can easily teach it. (Sec. 5)

Based on this awareness, one would expect to find changes of emphasis and varying degrees of difficulty in the lessons that Tetsugen wrote for disciples at different stages of Zen practice.

When comparing the lessons that Tetsugen wrote for beginners and those for advanced practitioners, one finds just this kind of appropriate variation in language and focus. In a lesson addressed to a relative beginner in the practice of Zen, the champion archer Hoshino Kanzaemon, Tetsugen used a bare minimum of Buddhist terms. In this case he preferred instead to borrow the language of archery to convey a simple message: perseverance in the practice of Zen meditation, as in archery, will lead to the desired goal.

> If you [shoot] an arrow with single-minded concentration, then you will hit the bull's eye. When your practice is already concentrated, then your mind

sees and your hand responds, so that you always hit the bull's eye. You eventually attain the skill of causing monkeys to cry [by just lifting your bow] and being able to shoot lice. The way of learning is also like this. When you have a single kōan in your heart and practice diligently night and day without ceasing, then your practice will ripen fully. When the time is right, and you are fully enlightened, then the mind transcending mind is illuminated and the thing transcending things is manifest. Right and left converge at the source. Warp and woof meet in the track. On the brink of life and death, you attain the great freedom. (Dharma Words 3)

Contrasting the terminology and simplicity of this message to that found in lessons for advanced practitioners demonstrates Tetsugen's ability to employ skillful means.

In writing a letter to Hōshū, his most advanced disciple, Tetsugen made free use of Zen terminology and employed numerous images from the Zen corpus of literature. Moreover, Tetsugen pushed Hōshū to take the final step toward enlightenment in terms that would perhaps have confounded a beginner.

> You must realize that you yourself Hōshū are the first and most recalcitrant delusion. When Hōshū is at the barrier, then the barrier becomes his prison. When Hōshū attains enlightenment, then enlightenment becomes a net of mistaken views. When Hōshū perfects the Way, then the Way becomes demonic and heretical. When Hōshū gives rise to understanding, then understanding becomes a shock wave [that disturbs the mind]. When Hōshū gives rise to compassion, then compassion becomes a love of spittle [that is, attachment to the self]. It would be better to slay this Hōshū, and be unfettered and at ease.

Tetsugen refers here to one of the most subtle of attachments, attachment to the Dharma itself, which afflicts only more advanced disciples. In writing a Dharma lesson for the Zen monk Shōchi (Dharma Words 4), Tetsugen again employs Zen terminology to address what appears to have been a specific problem the monk encountered in his meditation practice, discussing a phenomenon of depression and distraction encountered by advanced practitioners of *zazen*.

Tetsugen followed the example of Buddhist teachers throughout the tradition in using simple illustrations from everyday life to teach difficult and sophisticated concepts that the audience might not otherwise grasp. In some cases Tetsugen drew upon the common store of images and parables from the Buddhist scriptures, such as the story of the burning house from the *Lotus sutra,* the shining mirror, or the example of the water and the waves, which would have been familiar to much of his audience. He also supplemented this set with images of his own devising. He used familiar examples like conjuring tricks of magicians and the behavior of scavengers to express the intangible ideas of consciousness only and the interdependence of all things. It is not so much the originality of his examples as their effectiveness in expressing Buddhist concepts that marks his work.

Tetsugen quoted extensively from the sutras in his teaching materials. Although this fondness for scriptural quotations cannot be separated from Tetsugen's attitude toward the written Buddhist canon, a topic to be addressed directly in the next section, relevant here is the way in which he used the scriptures. To an extent unusual in the writings of Buddhist masters before the modern period, Tetsugen quoted directly and exactly from the sutras. No doubt this can be attributed to his own easy access to the texts as editor of the Ōbaku-ban. Most masters at the time gave rather loose renditions of whatever quotation they had in mind, conveying the general sense of the passage, sometimes without specifying the sutra. Tetsugen consistently named the sutras he quoted rather than using such generic references as "it says in the scriptures" or "as the Buddha said." There are only a few occasions when Tetsugen paraphrased a passage or failed to name his source. It is interesting to note that in every such case, Tetsugen alluded to passages from one of the Three Pure Land sutras, texts which he studied (and quite probably memorized) as a youth.[1]

As a rule, Tetsugen would first quote a passage in the original Chinese, or render it into classical Japanese, as he did in the *Dharma Lesson in Japanese.* Educated Japanese traditionally learn a style of reading off Chinese texts in classical Japanese (*yomikudashi*). Although such a reading already represents a form of translation, the text may not be readily understood by a general audience. This is especially the case with passages from the Buddhist scriptures that often contain technical language or obscure terminology. For this reason, Tetsugen would typically clarify the quotation with a paraphrase in simple Japanese. His lectures on the *Śūraṃgama sutra*, for instance, suggest that he sometimes did little more than provide a paraphrase of the original text in clear Japanese, followed by a short commentary to further elucidate the meaning of the text. Tetsugen wanted lay people to hear the teachings of the Buddha as directly as possible, and therefore concentrated on the primary source material. He, of course, made the editorial selections of the passages that he wished to stress, and so his choice of quotations tells us much about Tetsugen's primary themes.

FOCUS ON THE SCRIPTURES

Despite the popular assumption that the Zen school eschews the written word and devalues the Buddhist scriptures, Zen masters have traditionally held a wide spectrum of positions regarding the sutras. These range from the most radical views that appear to approach complete rejection, graphically illustrated by a master burning the scriptures, to far more positive attitudes of reverence for the sutras. The latter position is exemplified by the continued maintenance of scripture recitation and study as a part of Zen monastic practice. Tetsugen falls squarely in the category of Zen masters who took a positive attitude toward the scriptures.

In his written works, Tetsugen never directly recorded his understanding of the concept *zenkyō itchi*, that the truth realized through meditation and the truth expressed in the sutras is one. However, the *Deeds of Tetsugen* records one episode that effectively illustrates Tetsugen's understanding of the relationship between the teachings found in the sutras and those realized in Zen meditation.

> Someone once said, "Our sect values illuminating the mind and seeing one's nature, but [you] master are always preaching on the sutras and commentaries. Isn't that at variance with the teaching of 'direct pointing [to the mind, seeing one's nature and becoming Buddha]'?" Tetsugen laughed and said, "Isn't what you said a little simplistic? Meditation (*zen*) is the water and the teachings (*kyō*) are the waves. When you seize onto meditation and throw away the teachings, it is like seeking the water while rejecting the waves. The teachings are the vessel and meditation is the gold. When you seize onto the teachings and throw out meditation, it is like casting off the gold and looking for the vessel. The waves and the water are not separate. The vessel is itself the gold. Meditation and the teachings are not two things.

For those who had progressed sufficiently along the Buddhist path, Tetsugen never advocated giving preference to the study of the sutras over the practice of Zen meditation; for his own disciples he encouraged the single-minded pursuit of meditation on their kōan, fully aware that scripture study was a preliminary element in their monastic training, which was not likely in itself to inspire an enlightenment experience. Nonetheless, he did regard training in the scriptures as the necessary basis for monastic practice and the fundamental tool for spreading the Dharma among the laity, who could not always undertake meditation themselves.

Tetsugen's attitude toward the scriptures is best exemplified by his life's work of printing the Ōbaku edition of the scriptures, which made the texts accessible to ordained and lay Buddhists alike, in ways appropriate to their respective roles in life. In his very first essay on the need to increase the number of ready copies of the scriptures in Japan, "An Opportunity for Instruction," Tetsugen compared the sutras to medicine used by a great physician (the Buddha) and his nurses (the sangha) in order to relieve the suffering of sentient beings. In "Comments on an Opportunity for Instruction," he lamented that "in Japan, we have always had the Buddha and the sangha, but we have never had sufficient supplies of the curative Dharma. How, then, can the people's illness be healed?" Tetsugen regarded the scriptures as crucial for the promotion of Buddhism among the laity. His own style of teaching concurs with the role set out for monks in the above simile, that of a nurse administering medicine: Tetsugen lectured directly to the people on the sutras. Although he wrote more general lessons on Buddhist practice or Zen meditation for specific individuals, his public sermons were almost certainly extended commentaries on specific sutras that included paraphrases or translations of the Chinese texts into colloquial

Japanese. Not only did he preach, but he made the physical texts of the sutras accessible to scholar monks who had the skills to read them for themselves in order that they could better play their part in making the texts accessible to the common people through their lectures and writings.

KEEPING THE PRECEPTS

Just as there is a creative tension within Zen thought concerning the status of the written scriptures, there is likewise tension regarding the proper under-standing of the monastic precepts. Nearly all Buddhist schools, including the lineages of Zen as they were developed in China, share the common *Vinaya* tradition of monastic discipline. In the case of the Zen schools, older monastic codes are supplemented by a distinctive genre of literature, the "pure rules" or *shingi* of Zen monasteries. However, the same movement within Zen that cau-tions against reliance on an external Buddha or external scriptures takes aim at external codes of conduct. For example, the Sixth Patriarch Hui-neng con-ferred the "formless precepts" (*musōkai*) on his disciples, redefining the related terms in such a way that he elevated the discussion beyond the literal.[2]

> If in your own mind you rely on truth [the Dharma], then, because there is no falseness in successive thoughts, there will be no attachments. . . . If in your own mind you rely on purity [the Sangha], although all the passions and false thoughts are within your own natures, your natures are not stained.[3]

Based on this sort of passage, the tendency to uphold the freedom of enlight-enment in opposition to any external monastic code emerged within Zen Buddhism. In some extreme cases, this has led Zen masters to blatantly break precepts in order to illustrate their point. It is best to bear in mind that these extreme ideas and actions were typically situated within the context of monastic discipline. They were intended less as absolute denials of the precepts than as shocking reminders to disciples that even subtle attachments to the Dharma are a hindrance. Even those Zen masters who stressed the trans-literal meaning of the precepts continued to use those precepts to govern their monastic life.

Early in the Tokugawa period, the Rinzai sect in Japan was torn by an eruption of the recurring dispute over the proper understanding of the precepts. Once in Japan, Ōbaku masters became embroiled in the dispute, which pre-dated their arrival. The Chinese masters attracted to their ranks many Japanese monks who shared their view that the precepts had to be strictly preserved and further concurred that this was the best method for reviving Rinzai practice. Their opponents in the dispute were also dedicated to reviving Rinzai, but fa-vored a less literal interpretation of the precepts. Nonetheless, neither party advocated a literal rejection of the precepts in practical terms, and both sides continued to live and practice in accordance with the monastic codes.[4] Tetsu-gen came to this debate from a distinctive background for a Zen monk. As a former True Pure Land priest, Tetsugen had practiced within a tradition that did challenge the precepts on a literal and practical level. We might reasonably expect that his perspective on the relevant issues was somewhat different because of his unique personal history.

Tetsugen's strong dedication to strict monastic observance can be seen in his preference for the *Śūraṃgama sutra* as the most common topic for his sermons. In lecturing on the sutra, he gave heavy emphasis to the section of the text that addresses the necessity of keeping the precepts against sexual misconduct, killing, stealing, and lying. Although he followed the pattern and images of the sutra faithfully, he also expressed something of his own frustration with those monks who failed to uphold the precepts.

> Thieves don the robes of the Thus Come One [the Buddha], take on the appearance of a monk or nun, and so turn the Buddha into an object for sale and make him into the source of their livelihood. They create all sorts of [bad] karma, and say that it is all the teachings of the Buddha Dharma. Instead, they malign those monks who keep the precepts as followers of the Lesser Vehicle. They cause countless sentient beings to go astray, and cause them to lapse into the Gateless Hell. One must not take sutras that do not reveal the full meaning of the Dharma as one's own opinion and so cause those with less learning to err. (Mori Affidavit)

While Tetsugen may have been thinking primarily of his former True Pure Land colleagues, he was likewise concerned that Zen teachers were misleading beginners when they preached carelessly about the freedom of Zen.

Like other masters, Tetsugen believed that enlightened beings were free from any external constraints, and fulfilled the precepts as a natural result of their enlightened perspective. Enlightened beings "have great compassion, they [can look upon] all sentient beings as their own body, and regard them as their children" (*Dharma Lesson*, Sec. 2). They therefore cause no harm to other sentient beings without needing to manipulate their inclinations to conform to any external proscriptions like the monastic precepts. Nonetheless, beginners have not yet attained the shift in perspective necessary to fulfill the precepts organically, and it could be detrimental to their progress along the Buddhist path to hear prematurely about such freedom. As seen below in the discussion on the *Dharma Lesson*, Tetsugen encouraged not only monks and nuns to observe the monastic precepts, he likewise encouraged lay Buddhists to keep the first five precepts associated with lay practice. In stressing that keeping the precepts was the indispensable basis upon which to build the practice of meditation and strive for wisdom, Tetsugen was in substantial agreement with the standard Mahayana (and Theravada) understanding of the Buddhist way.

"HEMP BINDINGS AND PAPER BANDAGES"

Like many Zen masters of his day, Tetsugen was highly critical of some of his contemporaries who called themselves Zen masters. He believed that many so-called masters had fallen into a trap that all Zen practitioners face: having once attained some degree of proficiency in meditation, the practitioner may mistake this preliminary stage of realization for ultimate enlightenment itself and cease striving. In several of his writings, Tetsugen warned his own disciples against falling into this trap, which he regarded as a shallow understanding of the ultimate truth. For example, he wrote a strong response to Noritomi Tessen, a lay disciple who had expressed understanding of the Dharma using fairly common Zen expressions.

> Viewpoints like this look like the real thing, but they aren't. At the present time, those who practice Zen often produce this sort of view. They seek after these reflections and shadows, and take them to be the Master. Hemp bindings and paper bandages are taken to be the teaching received [when Bodhidharma] came from the West.

Tetsugen saw not only the problems that this shallow attainment implied for the mistaken individual, but the ramifications it could have for others as well if it were not recognized and corrected. If a Zen master were taken in by a practitioner's error, then the teacher might seriously compound the student's problem by attesting to the validity of the experience and thus perpetuate the pattern. "At the present time, many of those who teach Zen all over the place take this sickness to be the Dharma; they cannot recognize their error. In the long run, the blind lead the blind and end up pulling one another into the fiery pit [of hell]" (Dharma Words 2).

In Tetsugen's view, false masters posed a threat because they were able to pass themselves off as true masters by imitating the actions of the patriarchs described in the Zen literature.

> They raise their fists, point their fingers, raise their eyebrows, and wink their eyes. Some give a shout, and others wipe their sleeves. All of them are living in a demon's cave [of darkness and ignorance]. Their heels are not yet even on the ground. Their trumped up understanding is not the True Eye [of enlightenment]. On the contrary, they receive a white gourd [that is, false] *inka* and immediately bestow *inka* [on others]. They cause [their disciples] to seek after "clarity and spirituality" and to accept this as the teaching of the Patriarchs. In their rushing forward and shrinking back, they create an imitation and make a spectacle [of true Zen].

Having deceived their own masters, these charlatans then create the illusion of being true masters for their own aggrandizement. They cause harm to the next generation of practitioners who come to them sincerely seeking guidance. Tetsugen never indicated specific individuals that he believed were conferring "false *inka*," but his writings suggest that he felt it pervaded the Zen world of his day. He mentioned the problem in some way in almost all of his writings to advanced disciples. It would not be an exaggeration to say that Tetsugen viewed this problem as one of the greatest dangers facing Zen in his lifetime.

THE *DHARMA LESSON IN JAPANESE*
OF *ZEN MASTER TETSUGEN*

Tetsugen composed his *Dharma Lesson in Japanese* sometime toward the end of his life, though the actual date of the original text is unknown. His leading disciple Hōshū edited the first woodblock edition in 1691, adding a postscript that provides what information we have of the text's history. The full title of the woodblock edition is *Zuiryū Tetsugen Zenji kana hōgo,* The Dharma Words of Zen Master Tetsugen from Lucky Dragon Temple in the Vernacular. It was produced at Hōzōin as a part of the ongoing production of Buddhist texts that were appended to the Ōbaku edition of the scriptures. Unlike the woodblock style of the characters employed in all the other texts produced for the project, Tetsugen's *Dharma Lesson in Japanese* was designed to imitate the cursive style of calligraphy, using *hiragana* rather than *katakana.* The text includes phonetic readings (*furigana*) for all the Chinese characters throughout the text, even the most basic. Later editions were produced using the same woodblocks, changing only the frontpiece and portrait.[5]

According to Hōshū's postscript, Tetsugen wrote the lesson "for a woman deeply committed to Zen." The woman's identity is otherwise unknown; it is not known whether she was a nun or lay practitioner. One may surmise from the content that she was somewhat advanced in her practice, since Tetsugen wrote to her of the difficult problems related to the *alaya* consciousness, cited above. Nonetheless, it seems likely that Tetsugen had in mind a wider audience when he wrote this extended lesson. It was commonplace for longer examples of Dharma words to circulate among believers, often copied out first by hand and then later preserved in printed editions. Tetsugen himself had edited and published a number of Yinyuan's Dharma lessons, so he was fully aware of the possibility. Moreover, the text shows signs of careful planning and presentation, suggesting that Tetsugen regarded it as a formal composition.

In his shorter *hōgo* written in Chinese, Tetsugen generally used a very simple structure and concentrated on a single issue appropriate for the specific individual addressed. In contrast, he used a longer format with an intricate structure for the *Dharma Lesson in Japanese.* On the most obvious level, the entire work takes the form of an extensive commentary on a single verse from the *Heart sutra:* "When [Avalokiteśvara] realized that the five *skandhas* are all empty, he escaped from all pain and distress."[6] Following the pattern set by this verse, the *Dharma Lesson* divides naturally into six sections. After a very brief introduction in which Tetsugen introduces the verse and gives a preliminary explanation of its terms, there follow five sections addressing each of the *skandhas* individually. In these sections, Tetsugen strives first to define the *skandha* under consideration, to elucidate the delusions and attachments specifically associated with it, and finally to expose its underlying illusory quality. Through examples, parables, and quotations from scripture, Tetsugen describes the process by which one recognizes each *skandha* as empty. Beginning with attachment to form, which is the coarsest, and continuing along to attachment to consciousness, which is the most subtle, Tetsugen uses the five sections to describe a person's development along the Buddhist path from ignorance to enlightenment. Tetsugen's overall message for his reader can be encapsulated in a simple restatement of the verse: When you realize that all the five *skandhas* are empty, you will escape from all pain and distress. Indeed, variations on this theme serve as the concluding refrain for each of the five substantive sections.

The structure of the *Dharma Lesson* can be viewed in a number of alternative ways that elucidate other aspects of Tetsugen's teaching. In his introduction, Tetsugen reduces the five *skandhas* to two simpler categories: body and mind. "The five *skandhas* are form, sensation, perception, psychic construction, and consciousness. Although there are five items, they come down to just [two], "body" and "mind." First of all, "form" is the body, and the other four [*skandhas*] are mind." This suggests that on some level Tetsugen's full discussion of the five *skandhas* likewise falls into two distinct parts: the section on form (section 1), which addresses delusions related to the body, and the sections on sensation, perception, psychic construction, and consciousness (sections 2 through 5), which address those related to the mind. Tetsugen does indeed use this division to clarify the distinction made by Mahayana Buddhists between the Lesser (Hinayana) and the Greater (Mahayana) Vehicles. Those sentient beings said to be afflicted with delusions related to the body include both ordinary human beings who cannot rightly be said to be on the Buddhist path as well as those who follow the Lesser Vehicle, *sravakas* and *pratyekabuddhas*, who have made some progress beyond the confines of ordinary human ignorance. Tetsugen creates a contrast between those afflicted with delusions of the body, and the practitioners of the Great Vehicle, Bodhisattvas, who transcend the delusions of the body and progress toward enlightenment by eliminating the delusions of the mind.

In section 1, Tetsugen explains that ordinary human beings mistake the body for an eternally abiding self and become attached to this illusion of self. *Sravakas* and *pratyekabuddhas* are more advanced than this and have overcome the crude attachment to self. "Those in the two vehicles are wiser than ordinary people, and so they clearly recognize this body as a temporary configuration of earth, water, fire, and wind, and regard it in fact as white bones. They have no thoughts of attachment to their body in the least. Nor do they give rise to attachment to self or self-pride." Despite their understanding of no-self, they are still deluded by the body (form) on a more subtle level; *sravakas* and *pratyeka-buddhas* have not yet taken the further step and seen that all dharmas are likewise devoid of self. Bodhisattvas, transcending the delusions of ordinary people and of *sravakas* and *pratyekabuddhas* alike, understand the truth of emptiness. They recognize that they themselves and all dharmas are the *Dharmakāya*. In the traditional language of Mahayana Buddhism, they have realized that *samsara* and nirvana are one and the same. Or, in the language of the *Heart Sutra*, "Form is emptiness, and emptiness is form."[7] Tetsugen glosses this verse to mean "that this body is itself the *Dharmakāya,* and the *Dharmakāya* is itself this body."

Having dealt in section 1 with the preliminary stages of complete delusion and the limited progress of the Lesser Vehicle, Tetsugen then describes the path of Mahayana Buddhism proper, that is the path of the Bodhisattva, in sections 2 through 5. Although divided into four sections according to the number of *skandhas* related to the mind, the underlying structure of the text seems to fall into three rather than four parts. This recalls a number of common three-part archetypes used to describe Buddhist practice found throughout the scriptures, sometimes based on the threefold refuge of Buddha, Dharma, and Sangha, and other times based on the traditional divisions of precept, meditation, and wisdom. In the sixth fascicle of the *Śūramgama sutra,* a chapter for which Tetsugen showed an abiding predilection, we find an example of the latter.

> The Buddha said to Ananda, "You have always heard me explain in the *Vinaya* that there are three determined aspects in practice. That is to say, pacifying the mind is the precepts, then the precepts bring forth stillness, and stillness gives rise to wisdom. These are called the three pure [aspects of] study.[8]

In the case of the *Dharma Lesson,* Tetsugen follows a slightly different threefold pattern, namely the movement of Buddhist practice through discipline (keeping the precepts), teachings (the study of the Dharma), and finally meditation (transcending the intellectual, dualistic understanding of the Dharma experientially). This three-part movement roughly reflects Tetsugen's conceptualization of Zen training. Specifically, Tetsugen deals with issues of discipline in sections 2 and 3, with the teachings in section 4, and with meditation in section 5.

Tetsugen's use of source material and his style of argumentation support the three-part pattern. In sections 2 and 3, Tetsugen makes no direct reference to the scriptures, relying exclusively on examples drawn from human life to illustrate his points. In laying down the precepts as the foundation for all forms and levels of Buddhist practice, Tetsugen seeks to establish an intuitive understanding of the underlying principles rather than a scholarly explication based on the written canon. In section 4, Tetsugen changes his style and begins to introduce extensive quotations from the scriptures to frame his argument on psychic construction. At this stage, Tetsugen recognizes that a certain degree of understanding is attained by the believer, but that it is almost certainly an intellectual and therefore dualistic understanding. In section 6, Tetsugen finally introduces meditation, and for the first time makes use of the images and quotations characteristic of Zen literature. Naturally, Zen believers rely on the same basic pillars of precept and scripture as other Mahayana Buddhists, but Zen is distinguished by its focus on meditation as the ultimate form of Buddhist practice. In the monastery, the life of the Zen practitioner is not very different from that of other Buddhist monks; they follow the rule of monastic discipline to govern their communal life, and chant and study the sutras as a regular part of their daily practice. Tetsugen mirrors this pattern in his *Dharma Lesson* by leaving the specifically Zen discussion to the final section. Viewing the text in this manner helps to explain why Tetsugen, a Zen master, uses so little Zen vocabulary and so few references early on in the piece and reserves his discussion of meditation for the final pages.

In sections 2 and 3, Tetsugen turns his attention toward the Mahayana path leading to enlightenment. In the process of explicating the *skandhas* "sensation" and "perception," Tetsugen shows his concern for keeping the precepts, discipline being the first element in the practice of Buddhism. Although he mentions the Buddhist precepts against stealing, lying, and drinking liquor, he singles out the precept against killing in section 2 and, in a more subtle and indirect fashion, the precept against sexual misconduct in section 3. It is probably not accidental that he chose the very precepts that, for him, define Buddhist practice on the lay and monastic level, respectively. The two sections thus function as a single unit on discipline, but taken separately refer to the basic division in Buddhist practice between ordained and lay believers.

In his general discussion of the ideal of nonkilling, Tetsugen concentrates his attention on meat-eating. By singling out meat-eating among the many possible examples of killing, Tetsugen has chosen an instance that affected the lives of most of his audience. Moreover, he selected a behavior that anyone could change, even laypeople such as farmers who kill inadvertently in the normal course of their work. Tetsugen used graphic images like that of the crow eating rotten flesh to shock his reader into reinterpreting the commonplace activity of eating meat through the eyes of an enlightened being.

> [When] a crow . . . sees a dead cow or horse rotting or a human corpse festering, it thinks it is a rare treat. First it enjoys looking at it, then its enjoyment increases as it smells it and grasps it. It thinks this is the greatest of pleasures. Seen from the human perspective, this seems immeasurably impure and repulsive. If we were forced by others to eat such putrid things, it would be incomparable suffering. What is worse than being forced to eat them is that crows devour such things greedily, and think it is pleasant. Although it isn't [truly] pleasant, their minds are foolish and base, and so they think that pain is pleasure. What human beings find pleasurable is similar. Because of foolish minds, we are consumed by wife and children, are deluded by wealth, eat fish and fowl, and take this to be pleasant. Viewed from the perspective of Buddhas and bodhisattvas, this looks even more wretched than the crows seem to us from our human vantage. Conjecturing from this, [we see that] what deluded people find pleasant actually brings pain, they only believe it is pleasure.

Tetsugen teaches the most basic of all Buddhist precepts by explaining its rationale through example: We refrain from killing because like the Buddhas and bodhisattvas, we recognize that all sentient beings are our own children, our very bodies. What we perceive from our limited perspective as pleasant, is seen from a more advanced vantage point as suffering.

In the context of defining the *skandha* of "sensation," then, Tetsugen introduces a crucial element of the Buddhist understanding of the human condition, perception and misperception. Because sentient beings misperceive pain, confusing it with pleasure, like a moth going into the flame or a fish snatching the bait, they seek pleasure and reap pain. Tetsugen juxtaposes the human perspective of the crow's behavior with the perspective that an enlightened being would take of ordinary human behavior. It is when playing with these levels of perception that Tetsugen shows his reputed talent for language. His images in this section are by far his strongest, and his prose flows naturally without the interruption of quotations and their interpretation.

Appropriately, Tetsugen continues to develop the theme of perception and misperception in the section on the *skandha* of "perception." His dominant image in this section is the dream, which he uses to expose the fundamental unreality of waking thoughts.

> Everyone thinks that nighttime dreams are the only fabrications that lack a basis in fact, and that what they think about during the day is true. This is a terrible mistake. . . . Whatever we think of as hateful, lovable, reproachful, enviable, beloved, or dear, are all illusions that don't change the dreaming mind at all. Originally we have no such illusions in our true minds, which are like a shining mirror or pure water. Because we fail to realize our true mind, we leave the images of illusion reflected on our true mind. We believe they are true and become firmly attached to them, and so these illusions become increasingly extensive, and the delusions grow deeper and deeper.

In particular, Tetsugen exposes the illusion inherent in love, especially romantic love. He thus continues his development of the theme of the importance of the precepts by his subtle allusion to the precepts governing sexual conduct.

The monastic rules governing sexual conduct are based upon the realization that there is no basis for distinctions between loved and unloved from the perspective of the enlightened mind. Tetsugen explains this rationale by exposing to close scrutiny the sentiments of love that lead to romantic entanglements.

> Thinking that something is repulsive and thinking something is attractive are both figments of your own imagination. . . . As we gradually get to know someone, feelings of intimacy deepen toward a person we find compatible, and we create the feeling that they are attractive. It is precisely because of this circumstance that when we follow the paths of affection, however much it changes our lives, to that extent the ties of tenderness likewise increase. When you develop feelings of love in this way, love seems inevitable, and whichever way you turn it over in your mind, it is love without a trace of hatefulness. When love reaches an extreme, and you think that even if you were to live one hundred million *kalpas* your feelings wouldn't change, you are mistaken.

It is interesting to note that as Tetsugen continues his exploration of romantic attachments, he describes the inversion of love to hate.

> Though you are intimate friends, you will have some differences of opinion, and will quarrel. Then the quarrels grow into arguments. Or, as is the way of love, if your [lover's] feelings shift to another, however deep were your feelings of love at the beginning, that is how deep your hate will now become. These feelings of hatred and bitterness are so deep that you may even think that they will eventually kill you. . . . If the thoughts of love were not false in the first place, then you would probably not have changed your mind in a short time and decided it was repulsive.

According to Tetsugen, the process seems almost inevitable, love shifts readily to hate because both sentiments are based on an illusion. If from the beginning, one recognizes passing illusions like romantic love for what they are, then he suggests one can easily expel them. Precisely because one latches on to the feelings and allows them to pile up, they take on the appearance of reality.

In section 4, Tetsugen introduces the concept of "psychic construction," identifying it with the steady flow of ideas and images that run unceasingly through the mind. Ordinary people are deluded by psychic constructions and mistakenly identify this flow of ideas with the true mind. Tetsugen employs the familiar image of the mirror to explain the relationship between the true mind and the ideas that pass through it.

> When you see images reflected in a bright mirror all day long, it reflects the sky, the land, flowers, willow trees, people, animals and birds. All the colors change and the types of things [reflected] change without a moment's rest, but the true form of the mirror is not the birds and animals, or the people, or the willows, flowers, the land, or the sky. It is just the shining and unclouded mirror itself. Our original minds reflect and illuminate the ten thousand *dharmas*, but have no connection to their distinctions.

The mind, like the mirror, is independent of the images it reflects and remains unchanged by them. Therefore, there is no need to purify it of them. While it is possible to quiet the flow of psychic constructions in meditation, there remains a dualism inherent in the practice. For the enlightened mind, the mirror should be visible "even if images of blossoms and willows are reflected."

Tetsugen presents the twofold vision of the enlightened mind with an example that illustrates the Madhyamika teaching of the two levels of truth without employing technical philosophical language. Tetsugen invites the reader to consider an array of figurines made from gold. When regarded as shapes, they are each distinct, but when regarded as gold, they become indistinguishable. "The ten thousand *dharmas* are the same. When we look at them from the perspective of True Thusness, just as with the gold, there is no distinction at all. When we look at them from the perspective of the ten thousand *dharmas*, they are distinguished as different shapes." While the ordinary person is confused and deluded by the shapes, the enlightened person can see beyond the distinctions. The freedom to operate on both levels of the truth is the only difference between the enlightened and the ordinary person.

By breaking down the seemingly insurmountable distinction between ordinary sentient beings and enlightened Buddhas, Tetsugen undermines one of
the more subtle forms of delusion, attachment to the Dharma and the Buddha.
Tetsugen demonstrates that terms like "Buddha" and "nirvana" associated with
enlightenment are temporary designations used for convenience in teaching.
He applies the adjective "illusionary" identically to the vocabulary describing
both enlightenment and the pain and suffering of sentient beings in the six
paths. Aware that this kind of teaching may confuse some believers who will
mistake it for nihilism, Tetsugen hastens to reassure the reader that from the
perspective of enlightenment, this is not the case. The difficulty is almost always
one of perspective: What appears as food to an ordinary human being turns to
fire in the mouth of a hungry ghost. In a similar manner, when perfect enlightenment is the subject of the discriminating mind rather than a matter of direct
experience, it too becomes a hindrance.

Tetsugen continues to use simple, graphic illustrations to explain the more
complicated ideas in section 4, but he changes the style of argumentation to in-
corporate a large number of quotations from the sutras. Tetsugen quotes from
at least seven sources, showing a strong preference for those texts that support
the unity of the teachings and meditation, especially the *Perfect Enlightenment
Sutra*[9] and the *Śūramgama Sutra*. Yet despite his obvious enjoyment of sutra
explication, Tetsugen never loses sight of the need to transcend an intellectual
understanding of the Dharma. In the midst of arguing through proof texts,
Tetsugen moves the reader forward to his discussion of meditation by demonstrating the limits of the very scholarly approach employed.

> It says in the *Perfect Enlightenment Sutra*, "Since they have not yet escaped
> transmigration and realized perfect enlightenment, it is said that even per-
> fect enlightenment leads to transmigration." This means that while your mind
> is not yet enlightened, you use your discriminating mind to distinguish and
> consider perfect enlightenment itself, and so even perfect enlightenment turns
> into transmigration. In reality, if you think that you have realized enlighten-
> ment itself, and you do not cast off all intellectual understanding and clev-
> erness, if you do not stop thoughts of right and wrong or wickedness and
> correctness, it is just like coming face to face with a silver mountain or a wall
> of iron.

Tetsugen concludes this section with examples of monks who have taken the
teachings to the limits of intellectual understanding and then transcended
those limits with the direct experience of enlightenment. Here Tetsugen gives
us our first glimpse into the world of Zen Buddhism proper and so bridges the
discussion to the final section on meditation and enlightenment.

Tetsugen begins section 5, his commentary on the fifth and final *skandha*,
"consciousness," with a brief review of the material covered under the other
three rubrics related to the mind, sensation, perception, and psychic construction. This time, however, through image and example, he works backwards,

returning finally to distinctions like pleasure and pain associated with sensation. Generally speaking, Buddhist texts use descriptions of the five *skandhas* to explain the processes and workings of human life, starting with form and building to consciousness. By reversing the order, Tetsugen is inviting the reader to reverse the process, to deconstruct the false understanding of consciousness, and finally return to the original state of enlightenment. The means to accomplish this reversal is meditation.

Section 5 is the only opportunity that Tetsugen takes in the entire essay to focus on specifically Zen teachings. In particular, he describes various stages of meditation and the dangers inherent in them for the practitioner; he warns that the danger increases sharply after an initial breakthrough has occurred. The beginner remains trapped within the polar distinctions of good thoughts and bad thoughts. Transcendence of these distinctions marks the student's maturity in meditation.

> Once this happens, you must persevere in your meditation. If you sit in meditation intently without being negligent, at first your mind will clear for short periods, but gradually your mind will be clear while you meditate for one third of the time or two thirds of the time. Then it will be clear from beginning to end, neither good nor evil thoughts arise, nor is the mind indifferent. Like the clear Autumn sky or a polished mirror on a stand, the mind is the same as empty space, and you feel as if the Dharmakāya were within your breast. Nothing can compare with the coolness within your breast. This is the state of someone who has perfected sitting in meditation more than half of the time. In the Zen sect we call it "beating everything into one," "the realm of one form," "a person who has died the great death," and "the world of Fugen."

But Tetsugen explains that even though the student has become adept in this manner, it is possible to confuse this stage of significant progress with ultimate enlightenment, which has yet to be attained. Having fallen into this trap, the student may lack the motivation to forge ahead, blinded to the need for further effort. At this point, the student may even manage to deceive a Zen master and receive *inka* prematurely, thus compounding the danger by entangling another generation of students in the error.

Tetsugen identifies this intermediate stage of Zen meditation with the highest attainments achieved through Daoist and Neo-Confucian meditation. In Buddhist terms, he associates it with the *samadhi* of arhats and *pratyekabuddhas*. Practitioners at this level of meditation have become aware of what is known in Yogācāra thought as the *alaya* consciousness.

> All of the [above-mentioned attainments] are free from the distinctions of seeing, hearing, learning and knowing. They indicate a place of no-thought and no-mind like the one that the Buddha and the patriarchs mention. The place of no-thought and no-mind which is like the clear blue sky is known as "the eighth consciousness of sentient beings" [i.e., *alaya* consciousness]. . . .

Attachment to this advanced level of attainment constitutes the most subtle of all the hindrances that Tetsugen describes in the movement from attachment to form to enlightenment. The believer has reached the very precipice of enlightenment, but has not yet taken the final step.

According to Tetsugen, a master must take great care in instructing disciples about the *alaya* consciousness. Even the Buddha himself showed extreme caution at this critical juncture.

> Since this consciousness resembles the true original mind, but isn't the original mind, even the Buddha couldn't easily teach about it to foolish people. This is because, if he taught that this consciousness itself was the truth, then sentient beings would stop there, and thinking this [level of attainment] was sufficient, not persevere in their practice. [On the other hand,] if he taught that it wasn't true, then sentient beings would think that everything is completely void, doubt the existence of the original mind and fall into nihilism. Then they would indeed be unable to awaken to the original mind.

Awareness of the *alaya* consciousness is the final plateau in Zen meditation, after which, figuratively speaking, one must let go of the branch while hanging over a cliff or step off the end of a hundred-foot pole.

At the end of each section, Tetsugen states that by overcoming the delusions associated with the particular *skandha* under consideration, the believer attains enlightenment. This pattern becomes a kind of refrain that marks the conclusion of a section and restates the overall message of the entire *Dharma Lesson*. Tetsugen concludes section 5 with a similar, though much more extensive, version of this refrain, in which he elaborates on the theme of attainment. While Zen masters have always maintained that mere words cannot capture the experience of enlightenment, Tetsugen takes this opportunity to attempt a limited explanation of the experience. In order to describe an experience that transcends the confines of human speech, Tetsugen resorts to images such as a dawn of ten thousand suns rising simultaneously, seeing the Buddhas of the Three Worlds, and penetrating to the marrow of Sakyamuni and Bodhidharma.

Rather than conclude his essay with the description of enlightenment at the end of section 5, Tetsugen closes his lesson on a decidedly different note. He relates two enlightenment accounts designed to illustrate the way in which a Zen master can help a disciple take the final step toward enlightenment. In each case, the master diagnoses the illness, understands that the disciple believes he has attained enlightenment, and so provides a final challenge. Nothing can substitute for the face-to-face encounter between the master and the disciple. In the context of a written lesson, Tetsugen can only recommend diligent meditation and concentration on the kōan before and after one reaches the critical juncture. While his tone retains the positive element of hope and encouragement that with diligence the goal can be attained, his final words are a warning: You must not make a mistake and fall into a fox's cave.

THE *KŌMORI BŌDANKI* (THE FORGOTTEN WRITTEN ACCOUNT ABOUT BATS)

The *Kōmori bōdanki,* commonly attributed to Tetsugen, is a highly polemical text attacking the True Pure Land Buddhist practices and teachings regarding the Buddhist precepts. The text represents one side of an ongoing debate during the Tokugawa period over the True Pure Land practice of allowing clergy to openly marry and consume meat.[10] Tetsugen's actual role in this debate remains somewhat unclear. Without a doubt, he rightly earned a reputation as a vocal advocate of keeping the precepts in both his lectures and his written works. As a former True Pure Land priest, Tetsugen came to be seen by his former colleagues as a particularly heinous opponent, and on at least one occasion this led to open debate at one of his lectures in Edo.

I have chosen not to include a complete translation of the *Kōmori bōdanki* in this volume of Tetsugen's writings for several interrelated reasons. First and foremost, it seems doubtful that Tetsugen himself actually composed the *Kōmori bōdanki.* Second, the text stands out as distinct from Tetsugen's corpus of writings. Not only is it harshly polemical, attacking both the teachings and the members of a particular sect of Japanese Buddhism, its intended audience were the participants in the ongoing written debate rather than a broader Buddhist community. So while the *Kōmori bōdanki* is informative about the arguments relevant to that debate, it does not help contemporary readers to understand Tetsugen's teachings concerning Zen Buddhism or Mahayana Buddhism more broadly. Since the internal problems discussed below call Tetsugen's authorship into serious doubt, it did not seem responsible to include a text that would overshadow his other writings, writings that he and his disciples hoped to preserve for future generations.

Before moving on to discuss problems and issues related to the attribution of the *Kōmori bōdanki* to Tetsugen, a brief explanation of its title seems in order. The title is as polemical as the text itself. The expression for bats derives from the *Butsuzōkyō,* in which the Buddha applies the term to monks who would fail to keep the precepts after his death in the Final Age of the Dharma, long after the Buddha's death.[11] Bats are animals of ambiguous classification that can make a claim to be rats or birds as the circumstance suits them. In much the same way, the *Kōmori bōdanki* says that True Pure Land priests wear the robes and claim the privileges of Buddhist monks while behaving like laypeople. The term *bō,* variously translated as "forgotten" or "neglected," is commonly used in Chinese and Japanese compounds referring to individuals who neglect to fulfill various moral imperatives. To say that someone has "forgotten filial piety," for example, would be a harsh criticism.

The *Kōmori bōdanki* circulated under Tetsugen's name in manuscript form during the Tokugawa period. Tetsugen's disciples did not preserve the text as a part of Tetsugen's corpus of writings, and never published it in any form. In fact, to my knowledge, no manuscript copies are preserved at any Ōbaku temple or monastery. The two known copies are now preserved at True Pure Land institutions.[12] Modern Ōbaku scholars reject the attribution of the text to Tetsugen, arguing that it was a forgery.[13] Other scholars have accepted the attribution without extensive comment. While Ōbaku sectarian scholars of the past and present have their own apologetic reasons to deny Tetsugen's authorship, this does not mean that the attribution should be immediately accepted as factual. There were likewise several compelling reasons during the Tokugawa period for someone to attach Tetsugen's name to an anti–True Pure Land text such as the *Kōmori bōdanki*. First, Tetsugen enjoyed a rather high reputation within the Buddhist world because of his efforts to print the scriptures, and he was known as an outspoken proponent of strict adherence to the precepts. In addition, it was well known that he was a former member of the True Pure Land sect. Individuals directly interested and involved in the *nikujiki saitai* (clerical meat-eating and marriage) debates of the day[14] would have been well aware of the tensions that existed between Tetsugen and his former colleagues.[15] Attaching his name could have served the purposes of individuals on either side of the debate. Tetsugen's name could be seen to lend the weight of scholarly authority by someone who agreed with the text, perhaps even its author. Alternatively, True Pure Land proponents could have attached the name of one of their most despised critics to create a rallying point.

Setting aside possible apologetic or polemical motivations to attribute the *Kōmori bōdanki* to Tetsugen or not, certain internal problems with the extant copies call that authorship into question. The text includes an autobiographical preface that purports to describe Tetsugen's early experiences as a True Pure Land priest, particularly those events that compelled him to question the sect's practices and eventually to leave the sect. If authentic, the stories would provide information about Tetsugen's early life that is recorded nowhere else. However, the preface includes several autobiographical details that are at variance with all other evidence regarding Tetsugen's life. The first problem appears only in the Naikan Bunko copy of the manuscript, which locates Tetsugen's place of birth on Honshu rather than Kyushu.

> My first lineage was as the son of an Ikkō priest from Nagoya in Owari. When I was 13, I succeeded my father at the temple. . . . My temple is a large temple in Nagoya. . . .[16]

No corroborating evidence suggests that Tetsugen was born in Nagoya rather than in Higo province on Kyushu. Not only do all the biographies from the Tokugawa and modern periods agree that he was born on Kyushu, substantial physical evidence corroborates that fact. On the other hand, place names can easily be changed in copying a manuscript for any number of reasons, so this small item alone is in no way conclusive, and the other extant copy places these same events in the Higo province of Kyushu.

The second biographical error relates to Tetsugen "succeeding" his father at age thirteen. While the text is somewhat vague, the implication seems to be that Tetsugen had already been ordained before this time and that his father died, leaving him his position at the temple. According to the *Deeds of Tetsugen,* Tetsugen was first ordained at age thirteen, and at that time he was sent to study with another True Pure Land priest named Kaiun in a neighboring village. Tetsugen's father survived well into his career as an Ōbaku monk, dying in 1674, when Tetsugen was forty-four years old (forty-five by traditional reckoning).

The preface of the *Kōmori bōdanki* moves on to recount an experience that occurred at age fifteen, when Tetsugen was summoned to attend a memorial service for the local *daimyō.* At that time, the author says that he was dismayed that he and the other True Pure Land monks were required to sit at a lower level than the "pure monks" from other sects. True Pure Land monks and *yamabushi* were ranked together at such gatherings and seated below the level of the other sects, including, as the text observes, even Jōdoshū monks. According to the preface, this event prompted much study and soul-searching on the part of the young priest, and lead to Tetsugen's decision to abandon the True Pure Land sect.

> Therefore, night and day for three years I felt ashamed facing people and shed tears on my sleeve. I looked at various sutras and commentaries. In all the sutras the Buddha gave in 49 years, there was nothing about his disciples transgressing with women and eating meat. Again, night and day I thought about the three Pure Land scriptures that I explained to lay people. I rejected the Three Scriptures and decided that the 48 vows of Amida were meaningless. The Buddha never violated the notion that discipline, meditation and wisdom are One.... The Spring that I was 18, I begged my mother's leave. The Chinese monk Yinyuan had come to Japan and became the founder of Ōbaku in Japan. I joyfully went to see him and entered the Zen sect, and for the first time became a monk.[17]

There are several problems with the chronology suggested by this passage. First, the rather clear implication of the text is that Tetsugen decided to leave the True Pure Land sect at age eighteen, prompting a farewell visit to his mother before leaving home. In actuality, Tetsugen's mother died at about that time, many years before he abandoned True Pure Land and became a Zen monk. According to the *Deeds of Tetsugen,* she died sometime before he departed for Kyoto to continue his True Pure Land education there. Although the *Deeds* does not give the year of her death, external evidence from her memorial stone indicates that she died in 1650. At the time of her death, Tetsugen returned to his home village, presumably to attend her memorial services, and it was only thereafter that he left the region.

Finally, the suggestion that Tetsugen could have joined Yinyuan and become a Zen monk at age eighteen is anachronistic. According to traditional East Asian reckoning, Tetsugen was eighteen in the year Shōhō 4 (1647). Yinyuan did not arrive in Nagasaki for another seven years, in Jōō 3 (1654), and Tetsugen only went to meet him the following year, when he was twenty-six years old (twenty-five by Western reckoning). Tetsugen would have no compelling reason to alter such biographical details as the timing of his parent's deaths, nor his own age at conversion to Zen. At the very least, the preface to the *Kōmori bōdanki* appears to have been authored by someone other than Tetsugen, someone who was only vaguely familiar with Tetsugen's biography.

Identifying or dismissing Tetsugen as the author of other portions of the text is another matter. It is theoretically possible that the main body of the text was composed first and the preface added later by someone else. An analysis of the text, however, shows that the writing style and general vocabulary appear to be fairly consistent between the sections. On the other hand, the argumentation style employed in certain sections is somewhat reminiscent of Tetsugen's teaching style preserved in other contexts. It is certainly possible that even if he did not directly compose any portion of the text, he inspired parts of it through his public appearances or private conversations. However, there are significant differences between the writing style and vocabulary found throughout the main body of the *Kōmori bōdanki* and other works definitively attributed to Tetsugen.

The author of the *Kōmori bōdanki* directly attacks the True Pure Land sect in a harsh manner using caustic terms not found in any other of Tetsugen's writings. For example, the expression *nyobon nikujiki,* "trangressing with women and eating meat," is used throughout the *Kōmori bōdanki,* but does not appear in any of his other works, including those related to the True Pure Land sect. The fact that no other text in Tetsugen's corpus is polemical in nature could be said to explain this distinction. While the *Kōmori bōdanki* makes frequent use of a variety of Buddhist sutras and other Buddhist texts, which is typical of Tetsugen's style, the texts employed do not match the list of his usual resources. Most conspicuous by its absence is any significant use of the *Śūramgama sutra,* Tetsugen's favorite scripture for defending the crucial quality of precept observance. The only mention of that sutra is a brief comment at the conclusion, "Look to the *Śūramgama sutra.* Take refuge in it." Interestingly, the expression to "take refuge" in the *Śūramgama sutra* or any other sutra is foreign to Tetsugen's other writings.

CONCLUSIONS

Tetsugen's small body of teachings do not show him to be a creative force in Buddhist thought. Instead, his work presents in a clear, carefully crafted fashion, the Buddhist tradition as he understood it. His talent lay not in elucidating new ideas for the tradition, but in translating and presenting the existing tradition for believers of his own generation. Each generation of believers requires a similar translation of the tradition using the forms and language appropriate to the times. In his early life, Tetsugen immersed himself in the study of the scriptures as much as was then possible. Tetsugen excelled as a teacher, using the vernacular language in his writings and from the pulpit to foster belief among the common people of his day. Like many talented teachers, his energy was spent in spreading the Dharma in the present and preserving it for future generations. In his case, preserving the Dharma took concrete form in his edition of the scriptures. In that way, Tetsugen participated in the continuing process of Buddhist masters studying the scriptures and explicating them for lay believers in sermons and written texts.

CHAPTER FOUR

The Myth of Tetsugen

After his death, Tetsugen was venerated in the customary manner within the Ōbaku sect, particularly by his surviving disciples. The Ōbaku edition of the Buddhist scriptures continued to be printed and distributed for well over two centuries. This represented the only legacy that Tetsugen purposefully bequeathed to later generations of Buddhists, and it guaranteed that Tetsugen would be remembered within the wider world of Japanese Buddhism. With time, Tetsugen became the object of a small body of both devotional and popular literature. Given his position within the Ōbaku sect and his accomplishments, that is not surprising. What does come as a surprise is that today when his edition of the scriptures has faded in importance, Tetsugen's story has become something of a legacy in its own right.

Stories about Tetsugen come in a variety of forms and genres that can be categorized in a number of ways. There are at least three broad categories that will serve the purposes of analysis here: religious biographies, secular biographies, and polemical materials. The distinction between religious and secular as applied to this material refers primarily to the authorship and locus of publication. Religious biographies are those written by a believer for a Buddhist audience and typically published by a Buddhist press. Secular biographies are those that appeared in nonreligious contexts, including scholarly works. Neither the use of legendary materials nor a striving for historical accuracy characterizes one category over the other. While some religious biographers seek to use only verifiable historical facts, certain secular sources freely combine historical fact with legend. For the present purposes, the third category of negative material written to discredit Tetsugen is excluded from consideration, except to the extent that it influenced the creation of the more positive biographies.

RELIGIOUS BIOGRAPHIES

The religious biographies about Tetsugen begin with the sectarian biographies composed by Tetsugen's immediate disciples, of which the *Deeds of Tetsugen* is the primary example.[1] Within the Zen school, it is traditional for a disciple, especially a leading disciple or the primary Dharma heir, to compose a biography of the master. These sectarian biographies serve several purposes. First, they honor the memory of the deceased master and preserve his life story for his lineage. Second, by following certain relatively set patterns, they create an image of the master as an exemplary figure for others to emulate. In this latter capacity, biographies are pedagogical materials that teach proper conduct, and appropriate religious values and virtues and the like within the tradition.

Hōshū, Tetsugen's first and arguably most advanced disciple, wrote the *Deeds of Tetsugen* in time for the thirty-third anniversary memorial service of Tetsugen's death. He explained his reasons in the following way:

> I, Hōshū Dōsō, gratefully served Tetsugen the longest, and so am well informed about the details [of his life]. When I think about my debt of gratitude for his instructions, it seems no different from heaven sheltering us from above and the earth cradling us from below.
>
> The years have passed peacefully, and already thirty years are gone. Few among the young or the old know the story of Tetsugen's life. Now that thirty years have passed, most of the people who knew him have died. For this reason, without reflecting on my own incompetence, I have written this short summary in order to state it clearly for later generations.

Like many other religious biographies, the *Deeds* was written for an internal audience, in this case for later generations of Ōbaku practitioners.

Tetsugen's status as a famous Zen monk was firmly established by his successful completion of the scripture project, and this led to his reputation reaching beyond the confines of the Ōbaku sect to the broader Zen and Buddhist audiences. Beginning in the Tokugawa period and continuing down to the present, his biography came to be a regular item in the "famous monk" (meisō) collections. Compendia of biographies of important monks have long been characteristic of East Asian Buddhism, including many works focussed specifically on the Zen school. These biographical sketches tend to be short, often no more than a page or two in length, and to focus on specific accomplishments that make the monks extraordinary, such as founding a new school of Buddhism.

CRAFTING THE IMAGE

Commemorating Tetsugen's life gave Hōshū the opportunity to craft a fairly complete and detailed biography that nevertheless presented Tetsugen as a model Ōbaku master. He included a number of standard features that one commonly finds in Zen biographies of the day. The biography provides evidence of Tetsugen's childhood intellectual abilities and his promise as a Buddhist practitioner. It records the founder of Ōbaku Zen Yinyuan's initial evaluation that he was a "vessel of the Dharma" as well as descriptions of significant encounters

Tetsugen had with the other leading Chinese Ōbaku teachers. As one expects in any Zen biography, it details his exchanges between Tetsugen and Muan, especially the account of his Dharma transmission, and it includes Tetsugen's death verse. Like most Tokugawa biographers, Hōshū included what contemporary readers would regard as miraculous stories from during Tetsugen's lifetime and immediately after his death. These stories were standard elements in premodern Buddhist literature, and establish Tetsugen as a person of spiritual or karmic power.

While religious biographers often highlight specific details from a master's life that are especially instructive to believers, they just as frequently choose to edit out those elements that they deem uninstructive or detrimental to the overall portrait they wish to draw. Reading the sectarian biographies from the period, for example, one is left with the impression that Tetsugen passed the first twelve years of his monastic practice as a generic Buddhist monk without any sectarian affiliation. The biographers provide no specific details or stories that help one form an image of the young Tetsugen as a True Pure Land priest. Nor do they suggest possible reasons for his seeking out a Zen master and converting to Zen practice.

Biographies of the Chinese Ōbaku masters tended to stress the teachers' filial piety and early connections with Pure Land practice. In Yinyuan's biography, *Fushō kokushi nempu*, for example, the master is said to have encouraged his mother in her Buddhist practices by reciting the *nembutsu* with her daily in the years before he entered the monastery.[2] Similarly, Muan's biography details the master's early devotion to the bodhisattva Kannon (Ch. Guanyin) and his exposure to Pure Land teachings from his first Buddhist teacher.[3] Such is not the case with the sectarian biographies of Tetsugen. Although his early training in Pure Land teachings and practice could have been interpreted as paralleling the Chinese masters' lives, none of his early sectarian biographers followed the Chinese biographical pattern.

It would appear that for Tetsugen's early sectarian biographers, his extensive connection with the True Pure Land sect posed a problem for the image they wished to preserve. They either avoided the topic completely by glossing over his early years, or made only veiled references to it, as Hōshū chose to do in the *Deeds*. Rather than saying explicitly that Tetsugen's father was a True Pure Land priest, for example, Hōshū describes him as a fervent believer in Mahayana teachings and mentions that he joined the Lotus Society (*rensha*, short for *byakurengesha*) in his later years.[4] The Lotus Society did not exist as such in Japan, and the term appears to be a euphemism for Pure Land Buddhism. Nor does Hōshū make clear that Tetsugen himself was ordained as a True Pure Land priest, and that he traveled to Kyoto to study at the True Pure Land academy. This lacuna allows Hōshū to ignore completely any discussion of why Tetsugen chose to leave True Pure Land and convert to Ōbaku Zen.

Other facts related to Tetsugen's early life that would directly imply his True Pure Land affiliation are likewise omitted from the sectarian biographies.

Tetsugen's previous marital status is completely ignored in the sectarian sources, although it is quite likely that a twenty-five-year-old True Pure Land priest would already have been married. Moreover, secular sources specifically mention Tetsugen's wife. Since True Pure Land priests were the only Buddhist clerics who openly married at this time, a discussion of Tetsugen's married status would necessarily imply his previous affiliation. The sources likewise exclude mention of the Buddhist name Tetsugen used in his youth. Neither do they give any indication that either Yinyuan or Muan gave him a new name, although that was the common practice when a monk joined a Zen master's assembly. Moreover, the name Tetsugen is clearly of Zen origin[5] and it is easily recognized as one of a series of names in the Ōbaku community beginning with the same character. While it is possible that Tetsugen's first Buddhist name was not known by his biographers, it likewise possible that it was intentionally omitted, as an unnecessary reminder of his earlier affiliation.

SECULAR BIOGRAPHIES

Secular biographers of the day displayed no such scruples about discussing Tetsugen's early life. These sources were aimed at a different audience and designed to serve different purposes than the religious biographies. *Biographies of Unusual People of the Early Modern Period* (*Kinsei kijin den*) is one such secular source that includes a portrait of Tetsugen. The text is a compendium of biographical sketches of unusual individuals from all social classes and walks of life during the Tokugawa period. The text appears to have been intended for a wide reading audience, as it contains illustrations throughout and is written in very straightforward Japanese. Buddhist figures such as Tetsugen were not treated exclusively as saintly subjects; the author collected what information was available and presented it with an eye to creating an amusing and not just an edifying story.

The portrait of Tetsugen in *Biographies of Unusual People of the Early Modern Period* (hereafter *Unusual People*) includes some obvious errors in chronology as well as some popular stories that are impossible to check for historical accuracy. On the other hand, it provides anecdotal information about Tetsugen that helps to broaden our sense of the man himself. It begins with a direct reference to Tetsugen's True Pure Land affiliation and an explanation for his eventual disenchantment with the sect.

> The monk Tetsugen Dōkō was born in the province of Higo in a branch temple of Honganji. Although he was already married, he was dissatisfied that in the [True Pure Land] sect, people without talent or merit held high rank in the temple hierarchy. Therefore, he went up to Mount Ōbaku and followed [the instruction] of Muan.

The passage contains some minor historical errors. The reference to Mount Ōbaku is anachronistic, since Tetsugen first sought out Yinyuan in Nagasaki some years before the monastery was founded. In addition, Tetsugen only became Muan's disciple later, when Yinyuan left the majority of his Japanese disciples under Muan's instruction. Nevertheless, the passage is the earliest reference to Tetsugen's marriage that I have found in Tokugawa sources. The sketch continues with an entertaining vignette of Tetsugen hiding from his former wife.

> His wife came to [Mount Ōbaku] to find him, but he did not wish to meet her. So she camped outside the temple gate and watched for him to emerge. Finally, one day when he had no choice but to go out, she asked him to accompany her to their home province and return to their village. He escaped up the street and returned to the temple.

The veracity of this story is dubious, unless something similar actually occurred in Nagasaki, closer to Tetsugen's home village. Even if it were based on a historical event, one can readily understand why sectarian sources would have omitted any mention of it. The story poses several problems for a religious biography beyond revealing Tetsugen's True Pure Land affiliation. Not only does it undermine the dignified image that sectarian sources project, it suggests that Tetsugen did not have his wife's permission before he converted to Zen, a serious breach of the monastic code.

The story in *Unusual People* concludes with observations concerning Tetsugen's talents as well as his failings. It notes that Tetsugen failed to establish his own lineage within the Ōbaku sect, because "within his own group of disciples he was not forceful enough and so never designated a Dharma heir." It also reports that after his death there were problems with some of his disciples. This last piece of information is so vague that it is impossible to trace its source or to be certain what kind of problems are implied, but it is clear that the author made use of materials other than the sectarian biographies.

Despite the inclusion of unflattering material, the portrait of Tetsugen in *Unusual People* paints him as a highly virtuous and compassionate Buddhist.

> Since [Tetsugen] had set his mind on printing a woodblock edition of the Tripitaka, he collected funds. At that time, there was terrible starvation throughout the country. Tetsugen was troubled by this and distributed so much in alms that he had less than half of the money [he had collected] left. Just as before, he solicited funds and after several years collected it once again. For a second time, many people were dying of hunger because the grain crops had failed. This time as well he gave away all his money. However, due to his great virtue, the third time that he raised the money he completed the edition of the Tripitaka.

The focus here is clearly on Tetsugen's tremendous perseverance to fulfill his vow and his even greater compassion in placing the needs of others above his own plans. This version of the story represents an important turning point in the development of the myth of Tetsugen, as it is the earliest known written source of the legendary tale of Tetsugen thrice raising the funds to finance the scripture project.

The pattern of Tetsugen raising the funds three times and spending the money the first two times on the victims of natural disasters became the standard framework for many of the subsequent biographies. The location and nature of the disasters seems to shift from one version to the next—a flood in Uji, a famine in Kansai, an epidemic somewhere in the countryside—but in each case Tetsugen demonstrates his compassion and then perseveres to collect the funds for the final successful printing of the scriptures.

MODEL BUDDHIST TURNED MODEL JAPANESE CITIZEN

Testugen's fame was further enhanced by another secular version of his life story that appeared in an elementary school textbook produced by the Ministry of Education (Monbushō). Fukuda Gyōkai (1806–1888), a prominent Pure Land monk active in the Buddhist revival movement of the early Meiji period, originally composed the version of the story that was adopted for use in the lesson. It is interesting to note that, although he does not mention Tetsugen's attitude toward keeping the precepts in the story, Fukuda himself was a strong proponent of precept revival as a means to restore and revitalize Buddhism after the persecution during the early years of the Meiji period.[6] Fukuda may have found Tetsugen a compelling figure on several grounds, since Fukuda was also involved in a scripture project intended to provide translations and commentaries on the Chinese Buddhist scriptures in Japanese.

At a time when Buddhism was under attack by external critics as antisocial, otherworldly, and a drain on Japan's efforts to modernize, Fukuda could hold up Tetsugen as a fine example of a Buddhist monk who not only preserved and spread the Dharma but who behaved compassionately. His version contains none of the negative material found in the *Unusual People,* although it is otherwise similar in structure. In this sense it has more in common with religious biographies, as it may have been in its original context.[7]

Fukuda concentrates on Tetsugen's active and compassionate engagement with society. He spells out Tetsugen's reasoning in deciding to spend donations collected for printing the scriptures on disaster relief, carefully noting that Tetsugen sought and received the blessing of his benefactors. When a flood in Osaka caused tremendous property damage and human suffering,

> Tetsugen saw these conditions and felt disconsolate. Without hesitation, he decided, "When I determined to publish the Buddhist scriptures, it was in order to spread Buddhism. Spreading Buddhism is done for the sake of saving people in desperate straits. The money that I have received as donations will serve the same purpose whether I use it to finance the Buddhist scriptures or to save the hungry. Although it is necessary to spread the Buddhist scriptures throughout the world, saving people from death is even more urgent."

> Therefore, he told the people who had donated the money of his intention and received their blessing. He spent all the funds on relief efforts.

As in the story found in *Unusual People,* Tetsugen must raise the money three times before he can fulfill his original intention. The textbook lesson concluded with a direct quotation attributed to Fukuda, "Tetsugen published the complete Buddhist scriptures three times in one lifetime." Variations on this theme recur in later versions of the story.

As a Buddhist, Fukuda Gyōkai had reason to promote Tetsugen as an exemplary figure, but it was not his choice to include Tetsugen's story in a state-sponsored textbook. The Japanese Ministry of Education produced a series of national textbooks that were used in schools throughout the country from 1903 until 1945. The Tetsugen lesson appeared in the national-language textbook of two editions, those in print from 1918 through 1938. (The lesson was ultimately cut from the 1941 edition.) For approximately twenty years, virtually all Japanese school children (and their teachers) learned the story of Tetsugen. The lesson thus established Tetsugen as an important and well-known figure from Japanese history for generations of Japanese.

The national textbooks of the prewar years reflected the Monbushō's policy that moral values should pervade all of the curriculum, and not just the volumes dedicated specifically to ethics.[8] The Tetsugen story would have been included not only to introduce new kanji and other linguistic lessons, but also as a means to reinforce its moral content. Tetsugen presented an example of good citizenship. Japanese youngsters could be encouraged to persevere to attain their goals, even in the face of great obstacles. They could likewise be enjoined to always place the needs of society over their own personal goals.

Other stories about Tetsugen that appear in secular publications from the early modern and prewar years are primarily found in local histories and collections. This trend continues today. The city of Osaka, for example, includes Tetsugen's primary temple, Zuiryūji (listed under its more popular name Tetsugenji) as one of the city's historical sites. The website includes a brief biographical sketch of Tetsugen that mentions the scripture project as well as Tetsugen's relief work in the city during both the flood of 1674 and the famine of 1682.[9]

"PUBLISHING THE SUTRAS"

A quick search on the Internet verifies that Tetsugen, or at least his story, is better known today than ever. Accounts of him printing the scriptures and feeding the victims of flood and famine have spread far beyond the confines of the Ōbaku sect and Japanese Buddhism. The story appears in many different languages and in a wide variety of contexts. It has taken on a life of its own, freed from its original contexts and available to anyone with access to the Internet. It is obvious that in some cases people have altered the story to suit their audiences and to serve their own purposes. The process is not so different from the production of earlier renditions of Tetsugen's life.

In most cases, Internet versions of Tetsugen's story, whether in English, Spanish, French, German, or even Japanese, can be traced to a single published source, *Zen Flesh, Zen Bones,* a compilation of four earlier collections of stories. The small vignette about Tetsugen is called "Publishing the Sutras." It first appeared in 1939 in the small collection *101 Zen Stories,* compiled by Paul Reps in collaboration with the Japanese Zen teacher Senzaki Nyogen (1876–1958). The story follows the familiar three-part pattern, although there are significant differences in detail and it is therefore probably not based exclusively on any of the sources discussed above. It concludes with the comment, "The Japanese tell their children that Tetsugen made three sets of sutras, and that the first two invisible sets surpass even the last."[10] This line, reminiscent of Fukuda Gyōkai's statement quoted in the textbook lesson, indicates the shift in focus that one finds in the use of the Tetsugen myth. No longer the standard edition of the scriptures used in Japan, the Ōbaku edition had faded as a legacy. Now Tetsugen's legacy is the myth itself, which promotes compassionate action in the world as well as perseverance in fulfilling one's goals.

In this latest rendition from *Zen Flesh, Zen Bones,* Tetsugen's story gained popularity among Western practitioners of Zen. This occurred in large part because the tale suits one of the peculiarly Western inclinations regarding Buddhism. Many Buddhists from Western cultures, particularly Americans, are seeking a form of Buddhism that supports social action in its various forms. In keeping with that perspective, Tetsugen can be seen to represent a premodern example of socially engaged Buddhism. Nelson Foster, the Zen teacher at Ring of Bone Zendo in California and Diamond Sangha in Honolulu and a cofounder of Buddhist Peace Fellowship, has commented on this Western inclination toward activism and includes Tetsugen as one example from the Zen tradition's past.

> In an eagerness to find precedents and to feel continuity with my tradition, well before BPF's creation I had begun collecting historical instances of compassionate action taken by members of Ch'an and Zen sanghas.... The Ōbaku priest Tetsugen not once but twice furnished funds for disaster relief out of money gathered to publish the Buddhist canon....[11]

Foster lists Tetsugen as one among several examples of individual monks who provided practical assistance to others and thus inspiration for contemporary Buddhists like himself.

Not surprisingly, most of the Internet sites that make use of Tetsugen's story are Zen sites or more general Buddhist sites. The second largest category of Internet sites using the Tetsugen story, however, is inspirational sites, which include a wide variety of Buddhist, Christian, and New Age sites. The story also appears as an inspirational anecdote in a Christian sermon and a college commencement address that have been published online. It is interesting to note that Tetsugen's image shifts in many of these renditions. Just as the twelve-year project grows to twenty or thirty years in the retelling, so the nature of the project sometimes shifts from carving the woodblocks to translating the sutras from Chinese into Japanese. These small changes, made intentionally or not, make the scripture project at once more intelligible and more compelling for a Western audience, most of whom are unaware of the old woodblock style of publication.

In my work on Tetsugen, I have found no historical basis to support the three-part framework that typifies what I have come to call the myth of Tetsugen; and I have been able to establish the original source for the story. Perhaps it began as oral tradition and was later recorded and transmitted by texts such as *Unusual People*. It is not based on the earliest religious biographies written by Tetsugen's immediate disciples, although it has long since been incorporated into various later Ōbaku publications. In the *Deeds of Tetsugen*, Hōshū mentions relief work only twice, once in a very general recitation of Tetsugen's good deeds and once in his discussion of the Kansai famine of 1682. The latter effort occurred, it should be noted, only after the carving process was already completed. It is true that on that occasion Tetsugen interrupted his errand in Edo and rushed home to Osaka to lead the relief effort. It is quite likely that he spent some leftover funds originally collected for the scripture project for that relief effort. Whatever the myth's source and dubious status as historical fact, the inspirational story contains much that is true about the man Tetsugen and his work. Today, the myth of compassion and perseverance appears to be Tetsugen's final, unlooked-for legacy.

Translations

Part I

Teaching Texts

The *Dharma Lesson in Japanese* of Zen Master Tetsugen of Zuiryūji

Tetsugen composed the *Dharma Lesson in Japanese* for a Japanese woman "deeply committed to Zen."[1] The text takes the form of an extended commentary on a single line from the *Heart Sutra*. Tetsugen wrote the original text in Japanese. He uses parables and images from everyday life to explain basic teachings of Mahayana Buddhism, as well as teachings specific to the Zen school. He quotes freely from various scriptures, but explains the meaning of the Chinese passages in simple terms. The text would have been appropriate for a general lay audience of his day, which was probably his intention. Tetsugen's leading disciple Hōshū was responsible for publishing the *Dharma Lesson in Japanese*. His postscript is dated the twenty-second day of the eighth lunar month of Genroku 4 (1691). The present translation is based on a modern edition of Tetsugen's writings.[2]

The *Dharma Lesson in Japanese* of Zen Master Tetsugen of Zuiryūji

INTRODUCTION[3]

The *Heart Sutra* says, "When one realizes that the five *skandhas*[4] are all empty, one escapes from all pain and distress."[5] This means that the five *skandhas* are fundamentally empty, and when you realize that they have no abiding reality and grasp this truth clearly, then you will transcend all the suffering and misfortune of birth and death, and you will recognize yourself as the *Dharmakāya*, the body of *prajña*.[6]

The five *skandhas* are form, sensation, perception, psychic construction, and consciousness. Although there are five items, they come down to just [two], "body" and "mind."

SECTION 1: FORM

First of all, "form" is the body, and the other four [*skandhas*] are mind. Although all sentient beings are themselves fundamentally the eternal bliss of nirvana and embody the *Dharmakāya*, the body of *prajña*, they are deluded by the "form" and "mind" of these five *skandhas*, and so become ordinary people and wander aimlessly through the Three Worlds[7] [the realms of desire, form, and no-form].

To begin with, "form" is your body. Everything in the world with shape and color, the sky, the earth, the trees, and the grasses, are included in "form." The *Śūramgama Sutra* says, "Since time without beginning, all sentient beings have deluded themselves with things, and lost their original mind. They are turned by things."[8]

This means that since we don't realize that the ten thousand *dharmas*[9] are all the *Dharmakāya*, Ultimate Reality itself, and instead, think of them as the ten thousand *dharmas* [that have an abiding reality of their own], we become deluded by the perception of these *dharmas*. We exchange our [original] mind for the sake of things, and give rise to all sorts of illusory ideas.

In the past, people said that the *Dharmakāya* was concealed within the physical shell (*gyōkoku*). The physical shell is your body. Although your body is fundamentally the *Dharmakāya* itself, you don't realize this and think of it as the self. [This] means you look at the *Dharmakāya,* think of it as yourself, and then become deluded by this self, and so you create the afflictions such as greed and anger, and fall into the hateful paths.[10]

People are deluded and take the *tathagata,*[11] which is fundamentally the *Dharmakāya,* to be either the ten thousand *dharmas* or the self, and so have a twofold delusion.

The first kind of delusion [is as follows]. This body is created by a temporary configuration of the four great elements: earth, water, fire, and wind. Various parts of the body, such as skin, flesh, bones, and sinews, are earth. Tears, saliva, and blood are water. The movement and workings of breathing in and out are wind. Apart from these [elements of] earth, water, fire, and wind, there is nothing one could call the self. It is only momentary, and when your life ends and returns to its original earth, water, fire, and wind, you will become bleached bones, so there is nothing that one could rely on as the self even for the duration of dew.

Isn't it a pity that we think of these wretched white bones as the self, and for a thousand lifetimes and ten thousand kalpas are controlled by this skull. All we do is generate the karma [that leads to falling into] hell, and sink into the three paths [of hell, hungry ghosts, and animals].

Without realizing that the body is a temporary [configuration] of earth, water, fire and wind, we take it to be the self, and believe it will not die even in ten million years. We are firmly attached to this self. This is the first kind of delusion.

Those in the two vehicles[12] [*śrāvakas* and *pratyekabuddhas*] are wiser than ordinary people, and so they clearly recognize this body as a temporary configuration of earth, water, fire, and wind, and regard it in fact as white bones. They have no thoughts of attachment to their body in the least; and they do not give rise to attachment to self or self-pride. They neither lie nor flatter, envy nor slander.

Although they have achieved enlightenment of this kind, they still have not realized that they are themselves the *Dharmakāya,* the *Tathagata.* For this reason, the World Honored One generally despised them as the Lesser Vehicle. Since they do not realize that they are the *Dharmakāya* itself, with their two-vehicle wisdom they have not yet seen the inner realization of the Buddha or the realm of the bodhisattva, even in their dreams.

This is the kind of delusion characteristic of the two vehicles. Along with the delusion of ordinary people, we get two kinds of delusion. The delusion of those in the two vehicles concerning the *Dharmakāya* is one kind. Ordinary people are deluded about the *Dharmakāya* and are also deluded about what those in the two vehicles have understood, and so have a twofold [delusion].

Bodhisattvas transcend the twofold delusion of ordinary people, and see that this very body is the *Tathagata*, the *Dharmakāya*. [The Buddha] teaches this in the *Heart Sutra*, [saying] "Form is emptiness, and emptiness is form."[13] "Form" means this body. "Emptiness" means the absolute void; the absolute void is the *Dharmakāya*, and the *Dharmakāya* is the *Tathagata*. This means that this body is itself the *Dharmakāya*, and the *Dharmakāya* is itself this body.

Not realizing that the four great elements are originally the *Dharmakāya* itself, those in the two vehicles believe that the [four elements] are insentient beings.

When you see with the eyes of a bodhisattva, the four great elements are all the true body of the *Dharmakāya*. Therefore, it explains in the *Śūramgama Sutra*, "The nature of form is emptiness, and emptiness is the nature of form."[14] "Form" is the [element] earth. "Nature" refers to "the nature of form" because earth is fundamentally the *Dharmakāya* itself. Since it is the nature of form, it is empty.

Again, in the same sutra it says of water that "the nature of water is emptiness and emptiness is the nature of water"; of fire that "the nature of fire is emptiness and emptiness is the nature of fire"; and of wind that "the nature of wind is emptiness and emptiness is the nature of wind."[15] This means that just as with earth, water is itself the *Dharmakāya*, and the *Dharmakāya* is itself water. Fire is itself the *Dharmakāya*, and the *Dharmakāya* is itself fire. Wind is itself the *Dharmakāya*, and the *Dharmakāya* is itself wind. Since this is the case, the four great elements are not essentially the four great elements, but are the Mysterious Body of the *Tathagata*, the *Dharmakāya*. Ordinary people and those in the two vehicles are deluded and so think that they are the four great elements.

If you understand that the four great elements are fundamentally the Buddha, then not only will you see that your own body is from the start the *Dharmakāya*, but that everything even down to the heavens, the earth, the sky, and all of the universe is the mysterious body of the *Dharmakāya*. We say of the time when this enlightenment is achieved that "all dharmas are ultimate reality"[16] and "the grass, the trees, the nations, and the earth all without exception attain Buddhahood."[17]

Not only the grass, the trees, the nations, and the earth, but even the sky is the body of the *Dharmakāya*, but because we are deluded we think it is [just] the sky. When you achieve enlightenment, you will transcend the delusion of thinking it is [just] the sky and attain the enlightenment that all *dharmas* are one thusness.[18] Therefore, the *Śūramgama Sutra* says, "When a person gives rise to the truth and returns to the source, the sky in all ten directions temporarily disappears."[19] The *Perfect Enlightenment Sutra* says, "The infinite sky is illuminated by enlightenment."[20] In the Zen school we say, "The universe sinks and the sky crumbles."[21] Even those that teach that ultimate bliss is a land of gold[22] have changed the name for the sake of ordinary people.

If you open up and see this enlightenment, while the self is [still] the self, it is fundamentally the *Dharmakāya* itself, and so is not born. Since it is not born, it does not die. This is called "nonarising and nonperishing,"[23] and also "the Buddha of Immeasurable Light."[24] Seeing it as born and dying is referred to as the dream of delusion.

Since I am already like this, other people are as well. Since human beings are like this, even birds and beasts, grass, trees, earth, and stones are this way. The *Amida Sutra*[25] says, "Water, birds, trees and forests call out 'contemplate the Buddha, contemplate the Dharma, contemplate the Sanghá."[26] When it says, "The Buddhas in all ten directions speak with the Buddha's broad tongue to the three thousand great one thousand worlds, and teach the Dharma,"[27] it is also speaking of the time [of enlightenment]. The *Lotus Sutra* says, "All *dharmas* from their very origin are themselves eternally characterized by the marks of quiet and extinction,"[28] and "The endurance of the dharmas, the secure position of the dharmas, in the world ever abiding."[29] These are all places that express the attainment of enlightenment.

By practicing zazen and kōans very diligently, you will attain this kind of enlightenment, and by transcending the delusion of the *skandha* of form you will awaken to the *Dharmakāya,* Ultimate Reality itself.

SECTION 2: SENSATION

Second, "sensation" is a word for "reception," and means to take something in. This means that we take in the external objects of the "six dusts"[30] [that is form, sound, scent, taste, texture, and thought] with the "five roots,"[31] the eyes, ears, nose, tongue and body. We take in form with the eyes, sound with the ears, scent with the nose, taste with the tongue, and texture with the body.

Within sensation there are three types: pain, pleasure, and indifference. First, pain means to take in something unpleasant and painful with your eyes, ears, nose, tongue, or body. Pleasure means taking in something you enjoy very much with your eyes, ears, nose, tongue, or body. Indifference means to take in something that is neither pain nor pleasure. For example, waving good-bye when you are leaving is neither painful nor pleasurable. Seeing when nothing is the matter, hearing and tasting without anything being wrong, in the same way, are indifference.

Sentient beings are deluded by pleasure and pain, and think that they won't see with the eyes or hear with the ears painful things. They think that they will see, hear, smell, taste, and touch only pleasant things. Therefore, they trouble others, torment themselves, burn with the desire to steal, tell lies, covet things, sever the lives of fish and birds, and take into account only outward appearances in the world, so that day and night they generate only the karma [that leads to falling into] hell.

From a single moment of delusion about enjoying pleasure you give rise to immeasurable suffering. The [sort of people] in society who steal will also want to drink saké, eat fish, indulge in lust, love prostitutes, and even be extravagant in their clothing. From just a small desire for pleasure, they end up stealing, telling lies, and eventually their wickedness is discovered. They go to jail, are tortured, and lose their lives. [All of this] arises from a few thoughts of seeking out pleasure. This is what the old saying, "All craving is painful" means.[32] It is like a summer insect leaping into the fire or a fish in a pool craving the bait. For the sake of a fleeting covetous thought, they lose their precious lives.

The suffering of the one hundred thirty hells,[33] the hunger of the three grades and nine types of hungry ghosts,[34] the form of animals covered with fur and sprouting horns, the aspect of *asuras* bearing bow, arrows, swords, and staves,[35] all of these sufferings arise from covetous thoughts. Isn't it a wretched delusion to expect to get a drop of sweet pleasure and instead receive ten thousand *kalpas* of bitter suffering?

Even though what we think of as painful or pleasant aren't really pain and pleasure, because we are deluded, we end up thinking they are. The reason for this is that when a crow, a dog, or a fox sees a dead cow or horse rotting or a human corpse festering, they think it is a rare treat. First they enjoy looking at it, then their enjoyment increases as they smell it and grasp it. They think this is the greatest of pleasures. Seen from the human perspective, this seems immeasurably impure and repulsive. If we were forced by others to eat such putrid things, it would be incomparable suffering. What is worse than being forced to eat them is that crows devour such things greedily, and think it is pleasant. Although it isn't [truly] pleasant, their minds are foolish and base, and so they think that pain is pleasure.

What human beings find pleasurable is similar. Because of foolish minds, we are consumed by wife and children, are deluded by wealth, eat fish and fowl, and take this to be pleasant. Viewed from the perspective of Buddhas and bodhisattvas, this looks even more wretched than the crows seem to us from our human vantage. Conjecturing from this, [we see that] what deluded people find pleasant actually brings pain; they only believe it is pleasure.

If a man committed a great crime and for this reason his wife and children were executed before his eyes at the government's command, then [their bodies were] cooked and he were forced to eat them, how painful this would be! When people eat fish and fowl it is just the same as this. When seen through the eyes of enlightenment, even fish and birds are the *Tathagata*, the *Dharmakāya*, and fundamentally one body with all the Buddhas. Since all Buddhas and bodhisattvas have great compassion, they [can look on] all sentient beings as their own body, and regard them as their children.

Although all sentient beings are the same [that is, one with the Buddhas], such is the wretchedness of ordinary people that they say, "What good fish!" Tear its flesh, crush its bones, eat it, and take great pleasure in this. When this behavior is seen through the eyes of a Buddha, it looks no different than that of a demon. It is the same as cutting off your children's heads, tearing their flesh, and enjoying the sight, the smell, and the taste of it. We refer to this as the perversion of ordinary people.

Though we may think such a deed is pleasant, it is not truly pleasant. It is a great suffering. This kind of confusion between pleasure and pain is what we mean by the second *skandha* of sensation.

Such is the way with ordinary people wandering in the Three Worlds that they cannot escape from pleasure and pain. The reason for this is [as follows]. When we see blossoms in bloom, we find this pleasant, so that when in turn they scatter, we think it sorrowful. We enjoy seeing the moon as it rises, so when it sets behind the mountains, we find this sad. When we take pleasure in encountering something, then the separation is more painful. People who enjoy prosperity will also suffer times of decline. The poor suffer from not having. Wealthy people worry over what they have. Since currying favor is suffering, so in fact is living in luxury. Since loving is suffering, hatred is also suffering. How great are the two sensations of pain and pleasure! All sentient beings throughout the Three Worlds indulge in them and in the end cannot escape.

We refer to being born as "the suffering of birth," to aging as "the suffering of old age." Being ill is "the suffering of sickness," and dying is "the suffering of death."[36] Men suffer, and women also bear much pain. Farmers suffer, and so do all the craftsmen and merchants. Those who serve a lord suffer, and so do [those who have no lord], the *rōnin*. Retainers suffer, and their lords are not immune from it. Not only householders suffer, but so do monks and nuns.

Under these circumstances, when our suffering lightens a bit, we become confused and think that this pause [in the pain] is pleasure. For example, it is like a person carrying a heavy load putting it down and thinking that is pleasure, or when a seriously ill person gets better, they call that pleasure. Although we cannot say that [these experiences] are especially pleasurable, we do think of a pause in our suffering as pleasure.

Moreover, when we believe that drinking saké, eating fish, and indulging in lust is pleasure, we are like a person suffering from itchy boils who warms himself by the fire and washes himself with hot water, and thinks that this is pleasure. Although itching cannot compare to an illness, in fact it is also painful. Thinking of warming or washing oneself as pleasurable is actually taking pain to be pleasure. In fact, for anyone not ill with boils to find warming oneself agreeable is not perverse, it really is a pleasure. If you realize this truth and transcend pleasure and pain, then you will escape from the second *skandha* of sensation, and attain the true pleasure of nirvana.

SECTION 3: PERCEPTION

Third, "perception" means thoughts, and refers to the illusions that arise in people's minds every day and every night. Daytime becomes illusion, and nighttime a dream. Everyone thinks that nighttime dreams are the only fabrications that lack a basis in fact, and that what they think about during the day is true. This is a terrible mistake. The thoughts of deluded people, even what they think about during the day, are the same as dreams. Since they don't realize that these are all illusions without foundation, they believe them to be the truth.

Illusions are empty and false. Anything that is actually without substance but that seems to exist we refer to as an illusion. For example, a shadow has the appearance of a figure, just like something that seems real in your dreams. Although they are all completely nonexistent, they seem to exist in the dream. Although a shadow is nonexistent, if you stand in the light of the sun, the moon, or a lamp, a shadow immediately takes on your shape. When you move, the shadow also moves; when you stop, the shadow also stops. Images reflected in a mirror or in water are the same. Fundamentally they do not exist, but they certainly seem to.

In the same way, people's illusions are truly nonexistent, but when they come to mind, they certainly seem to exist. Whatever we think of as hateful, lovable, reproachful, enviable, beloved, or dear are all illusions that don't change the dreaming mind at all. Originally we have no such illusions in our true minds, which are like a shining mirror or pure water. Because we fail to realize our true mind, we leave the images of illusion reflected on our true mind. We believe they are true and become firmly attached to them, and so these illusions become increasingly extensive, and the delusions grow deeper and deeper.

Thinking that something is repulsive and thinking something is attractive are both figments of your own imagination. We label these figments of imagination "illusions." The reason that both repulsion and attraction result from our imagination is that, even in the case of a person you now find repulsive or attractive, before you got acquainted, the person was neither. In addition, when you first met, while you were still casual acquaintances who didn't know each other very well, such feelings did not yet exist.

As we gradually get to know someone, feelings of intimacy deepen toward a person we find compatible, and we create the feeling that they are attractive. It is precisely because of this circumstance that when we follow the paths of affection, however much it changes our lives, to that extent the ties of tenderness likewise increase. When you develop feelings of love in this way, love seems inevitable, and whichever way you turn it over in your mind, it is love without a trace of hatefulness.

When love reaches an extreme, and you think that even if you were to live 100 million *kalpas* your feelings wouldn't change, you are mistaken. Though you are intimate friends, you will have some differences of opinion, and will quarrel. Then the quarrels grow into arguments. Or, as is the way of love, if your [lover's] feelings shift to another, however deep were your feelings of love at the beginning, that is how deep your hate will now become. These feelings of hatred and bitterness are so deep that you may even think that they will eventually kill you.

If you conjecture based on these truths, [you will see that] thinking something is attractive is an illusion. Since these [thoughts of love] are false like your dreams, thinking something is repulsive is also an illusion. If the thoughts of love were not false in the first place, then you would probably not have changed your mind in a short time and decided it was repulsive. Likewise, if the feelings of repulsion were true, then you would not have thought it was attractive at the beginning. Since both attraction and repulsion are illusions, the mind is undetermined and shifts and changes just like a dream.

It is a wretched delusion to have these dreams of illusion bewilder us so that they burn our hearts, trouble our bodies, and if they are strong enough, kill us.

Since lovable and hateful are illusions in this way, then so are regrettable and desirable. To detest, to envy, to enjoy, to be sorrowful, are these not all illusions? Because we are deluded by illusions, we say that another person is our superior or inferior, an acquaintance or stranger, old or young, male or female, and do nothing but generate the seeds of hell.

We don't recognize these illusions are dreams, and so from the distant past without beginning down to this very life today, we have transmigrated without cease, fallen into hell, become hungry ghosts, been born as animals, and become *aśuras*. Accordingly, if you ask the origin of becoming a Buddha or falling into hell, it comes down to whether or not you have these illusions. You must pay close attention and understand that these illusions cause harm; you must make it clear that they are just illusions and completely devoid of reality.

Although it is foolish from a worldly perspective, if you steal and suffer the government's orders, then you will expose yourself to shame in this life and a long fall into hell in the next. All of this results from a momentary illusion of coveting something. If a person plots rebellion and schemes to overturn the whole country, he falls into serious sin and exposes his family, wife, children, and siblings to endless suffering. This is the result of just one moment of illusion. The first momentary thoughts of plotting rebellion are merely a momentary illusion, like the thin haze of tobacco smoke.

You don't realize that these momentary illusions are the origin of evil, and pile them up intently, so that in the end they become like clouds that fill the whole sky and it becomes increasingly difficult to stop them. If at the moment of the first thought, you could see clearly that "This is an illusion!" then blotting it out of your mind would be the easiest thing of all. [As Laozi said,] "Even a tree that can fill the span of your arms started as a sprout."[37] Even a tree as big around as five or ten arm spans was like the tip of a needle when it started growing, a mere seedling. When this seedling [first] appears, you can easily pull it up with one finger. When it has grown into a large tree, even with the strength of one thousand or ten thousand men you can't readily pull it up.

Illusions are the same way. At the first moment, you can quickly dispose of the thought. Illusions that cause evil are also like this. If you pile them up intently, they come to cause great harm to the country. When this happens, there are many troubles. Like a large tree, when [illusions first] take shape they are not difficult to abolish. Even if they have been piling up, when you decide to dispel them and cast them from your mind, just as the rising sun dispels the darkness, you have no trouble at all. We can compare this to lighting a lamp in a room dark for a thousand years. Although the darkness lasted a long time, when you light a lamp, you have no difficulty dispelling it. Illusions are just like this. When you change your mind for one moment, even delusions from the distant past with no beginning are dispelled in an instant. By understanding this truth and casting off your dreamlike illusions, you can ground yourself in the mind of enlightenment.

If you don't cast off these delusions, and continue piling them up single-mindedly, there are many examples of people turning into demons and snakes[38] [in this lifetime], not to mention future lives. Women are said to be especially sinful because they are unwilling to cast off their deluded minds.

Even the ten billion triple-thousand great one-thousand worlds arise from the illusions of sentient beings. The one hundred thirty-six hells are also created by human illusions. We possess the wretched lot of ordinary human beings be-cause we ourselves gave rise to an illusory fire and then for one hundred million *kalpas* have burned ourselves with it. If we cast off these illusions and transcend the third *skandha* of perception, then we can attain the land of enlightenment.

SECTION 4: PSYCHIC CONSTRUCTION

Fourth, "psychic construction" means that your mind moves and changes, arises and passes away; as they say, "Psychic constructions move and flow."[39] Since you have illusory thoughts in your mind, it never rests even for a moment, but constantly moves and changes. It is, for example, like water that flows endlessly without a moment's rest, or like a lamp flame that every instant is extinguished, yet while it flickers, never stops [shining]. From morning until night, people are constantly thinking about something, and you should examine closely [the mind's] movement and change. Just like a flash of lightning, it changes instant after instant and never stops.

Since all phenomena, that is all delusionary *dharmas*, are the change and flow of psychic construction, they are impermanent and change with every thought. Moment after moment, they arise and pass away without stopping for an instant. Although violent [degrees of] arising and passing away within the mind are apparent even to the foolish minds of ordinary people, subtle [de-grees] that change with every passing moment are not, and they are not visible to the eyes of those in the two vehicles. This kind of arising and passing away [goes on] in their minds, so that when various *dharmas* arise from the mind, they also see the ten thousand *dharmas* change.

When the *Perfect Enlightenment Sutra* says, "When the clouds are swift, the moon moves. When the boat leaves, the shore shifts,"[40] it means the [fol-lowing]. When the movement of the clouds is swift, it looks as if the moon were moving, and when the boat moves quickly, it seems as if the shore and mountains were also moving. It isn't that the mountains are moving, it is because of the movement of the boat in which we are riding.

Since the clouds in our minds are swift, it looks like the moon of True Thusness is moving. Though all *dharmas* are fundamentally reality, and of themselves always have the marks of "quiet and extinction,"[41] the Three Worlds seem to move and change, the changing of the four seasons never seems to stop. All of this is the delusion of psychic construction.

When the *Nirvana Sutra* says that, "All conditioned things are impermanent. This is the Dharma of arising and perishing,"[42] it means the [following]. "All conditioned things" means psychic constructions. Because psychic constructions arise, pass away, move and change, this means that all the ten thousand *dharmas* move and change without stopping for even an instant. If all *dharmas*, that is, the delusions of phenomena that arise and pass away, entirely ceased to pass away, then there would be no tranquillity and no extinction of the uncreated, no great pleasure of nirvana. When the arising and passing away of the *dharmas* stops completely, that is when the *Dharma* of tranquillity and extinction will appear before your eyes, as will the wondrous pleasure of nirvana in which "the ten thousand *dharmas* are one, and all *dharmas* are ultimate reality."[43] [The Buddha] taught this saying, "When arising and passing away are themselves extinguished, then quiet and extinction constitute pleasure."[44]

Therefore, although our bodies and minds and all ten thousand *dharmas* are the eternal *Dharmakāya* itself, and originally there is no such thing as "arising and passing away," we do not perceive ultimate reality itself, and end up thinking that the ten thousand *dharmas* arise and pass away in the Three Worlds due to the delusions of psychic construction.

When you transcend the delusion of psychic construction, first your mind is eternal and nothing moves or changes. When your mind does not move and change, neither do the *dharmas*. Therefore, your true mind not moving and changing is the same as the true form of a mirror. When you see images reflected in a bright mirror all day long, it reflects the sky, the land, flowers, willow trees, people, animals, and birds. All the colors change and the types of things [reflected] change without a moments rest, but the true form of the mirror is not the birds and animals, or the people, or the willows, flowers, the land, or the sky. It is just the shining and unclouded mirror itself.

Our original minds reflect and illuminate the ten thousand *dharmas*, but have no connection to their distinctions. The fact that [the mind] never participates in arising and passing away can be understood through the example of the mirror. Deluded people only see the reflections moving in their minds, they cannot see the mirror of the original mind [itself]. When the *Perfect Enlightenment Sutra* teaches that, people "take the phantoms of the six dusts to be the aspect of their minds,"[45] that is what it means.

All the images reflected in the mirror are completely empty and nonexistent, so only a foolish person would decide to purify [the mirror], cast off these images, and thereby see the mirror for the first time. Even if images of blossoms and willows are reflected, you should be able to see the shining mirror which itself has no coming or going, no form or scent.

We name this the *Dharmakāya*, we call it "true thusness." When the *The Discourse on Consciousness Only*[46] says, "The Truth refers to things as they really are, without any falsehood or delusion. Thusness refers to intransience, without any change,"[47] it means the wondrous body of true thusness. In the *Diamond Sutra*, when it says, "The *Tathagata* is without coming and without going,"[48] it is talking about the *Tathagata*, the *Dharmakāya*.

Since our original minds are already like this, the ten thousand *dharmas* are as well. When we see them as heaven, earth, and everything in the universe, these are actually reflected images. The ten thousand things are themselves the shining mirror. Someone deluded by these images is an "ordinary person" and someone who sees the mirror is a "saint."

Let me explain this with an example, it is like making the shapes of various things out of gold. When we look at them as shapes, the demons are terrifying and the Buddhas venerable, the old are wrinkled and the young charming. The crane has long legs and the duck short legs. The pine grows straight and the brambles twisted, the willow is graceful and the blossoms elegant. When we look at them as gold, the demon is gold and so is the Buddha. Male and female have no distinction, and there is no superior and inferior between lord and retainer. If the long-legged crane is gold, so is the short-legged duck. Blossom, willow, pine, and bramble are all just gold, and not even the slightest distinction can be found.

The ten thousand *dharmas* are the same. When we look at them from the perspective of True Thusness, just as with the gold, there is no distinction at all. When we look at them from the perspective of the ten thousand *dharmas,* they are distinguished as different shapes. Sentient beings are deluded by these shapes. All the Buddhas recognize that they are thusness. When you realize that the gold is thusness itself, all the distinct shapes are equal and undistinguished just as they are.

There are no demons you should hate, no Buddhas to venerate. Since there is no one with whom you should be friendly, there is likewise no one you should slight. What is there to hate or to like? Whom would you censure or praise? There is neither bitterness nor envy. Although you don't intentionally stop them, all the afflictions pass away of themselves. For example, when the sun rises, although it isn't intentionally done, the darkness is naturally dispelled. Although you don't intentionally dispel the afflictions, there is only one ultimate reality, so delusion naturally is unattainable. Long ago, the Second Patriarch [Huike] stilled his mind by realizing this.[49] The Sixth Patriarch [Huineng] realized it and received the robe [of Dharma transmission].[50]

The *Diamond Sutra* says, "The Three Worlds are unattainable,"[51] and the *Lotus Sutra* says, "All phenomenal things are themselves the ultimate reality."[52] These are two aspects of the [same] idea. Because the Three Worlds are unattainable, all phenomenal things are themselves ultimate reality. Because all phenomenal things are themselves ultimate reality, the Three Worlds are unattainable. How wondrous are the golden words of the Tathagata!

You should try to quiet your mind. If you separate your original mind from arising and passing away, coming and going, and clearly realize what is intransient, the images reflected in your mind will also be intransient and unperishing. The reason for this it is that the distinctions between all the things in the universe, the arising and passing away of past and present, coming and going, are fundamentally false and illusory. Nothing comes, nothing goes. Nothing arises and nothing passes away. Of course, if nothing arises and passes away, or comes and goes, there is nothing that possesses all the distinctions. You should understand this from the [example] of reflections in the mirror.

When you first see something reflected in a mirror, it's not a matter of the image entering into the mirror. From the beginning, the image has not entered [the mirror], so there is nothing to get rid of. Since originally the object does not enter and leave, or come and go, the mirror is just the mirror, and does not eventually become the image. Since the mirror does not become the image, but reflects it, there is nothing in the universe that ceases to be distinct. It is difficult to say what is reflected and what is not. Various shapes made out of gold are not demons or Buddhas, but they take on the shapes of demons and Buddhas.

It is hard to say whether or not these [reflected images] exist. We refer to them as the phantomlike ten thousand *dharmas,* since "phantoms" are living things created with the magical arts. If a living thing has been produced by magic, then it's hard to say whether or not it exists. When we try saying it doesn't, then right before our eyes, it becomes a bird or animal and flies or runs around. When we try saying it does exist, then [we see that] it isn't a real bird or animal. Actually it is a piece of wood or a hand towel that has been changed into a living thing by magic.

Now, in the Three Worlds, this [view] extends to the entire universe, the ten thousand *dharmas,* as well as human beings. From the perspective of one mind[53] itself, we see that, in fact, there is not a single thing,[54] and ultimate reality does not set up so much as one object of perception.[55] Therefore, there are no Buddhas, no sentient beings, no past, no present, nothing in heaven, nothing on earth, no self, and no other. This is the one mark of the *dharma-dhatu.* It is similar to looking at things made from gold from the perspective of gold. We refer to this as "the aspect of mind as true thusness."[56]

When we look at things from the perspective of the ten thousand *dharmas,* we make distinctions between heaven and earth, sun and moon, and distinguish all the various things in the universe. Flowers are always crimson and willows always green. Fire is hot, water cool; the wind moves and the earth is at rest. The pine is straight and the brambles twisted. The crane is white and the crow black. The sky is high and the earth low. There are Buddhas and sentient beings. We speak of "self" and "other." There are the four seasons, and the colors blue, yellow, red, and white, each without any confusion. It is as if we saw things from the perspective of the individual forms and didn't see the gold [from which they are made]. We refer to this as "the aspect of mind as arising and passing away."[57]

All sentient being are deluded by the aspects of the ten thousand *dharmas*, so when they see something, they covet it; when they hear something they argue over it; when they smell, taste, or touch something they become greedily attached to it. They have no conception at all that these *dharmas* are like dreams and illusions, or foam [on the water] and shadows. Like reflections in a mirror or the moon [reflected] on the water, they are illusory manifestations and empty delusions.

[As a result], they take on the four kinds of birth, from the womb, from an egg, from moisture, or by metamorphosis; they are transformed by the four marks of arising, abiding, changing, and passing away,[58] they become attached to the objects of the five desires,[59] create the evil karma of the six senses, and for one thousand lifetimes and ten thousand *kalpas* their bodies burn in the flames of hell or [suffer] as hungry ghosts. Birth after birth and lifetime after lifetime they sink into suffering as animals and *asuras*. Even if they are born as human beings, they believe that their body formed by the union of the four great elements is the self, and because they take the external objects of the six senses to be their mind, they are constantly afflicted by old age, sickness, and death. They move through the four seasons, their black glossy hair becomes completely white, just as the sweet fragrance of the blossoms eventually withers, the morning dew disappears in an instant, and the evening mists lift.

In this floating world of transience and transformation, our lives are like a flash of lightning, not enduring for even a short time. We are not at peace for a moment, like constantly flowing water. We are like the flame that is extinguished every moment. Surely this is the shape of the *skandha* of psychic construction.

However, while sentient beings are transmigrating through the Three Worlds, they do not know that the ten thousand *dharmas* are illusory manifestations, and so become greedily attached to the dreams and illusions that are the objects of the six senses, and produce the illusory karma of the ten evil acts[60] and the five serious sins.[61] Therefore, they receive the illusory fruits of [falling into] hell and [becoming] hungry ghosts.

Your body is fundamentally an illusion, as is your mind. Since your mind is already an illusion, the afflictions are also illusions. Since the afflictions are fundamentally illusions, all evil karma is also illusion. Since evil karma is entirely illusion, so are the painful fruits of the three [lower] realms. Since the three [lower] realms are already illusion, the realms of heaven and of human beings must also be. Since birth and death in the Three Worlds are illusion, the causality of the four kinds of birth are also completely illusory, and so there is nothing within the entire *dharma-dhatu* that is not an illusion.

Because sentient beings create illusory karma and receive illusory suffering, all Buddhas extend their illusory compassion and teach the illusory *Dharma*, saving [sentient beings] from their illusory pain and offering them illusory pleasure. We refer to this as the supreme pleasure of nirvana.

You receive this supreme pleasure when you understand the illusory *Dharma*. Sentient beings are deluded about this illusory *Dharma*, so they receive illusory suffering from their illusory karma. The Buddhas have awakened to this illusory *Dharma*, and so escape from illusory suffering and turn it into illusory pleasure. Sentient beings are deluded by the illusory *Dharma* and befuddled by the dreams and illusions of arising and passing away, and so undergo birth and death, the unending suffering of impermanence,[62] and create the transmigration of psychic construction. The Buddhas, awakened to the illusory *Dharma*, turn these dreams and illusions of birth and death into nirvana, destroy the suffering of impermanence, and attain eternal pleasure. It is not especially difficult to see how to turn this suffering of impermanence into the eternal pleasure of nirvana. It is simply a matter of realizing that the transmigration of the ten thousand *dharmas* and the truth of birth and death are both dreams and illusions through and through.

Therefore, the *Perfect Enlightenment Sutra* says, "When you realize that it is illusion, then you escape it. Without using expedient means, you escape from illusion and so are enlightened. It is not a gradual process."[63] This can be explained as follows: The ten thousand *dharmas* of the Three Worlds are already illusion, so illusion originally does not arise. If the ten thousand *dharmas* don't arise, when would they pass away? If they have no connection with arising and passing away and coming and going, then wouldn't this be the nirvana of not-arising and not-passing away?

Originally, there is no birth and death, so "nirvana" is just a temporary name. Since there is neither birth and death nor nirvana, nor is there a distinction between affliction and enlightenment, nor a difference between sentient beings and Buddhas. Worrying about birth and death is an affliction. Since there are no afflictions, there is no enlightenment. Since there are neither afflictions nor birth and death, what should we refer to as sentient beings? We call a sentient being who becomes enlightened a Buddha. Since originally there are no sentient beings, there is nothing we can call a now-enlightened Buddha. Therefore, what we call enlightenment is the certain discovery that in this way people are not fundamentally deluded, and [enlightenment] is merely their original form.

That is what it means in the *Perfect Enlightenment Sutra* when it says, "For the first time you understand that sentient beings are fundamentally perfected Buddhas (*honrai jōbutsu*)."[64] "Fundamentally perfected Buddhas" means being a Buddha from the beginning. Since originally they are not sentient beings, there is no particular need to call them Buddhas, but [in order to show that] they are not fundamentally deluded sentient beings, perforce we refer to them as Buddhas. Therefore, although there is no birth and death nor nirvana, we never say that there is no wondrous enlightenment, which ordinary people would find impossible to fathom.

For example, in the *Laṅkāvatāra Sutra*[65] there is a saying, "Just as the na-ture of a horse is not to be a cow, and the nature of the cow is not to be a horse, [so all *dharmas* have their own natures]."[66] For instance, just because we say [a horse] isn't a cow, doesn't mean that there is no horse nature. And when we say [a cow] isn't a horse, that doesn't mean the cow has no nature.

This is the same as saying there is no birth and death, no nirvana, no afflic-tions, no enlightenment, no sentient beings and no Buddhas. It is all the same as saying [a horse] is not a cow. In the same way, when we say birth and death and nirvana are not cows, that doesn't mean that the horse of the mysterious and wonderful enlightenment has no nature.

It is like turning to someone who is dreaming and saying, "None of the things you see are real. The earth and sky you are looking at aren't the real earth and sky. The grass, trees, and land that you see aren't the real grass, trees, and land. What you see as yourself and as others, what you think of as sorrow and pleasure, none of these is real." [When you do this,] the dreaming person hears you and says, "Well then, if there is no earth and sky, no grass, trees, and land, no self and no other, then does the awakened truth mean empty space?"

We say that it isn't this and it isn't that [for the following reason]. The things we see in dreams are all unfounded delusions. Although they aren't real, in the mind of the dreamer they are taken to be. The dreamer clings to them and thinks of them as suffering or pleasure. Therefore, we wake them from their dream to show them the real heaven and earth of waking hours.

Now, when you turn to deluded people and say that there is no birth and death, no nirvana, no sentient beings, and no Buddhas, they wonder whether this is complete nihilism,[67] if you are saying that true enlightenment is empti-ness. This resembles the dreaming person saying, "When you say that nothing I see is real, are you saying that heaven and earth are empty and the real waking world is a place devoid of anything at all?" If you have never been enlightened and awakened from the dream of delusion, then you cannot know for certain what enlightenment is like.

In the *Lotus Sutra*, when [the Buddha] says of [the ten thousand *dhar-mas*], "the suchness of their marks, the suchness of their nature, the suchness of their substance, the suchness of their powers, the suchness of their function, the suchness of their causes, the suchness of their conditions, the suchness of their effects, the suchness of their retributions, and the absolute identity of their beginning and end,"[68] this [describes] the moment you awaken from the dream of delusion. "The dharmas abide in the secure position in the world ever abiding"[69] also refers to it.

In addition, [the Buddha] also said, "When sentient beings see the *kalpa* ending and being consumed by a great fire, this land of mine is perfectly safe, ever full of gods and Buddhas."[70] This means that when the *kalpa* comes to an end and this world is being destroyed, in the eyes of deluded people, it seems that a fire from *avici* hell[71] has broken out and is burning everything as far as the First Meditation Heaven.[72] Yet in the eyes of the *Tathagata* Śakyamuni this world looks safe and filled with divine and human beings. Among the countless pleasures [he sees] there are various halls and pagodas in the garden adorned with all kinds of treasures, jewel trees laden with blossoms and fruit, and sentient beings amusing themselves there. Heavenly beings beat drums and continually play beautiful music. Heavenly blossoms rain down and scatter over the multitude, summoning the Buddhas.

[In the same way] although it is one and the same water, to the eyes of hungry ghosts it looks like fire, but human beings naturally see water. Although the Three Worlds are the tranquil Pure Land and not a burning house[73] if you are not deluded, just as the hungry ghosts see water as fire, for the deluded the Three Worlds look like the six paths.

Question: When you hear a truth as detailed as this, you understand for the most part and have no doubt that you yourself are originally a Buddha and that since the ancient past the world has been the Pure Land. Be that as it may, when you observe the changes in the phenomenal world, and associate your body with birth, old age, sickness, and death, it will seem as if you have not escaped from the suffering of impermanence, arising and passing away. How can you escape this suffering of impermanence and attain no-arising and no-passing away?

Answer: This kind of comprehension is known as faith and understanding. Although it seems that by careful conjecture you can understand the state of enlightenment a little bit, because true enlightenment still hasn't been disclosed, you have not yet awakened from the dream of ignorance. Since that is the case, while you know the gist of this truth, you have not escaped attachment to self or self-pride within your dreamlike body, and [your thoughts of] hate and love or right and wrong are still deep. Deluded as you are within the realm of dreams and illusion, you are apt to arouse thoughts of gain and loss or benefit and harm, and create the karma of the three [lower] paths. All of this is a form within a dream.

The *Perfect Enlightenment Sutra* says, "Since they have not yet escaped transmigration and realized perfect enlightenment, it is said that even perfect enlightenment leads to transmigration."[74] This means that while your mind is not yet enlightened, you use your discriminating mind to distinguish and consider perfect enlightenment itself, and so even perfect enlightenment turns into transmigration.

In reality, if you think that you have realized enlightenment itself, and you do not cast off all intellectual understanding and cleverness, if you do not stop thoughts of right and wrong or wickedness and correctness, it is just like coming face to face with a silver mountain or a wall of iron. Indeed, you will give rise to a firm intention and focus on a single kōan, and without turning to look ahead or behind, to the right or the left, you will forget about sleeping, eating, cold and heat, and come to doubt. Therefore, when the [proper] time comes and the causes [are ripe], you will suddenly overcome the darkness of ignorance [that has surrounded you] for innumerable *kalpas*. For the first time you will wake up from the long night of dreaming. You will clap your hands and laugh out loud. You will reveal your original face[75] and illuminate the landscape of the original state.[76] You will be able to accomplish the true desire of one thousand lifetimes and ten thousand *kalpas*. If you do not give rise to the thought of great truth, only then is it impossible to overcome ignorance.

Long ago, the venerable Changshui[77] wondered about the meaning of the passage in the *Śūraṃgama Sutra*, "How does pure nature suddenly gives rise to mountains, rivers, and the land?"[78] He asked Master Huijue[79] of Langye, "What does this verse mean?" [The master of] Langye answered, "How does pure nature suddenly gives rise to mountains, rivers, and the land?"[80] Upon hearing these words, Changshui suddenly attained great enlightenment just like the bottom of a bucket dropping out. Certainly this is a figure who overcame the skandha of psychic construction.

The meaning of that passage from the *Śūraṃgama Sutra* is [as follows]. "Pure nature" means that this world is originally the Pure Land of pure nature. When the World Honored One taught the *Śūraṃgama Sutra,* the venerable Pūrṇa[81] asked, "As the *Tathagata* said, this world is the Pure Land of pure nature, so how is it that it suddenly gives rise to mountains, rivers, the land, and all phenomena, and so constantly changes, arising and passing away?" Before Changshui asked [his question], he had not awakened from the dream of psychic construction, and so the verse caused him great doubt. However, when he brought it up and asked, as a result of Master Langye's answer, he awoke from the dream for the first time and saw his pure nature.

Long ago there was a monk who asked a virtuous old monk, "What should I do if [thoughts] won't stop arising and passing away?" The old monk answered, "You must immediately make them into cold ashes and a withered tree." [The monk then] asked another virtuous old monk, "What should I do if [thoughts] won't stop arising and passing away?" The old monk answered, "Blind fool, where do they arise and pass away?" It is said that upon these words the monk attained great enlightenment. These are all people who attained the realm of their original portion by means of [overcoming] psychic construction.

SECTION 5: CONSCIOUSNESS

Fifth, consciousness is basis of the four other [*skandhas* that we have already considered], namely matter and form, sensation, perception, and psychic construction. It produces the Three Worlds and the six paths; it is the root of delusion that produces everything from the human body to the universe as a whole, the heavens, earth, and sky. This consciousness is itself the original mind, and although in itself free from distinctions, because of the misfortune of ignorance, we refer to it as consciousness. If it weren't for this misfortune of ignorance, then it would be the original mind. As Guifeng[82] said, "Consciousness is like an illusion or dream, [actually] it is just one mind."[83]

What we call "consciousness" is just like the illusions that a magician makes when he takes a piece of wood and turns it into a bird or beast. No doubt it becomes an animate thing, flying or running about, but a piece of wood is fundamentally a piece of wood and not a bird or beast. Showing it turn into something that doesn't exist is the power of the magician. In much the same way, through the magical power of ignorance, consciousness shows the original mind as something that changes, but the original mind itself does not change.

As a different example, [let me suggest that] consciousness is like people dreaming. When you aren't sleeping, you don't see dreams. When you are asleep, you see all kinds of dreams, and it seems as if all sorts of things that don't exist do. Consciousness is the same. When the original mind is not sleeping the sleep of ignorance, there are no distinctions between Three Worlds, there are no six paths, no hell, no heavenly realm, and nothing known as *saha*.[84] In that case, what would we refer to as "ultimate pleasure"?

Since originally there is no birth and death, we cannot apply the name "nirvana." From the start, afflictions do not arise, so we need not seek enlightenment. Originally, we do not become sentient beings, so we don't need to become Buddhas. Since the mind has never been deluded, to what should we be awakened now? Everything is just like this, and the splendid original mind itself does not express it in words. We pointlessly give [this level beyond all expression] a name, and refer to it as "original portion"[85] or "original face." Affixing the sleep of ignorance to this original face is known as the root of ignorance. It is the beginning of ignorance. Because we affix the sleep known as the root of ignorance, we see all sorts of dreams. First of all, we see that there is emptiness, and this is the beginning of the dream.

In the *Śūraṃgama Sutra*, when it says, "Darkness makes emptiness"[86] or "There is emptiness in delusion,"[87] it means [the following]. Because we see that there is emptiness, it seems that within emptiness is heaven and earth, within heaven and earth are the myriad things, among the myriad things are human beings, and among human beings is the self. Since there seem to be people, birds, animals, the moon and the blossoms, there are repulsive things, attractive things, things you like, and things you don't. Thereupon, there are things you desire and others you regret, and so you produce the dream of the eighty-four thousand afflictions.[88] Because of these afflictions, you kill, steal, feel lust, lie, and do other evil things with your body. You are driven mad with these afflictions and this is the evil karma you produce.

When you create all this evil karma, you fall into one of the three evil paths, hell, [the realm of] hungry ghosts, or [the realm of] animals. For innumerable *kalpas*, your body is burned in raging flames, or your bones are frozen in the ice of the Crimson Lotus Hell and the Large Crimson Lotus Hell.[89] Or, you sink into the tortures of hungry ghosts, which are difficult to stop, and for ten million *kalpas* you won't so much as hear the names of food and drink. When you come upon water and try to drink it, the water will turn to fire instead, and burn your throat. Even when you endure this kind of suffering, it is all just a dream within the sleep of ignorance.

On the other hand, if human beings reverse this evil karma, keep the five precepts[90] and [practice] the ten good acts,[91] they will escape from the three evil paths and attain a life as a human or heavenly being, and be born in their next life in a splendid body. Depending on the degree of their good karma, they will receive this or that pleasure. Be that as it may, they are still within the Three Worlds, inside the dreams within the sleep of ignorance. So, even though they are called pleasures, they aren't real pleasures. Though at the root they are suffering, because we are deluded, we think they are pleasure. Moreover, human beings endure the eight types of suffering[92] and heavenly beings the five marks of decline.[93] Since this suffering does not cease, [the human and heavenly realms] are not places where you can stop thoughts [of craving and desire]. [Instead, they are] worlds you should grow weary of and cast off at once.

If persons understand this truth, they will realize that though the pleasures of human and heavenly beings resemble pleasure, they still lie within the transmigration of the six paths. Theirs is still the transitory pleasure of phenomenal existence, and so is the ephemeral pleasure within the dream of ignorance. [Those who understand this] will give rise to belief in the Great Truth. When they sit in meditation and work on kōans, within their minds they will produce these three qualities: good, evil, and indifference. "Good" means the mind is thinking about good things. "Evil" means that evil things float through the mind. "Indifferent" refers to a mind that is neither good nor evil, but does things absentmindedly and idly.

You never stop giving rise to these three kinds of thoughts. If you aren't thinking about something evil, then you are thinking about something good. If you aren't thinking about something good, then you are thinking about something evil. The short periods of time when you aren't producing good or evil thoughts are known as indifference; indifference [refers to] a mind that acts absentmindedly without thinking anything, a state of idleness. Evil thoughts are the seeds of hell, hungry ghosts, and animals; good thoughts are the seeds of becoming a human or heavenly being; and indifference is the form of foolishness and ignorance that has not yet distinguished good and evil.

In this way, while you are not yet free from good, evil, and indifference, you are a beginner who has still not mastered sitting in meditation. When you are no longer concerned that such thoughts arise, your intention will deepen more and more, and you will sit in meditation intently, without boredom. Then as your zazen matures a little, at times neither good nor evil thoughts will arise, nor will the indifferent mind act idly. Your mind will be perfectly clear, and for a little while you will produce a mind like a highly polished mirror or crystal-clear water. This zazen mind is a sign that appears as long as the dew.

Once this happens, you must persevere in your meditation. If you sit in meditation intently without being negligent, at first your mind will clear for short periods, but gradually your mind will be clear while you meditate for one-third of the time or two-thirds of the time. Then it will be clear from beginning to end, neither good nor evil thought arise, nor is the mind indifferent. Like the clear autumn sky or a polished mirror on a stand, the mind is the same as empty space, and you feel as if the *Dharmakāya* were within your breast. Nothing can compare with the coolness within your breast. This is the state of someone who has perfected sitting in meditation more than half of the time. In the Zen sect we call it "beating everything into one," "the realm of one form," "a person who has died the great death," and "the world of Fugen."[94]

When this has happened, after a while the beginner wonders if he or she is already enlightened, or even if he or she is the equal of the Buddha Sakyamuni or Bodhidharma. This is a terrible error. It is just this kind of situation that we refer to as the fifth *skandha* of consciousness.

The *Śūraṃgama Sutra* says, "Entering deeply and encountering depth is the limit of consciousness."[95] This means [the following]. There are some people in this world who practice zazen diligently. When they encounter this [level of experience], they immediately believe it is enlightenment, and may even deceive Linji[96] or Deshan.[97] They spread it about that they have attained their original face and arrived at their original portion. They bestow *inka*[98] on many other people, make use of the [master's] rod, shout "*Katsu!*"[99] and in this way imitate the behavior of the patriarchs. But they have neither yet realized the inner enlightenment of the patriarchs, nor reached the root of One Mind.

Not yet having attained [enlightenment], they believe in all sorts of truths and think that this is enlightenment. Or they say that enlightenment is a place of complete emptiness, or that it is a matter of moving one's eyes and mouth and working one's arms and legs. There are those who will grant permission [i.e., *inka*] even to people such as these. They are all far from the mind of the patriarchs.

Now those who are deluded by consciousness and think it is enlightenment are quite different from people [just described] who have such a shallow understanding. They [seek] the truth, and even though their practice climbs to this level [of sitting in meditation without thoughts arising], they don't understand transcending consciousness. Therefore they are deluded by consciousness and take it to be their original mind, because they have not yet attained [true] practice.

The *Śūraṃgama Sutra* says, "When there are no distinctions of this sort at all, then there is no form and no emptiness. Makkali Gosāla[100] was deceived and what he took to be the basic substance of existence has no distinct nature apart from all *dharma* causes."[101] It also says, "Even if you extinguish thinking, hearing, learning, and knowing,[102] and preserve your internal quiet and seclusion, this is still a contrived notion of distinction, an object of the mind."[103]

As virtuous monks of the past have taught, whenever this interior quiet and seclusion is preserved, in the end some wise and holy people are overwhelmed [by the experience of nothingness and cannot escape]. When we look at the Song Confucian disposition in which joy, anger, grief, and pleasure have not yet appeared,[104] it is merely within this realm. Laozi's attainment of extreme emptiness and his preservation of tranquillity and kindness are also within this realm. In Buddhism, the entry of *arhats* and *pratyekabuddhas* into *samadhi*, and the fruits of their enlightenment are also said to be in this realm.

All of the [above-mentioned attainments] are free from the distinctions of seeing, hearing, learning, and knowing. They indicate a place of no-thought and no-mind like the one that the Buddha and the patriarchs mention. The place of no-thought and no-mind that is like the clear blue sky is known as "the eighth consciousness of sentient beings"[105] (i.e., *alaya* consciousness) and is the source that produces the delusions of the Three Worlds and the six paths. It is from [the *alaya* consciousness] that we create heaven, earth, sky, and all sentient and insentient beings in them. It is just like seeing all kinds of dreams when you are asleep. This is what the Buddha meant when he taught that the Three Worlds are consciousness only.[106] It is also what it means to say that *alaya* consciousness "is the basic sense organs, the seeds [of consciousness] and the perception of the physical world."[107] He also taught in the *Śūraṃgama Sutra*, "The *alaya* consciousness is the consciousness of detail. It makes habitual feelings continue without cease. Afraid of confusing truth and untruth, we never begin."[108]

As virtuous monks of the past explained, if the Buddha had taught one-sidedly that [the *alaya* consciousness] was true, then sentient beings would not progress in their practice, but fall into the pride of their own superiority. If he had taught one-sidedly that [the *alaya* consciousness] was untrue, then sentient beings would fall into self-despair and self-rejection, and give rise to nihilistic views. Accordingly, it is said that he never taught ordinary people or [*śrāvakas* and *pratyekabuddhas* in] the two vehicles about it.

Since this consciousness resembles the true original mind, but isn't the original mind, even the Buddha couldn't easily teach about it to foolish people. This is because, if he taught that this consciousness itself was the truth, then sentient beings would stop there, and thinking this [level of attainment] was sufficient, not persevere in their practice. [On the other hand,] if he taught that it wasn't true, then sentient beings would think that everything is completely void, doubt the existence of the original mind, and fall into nihilism. Then they would indeed be unable to awaken to the original mind. That is what I mean when I say that this is a very great matter, and not even the Buddha can easily teach it.

Although this consciousness is the original mind itself, because we are asleep and attached to ignorance, it is difficult to say that it is. Although it is difficult to call it the original mind, just because all deluded thoughts have not instantly disappeared, doesn't mean that we can say it is totally delusion. If practitioners arrive at this level, they will produce more and more energy for practice. Before long, they will [attain] true enlightenment of the sort previously described.

This is like the night growing light even before the sun has risen. Although the darkness of night will soon be lifted, for some reason, you don't realize that this will happen and the whole world will become bright. If you see the darkness dispelled and still ignore the fact that it has happened, then you will not be able to see the sun. If the darkness of delusion has been lifted, and you notice that your heart is perfectly bright and clear, and still ignore the fact that you are enlightened, then you cannot see the sun of *prajña.*

Although the darkness of delusion has been dispelled, you still don't believe this is [enlightenment], so you don't let it alone or enjoy it. Thinking this isn't the mind of enlightenment, but just no-thought and no-mind, you continue striving single-mindedly. Then, suddenly, real enlightenment appears, and the ten thousand *dharmas* will all be illuminated, just as if one hundred thousand suns had come up all at the same time. We say this is "seeing your [original] nature and becoming a Buddha,"[109] and call it "the Great Enlightenment and Great Penetration,"[110] and "the nirvana of pleasure."[111]

At that time, you will see all the Buddhas in the Three Worlds and will understand the marrow of Śakyamuni and Bodhidharma. You will see the original nature of all sentient beings, and penetrate to the origin of heaven, earth, and the myriad things. Nothing can compare to such a joyous event. Therefore, the *Śūramgama Sutra* says, "Purity comes to perfection, and light is transmitted. Tranquillity and illumination encompass emptiness. When you return to look at the world, it is still like something in a dream."[112]

When this enlightenment has completely developed, your *Dharma* nature and the *Dharmakāya* are tranquil and illuminating. They are one, and not two, like the land and the sky. Everything in the universe is one, and there is nothing that is not within your original mind. For this reason, the *Śūramgama Sutra* says, "Although what you see and perceive seem to be in the world before your eyes, from the beginning it is your own creation."[113]

"What you see" only mentions one of the six sense organs, the eyes, but it represents the other five as well. "What you perceive" means the realm of the six dusts, [that is] all the ten thousand *dharmas.* This teaches that the self and the ten thousand *dharmas* are just the one original mind, wondrous enlightenment itself. As they say, "The land is changed into gold, and the long river is churned into whey."[114] This is the true world of ultimate bliss.

Long ago there was a monk who asked Yunmen,[115] "When you don't give rise to a single thought, what is it like?" Yunmen answered, "Mount Sumeru."[116] There was another monk who asked Zhaozhou,[117] "How would it be if I came carrying nothing at all?" Zhaozhou said, "Set it down!" The monk replied, "But I am already carrying not one thing. What would I put down?" Zhaozhou answered, "If you have set it down, then take it up again!" Upon these words, the monk attained great enlightenment.[118]

One [monk] spoke of "not giving rise to a single thought," and the other of "not carrying a single thing." Both monks had reached the level of no-thought and no-mind. They believed that this was enlightenment and questioned Yunmen and Zhaozhou [respectively]. Knowing that they were ill, the [masters] answered them as they did. When they could penetrate "Mount Sumeru" or

"Set it down!" for the first time they arrived at their original portion and could see eye to eye with Yunmen and Zhaozhou. By practicing kōans diligently you should reach this level.

For this reason, people from the distant past said, "When hanging off a cliff, you should let go your hand of your own free will. After the end, when you come back to life a second time, no one will be able to deceive you."[119] They also said, "Take one step off the end of a hundred-foot pole and your body will appear in all the worlds in the ten directions."[120] All these [sayings] express the moment of enlightenment. By diligently sitting in meditation and practicing kōans, you should attain this level. You must not make a mistake and fall into a fox's cave.

Instructing the Community

Jishu, or instructions for the community, are short pithy statements about the Buddhist teachings. Zen teachers composed these verses for their monastic community, in order to promote contemplation in the students. They are not sermons in the usual sense, but rather statements of the master's understanding of the Dharma, which served as challenges to disciples. The genre of *jishu* is preserved in the recorded sayings of various Zen masters. It is closely related to other types of genre of Zen teachings, such as *suigo.*

Tetsugen composed the following verses for his disciples at his home monastery, Zuiryūji, in Osaka. He used formal language, writing in stanzas of four lines, comprised of either seven or five Chinese characters. He obviously prepared the verses in advance for specific occasions; they do not represent spontaneous remarks. In most cases, the verse includes information about the occasion on which Tetsugen presented it, although none of the verses are dated. The terminology is generally quite technical, including many references to various scriptures and allusions to Zen texts.

The translation of these texts is based on the version found in the *Tetsugen Zenji Yuiroku,* first fascicle, pp. 1a–2b.

Instructing the Community

On the Buddha's birthday[1] [the master] instructed the community:

> In ice and snow, the body is pure, gone beyond dirt and dust.
> From a fragrant bath, one emerges even more fresh and clean.
> Within the womb of Maya,[2] expansive from the beginning,
> [Buddha nature] gives birth to 30,000,000,000,000 beings.

※※※

[The master] instructed the community:

> Life and death are empty; they transcend past and present.
> Throughout the country in the ten directions, you cut off inquiry.
> The sound of the water, the color of the mountains are not distinct things.
> Truly you yourself are Kannon.[3]

※※※

[The master] instructed the community:

> The four great elements[4] have yet to come together.
> Your mind discriminates and foolishly brings up the passions.
> Limitless life and death, how many lifetimes?
> In the end, you have not received even a single life.

※※※

[The master] instructed the community:

> Sitting idly on the cushion for twenty years,
> I do not grasp the Zen of the Patriarchs.
> In daily practice I know nothing of samadhi.[5]
> When I am hungry, I eat, and when weary, I sleep.

❋❋❋

[The master] instructed the community:

> Life and death are always said to be the great matter.
> I ask, "Where is life and death?"
> The cataract deeply formed is not yet removed;[6]
> Mistakenly, within my eyes, it causes flowers to appear in the sky.

❋❋❋

On the anniversary of the Buddha's death[7], he instructed the community:

> The wind is still, the clouds gather, and the moon is just full.
> Grasping onto the corpse today teaches Nirvana.
> The Buddha's body is not originally different from the earth.
> In the middle of February, the weather remains cold.

❋❋❋

[The master] entered the new Meditation Hall and instructed the community:

> Within the individual, extinction (nirvana) already has a place.
> The dust of this world is distant, and one transcends self without limit.
> If the subjective mind does not darken the eyes of one born of a mother,
> Then sitting, lying down and chanting the sutras are not hindered.

❋❋❋

On hearing of a death, [the master] instructed the community:

> The causes of the myriad things are all illusions.
> Who can escape from this?
> In the span of one lifetime, you have already received the body of the
>   Unborn;
> On the day of one's death, you return to see the body of the Undying.[8]
> The cataracts on both your eyes are extinguished and come to an end;
> Reflections of flowers throughout the whole sky evaporate of themselves.
> The heel complies, and cuts off the silk thread.[9]
> To the West and to the East, you roam without hindrance.

※※※

[The master] instructed the community:

> Your original face has not been concealed.
> Yajñadatta lost his head and needlessly drove himself insane.[10]
> The great dream suddenly returns and that state of mind comes to an end.
> Flowers in the sky and the myriad things are all themselves the wondrous
>   illumination [of Buddha nature].

※※※

[The master] instructed the community:

> On entering the stream, you forget the place and attain full realization.
> All things in nature transcend distinction.
> From an upper branch, a warbler sings; rain [falls] on the willows.
> A butterfly dances among the flowers; wind [blows] through the plum and
>   the peach trees.

※※※

After looking at a flower, [the master] instructed the community:

> One hundred flowers are all alike; each has its own truth.
> Only in compliance with your affections do you create the dust of form.
> When the error of affection has ended, then the form of dust comes to
>   an end.
> Just then one realizes the innate eternal Spring[11] [of enlightenment].

※※※

[The master] instructed the community:

> Half of the three-month retreat[12] is already passed.
> You yourself, how are you?[13]
> Low spirits conceal the brightness and your eyes grow cloudy.
> Scattered [thoughts] confuse the mind; the clues are too numerous.
> From the beginning, your head is not hidden from you.[14]
> The image of the dragon,[15] why doesn't it enlighten others below?
> If you remove delusions and seek a new nature,
> The fetters pile up above you more and more, and compound the iron
>   shackles.

⁂

[The master] instructed the community:

> All the Buddhas take compassion as the body.
> Ordinary people take the mind as the [true] self.
> The universal gate[16] opens here and there.
> Wondrous forms appear within the six dusts.

⁂

Upon seeing cherry blossoms, [the master] instructed the community:

> Searching for Spring, the traveler is vexed by a poetic spirit.
> At the outer porch, he once again encounters a solitary cherry tree.
> Its elegance is similar to Yangfei[17] approaching a mirror and smiling.
> Its beauty is like Sichuan brocade[18] cast aside lightly.
> When the [blossoms] open, you do not understand their fleeting and empty
>   form.
> When they fall later, you understand how uncertain and fragile their
>   appearance.
> When will you attain the true eye of Lingyun?[19]
> The very moment you make empty all things in nature and create the
>   wondrous light [of wisdom].

Dharma Words

Hōgo or Dharma Words are short lessons prepared by a Zen teacher, usually for a specific disciple. In Japan, Zen teachers generally composed their *hōgo* in Chinese, which was the written language of educated Japanese for most religious, scholarly, and government purposes. When writing for women or a broader audience, teachers sometimes wrote in Japanese, as was the case with Tetsugen's Dharma Lesson in Japanese. Because *hōgo* were addressed to a single individual, the master had the opportunity to shape the lesson to meet the special needs and circumstances of his student. For this reason, some may contain a wealth of technical Buddhist language and Zen images, while others may be written using simpler terminology.

Only three *hōgo* written by Tetsugen are preserved in the *Yuiroku,* The Preserved Writings of Tetsugen;[1] none of them are dated. Tetsugen addressed the first two of these texts to a layperson named Kyogoku Hyōbun, about whom nothing is known. He composed the third for Hoshino Kanzaemon, a famous archer of the day. In this case, we can easily see that Tetsugen selected a vocabulary appropriate for his audience. An additional *hōgo,* not published with the others, was preserved at a temple called Jōkanji. This lesson, signed by Tetsugen and dated the twelfth lunar month of 1678, was addressed to a disciple named Shōchi, a Zen Buddhist monk. In this case, Tetsugen seems to address a serious concern related to Shōchi's meditative practice. Knowing that his audience was a monk familiar with Buddhist concepts and texts, he made use of extensive Buddhist terminology and Zen allusions. The translation is based on the version preserved in Yoshinaga Utarō's compendium *Tetsugen Zenji.*[2]

In this case, the term *hōgo* is translated as Dharma words instead of Dharma lesson in order to distinguish in English between the texts originally composed in Chinese and Japanese.

HŌGO 1

The self, the light of *prajña*,[3] is not within or without. It is not the phenomenal world, it is not the mind. It has no right and no wrong. It is not past or present. It is not truth and it is not delusion. It is not in motion and it is not at rest. It is not the place where one distinguishes all thoughts. The senses and their objects are far removed from it; it is bound by heaven and earth. It is spread throughout past and present. Shining brightly between thought and perception, it is exposed beyond all things.

What's to be done about all the people who are deceived by the deluded senses and their objects and so cannot awaken completely? Even someone who knows a little about practice cannot cut off the minute distinctions of consciousness and feeling. Therefore the mind that perceives subject and object is never at rest. How can the Original Mind of tranquillity and extinction ever be manifest?

Fortunately, you are deeply affected by residual causes.[4] I tell you, strengthen your firm resolve and you will personally attain the level of enlightenment of the ancient [masters]. Never be satisfied with petty knowledge and petty understanding. I send you my regards.

(Sent to the layperson Kyogoku Hyōbun)

HŌGO 2

The ignorance of innumerable kalpas lingers on, and one enters into the field of the Eight Consciousnesses.[5] One comes into contact with things, and so they exist. Encountering the realm of love and hate, one cannot stop changing. Rather one changes all the more because of things. Although one may possess [worldly] wisdom and discernment, they are completely useless. One cannot attain freedom [with them]. Perhaps this is because one's practice is not yet mature, and so one cannot overcome the consciousness arising from ignorance.

At the present time, many of those who teach Zen all over the place take this sickness to be the Dharma; they cannot recognize their error. In the long run, the blind lead the blind and end up pulling one another into the fiery pit [of hell]. If one does not possess the eye of Zen and carry an iron-like resolve, how can one skillfully attempt [to teach others]? Earnestly search carefully. Never regard shallow discernment as one's Original Portion.[6]

HŌGO 3

If the pathway has too many branches, you lose the sheep. If you [shoot] an arrow with single-minded concentration, then you will hit the bull's-eye. When your practice is already concentrated, then your mind sees and your hand responds, so that you always hit the bull's eye. You eventually attain the skill of causing monkeys to cry [by just lifting your bow] and being able to shoot lice. The way of learning is also like this. When you have a single kōan in your heart and practice diligently night and day without ceasing, then your practice will ripen fully. When the time is right, and you are fully enlightened, then the mind transcending mind is illuminated and the thing transcending things is manifest. Right and left converge at the source. Warp and woof meet in the track.[7] On the brink of life and death, you attain the great freedom. In heaven above and earth below, you alone are revered.[8] Oh what pleasure!

You, the layman Hoshino Kanzaemon[9] of Owari have studied archery since you were small, and have truly attained that skill. Indeed, you have an arm that can pierce a willow from one hundred paces. In the seventy provinces, there is no one who surpasses you. In the Autumn of 1676, we met in Taihei, and our conversation extended to the Way. Therefore, I took out paper and sought for [the right] words, and eventually wrote this to aid you in your practice.

(Sent to the layperson Hoshino Kanzaemon)

HŌGO 4

As a rule among practitioners of Zen, many experience darkness and distraction,[10] and these two demons cause them grief. Therefore, their practice cannot be pure. This is nothing other than the result of the mind that rises and passes away not cutting through [the darkness and distraction]. If the mind that arises and passes away does cut through them, it is because you are stubbornly maintaining your determination, like a soldier [keeping watch] on a high castle wall. The five desires [that arise in response to] the objects of the senses cannot enter the gate. There is no need to remove "sinking into darkness and being disturbed by distractions." They recede of themselves. If unfortunately the darkness and distraction cannot be dispelled, and when you make up your mind that you want to remove them, then you increase your delusion and anguish more and more.

In general, within the minds of deluded sentient beings, thoughts are either good, evil, or neutral in character. When the mind is not thinking good [thoughts], then it is thinking about evil. When it is not thinking about evil, then it is thinking about good. Choosing between the two opposing concepts of good and evil, one goes beyond external running about, and internally gathers one's thoughts. We call this the disturbed [mind]. If [the mind] is not thinking about good or evil, then thoughts have no place to cling. Inside the mind is vast, indistinct, and dark, and there is no place to hold memory. We call this no-memory. Furthermore, it is called depression. This unsettled mind is dualistic. Shadows cover and conceal the perfectly illuminated pure Dharma eye. For this reason, one is not able to return to one's original shining mirror, one's original face.[11]

All sentient beings follow a succession of thought after thought without beginning. If one has not yet departed from thoughts, then one cannot by means of this departure from thoughts have the mind and body draw near to realization. If by means of mutual correspondence for a brief time one separates from sense objects, then there is no place to attach to thoughts. Externally, one already has given up the connection between subject and object. Internally, one has not yet seen the tranquil and penetrating mysterious wisdom. On this account, [the mind] is dark and confused, without discrimination, and nowhere fully distinct. Ordinarily, one would fall into a dark pit of depression. In that case, one gives rise to anxious thoughts and rushes [back] toward the region of good and evil, thus entering all the more deeply into disturbed mind. The realm of dust [that is the senses] turns one around and is troubling, like a region where monkeys are endlessly dashing up and down tall trees. Like a loose horse roaming through a wilderness, far and near one follows the mind [as it wanders].

This mind originates in delusion, like an image in a mirror or the moon [reflected] on the water. Again, it is like imaginary flowers one sees in a dream. The changing mind of those stuck in the rut of ordinary people dwells perpetually in the defiled triple world.[12] Those in the two vehicles[13] entrusted to praise and blame still fall into the deep hole of nonactivity.

This mind that is without reality is not separate from the true mind. From the beginning, it is the formless true origin. It turns and creates the discriminating mind of sentient beings, just as wind raises up waves on the clear water of a pool. Although it moves, at the source it always abides and does not move. It is like [diseased eyes][14] giving rise to flowers in the realm of emptiness. Although they appear, they do not [exist][15] and have the characteristic of emptiness. Shenguang [Huike] sought this discriminating mind and was unable to attain peace of mind with it.[16] He remembered that Ananda seized on this thought and its appearance caused the truth to be hidden, and he was upbraided for acknowledging the thief.[17] He was not able to make up his mind to remove them. Removing them, moreover, gave rise to a heavy hindrance. He was not able to find it and went rushing one place and another. He set fire to the five desires, and the fire took hold. He was unable to forsake it and so was unable to burn the deceptive illusionary flowers. What suffering seized hold of him! Therefore, it is said that all the more if you contemplate wandering thoughts, in the end you won't give rise to it [the true mind of enlightenment]. In accordance with the three time periods, if you seek it, you will not find it. Facing the ten directions, you will search for it without [finding] a trace. You still are unable to give rise to this mind. Likewise, in no place is there a trace of it passing away. Arising and passing away are completely separate [from it]. Likewise, the empty mind is a clear mirror. Still, its name is the way of seeing.

If you cannot directly penetrate and see, just exert yourself and offer up a single verse on your kōan. Until your practice is mature, you cannot remove it. It removes itself just as darkness passes away on its own when the sun has risen. Do not worry that deluded thoughts do not go away. Only worry that your practice does not cut through [the darkness and distraction]. Just when your practice cuts through them, then delusions of themselves will desist. When delusions desist, the mind is empty. True wisdom of itself appears. True wisdom, unknowing, is always shining, always manifest. The Iron Mountains[18] cannot hide its brightness. The vast sky cannot compare to its form. Not pure and not coarse, the myriad things cannot conceal their truth. Not abiding and not dependent, the burning of defilement cannot change its nature. How wonderful! The earlier defilements manifest brightness. The opposing objects [of the senses] give rise to wisdom. Naturally tranquil and penetrating mysterious wisdom is deep. It burns without limit. Then the darkness sinks and makes limitless light. You cast off the senses and their objects and attain supernatural light without hindrance. How sudden! How joyous!

Strive on! Strive on!

Given in the 12th lunar month of 1678 to my disciple Shōchi.

Tetsugen of Zuiryuji Temple

Response to the Lay Buddhist
Noritomi Tessen

Tetsugen wrote this letter to a lay practitioner named Noritomi Tessen, apparently in response to a letter Noritomi had addressed to him. Noritomi's letter is not extant. Nothing is known about Noritomi, except what can be gleaned from internal evidence. His personal name is Buddhist, and was almost certainly given to him by a Zen teacher. Noritomi appears to have had a master-disciple relationship with Tetsugen. He seems to have stated his understanding of the Dharma in his original letter, and in this response, Tetsugen warns him that it was not yet mature.

Tetsugen's letter was composed in Chinese and the existing versions are undated. The following translation is based on the version found in the *Yuiroku*, The Preserved Writings of Tetsugen.[1] In addition to this response, Tetsugen also addressed at least one poem to Noritomi Tessen.

Response to the Lay Buddhist
Noritomi Tessen

I received your letter. "One's original spiritual nature neither arises nor passes away." "What one sees, hears, thinks, and knows is not the Master.[2]" "Birth and death are themselves Nirvana; the afflictions are themselves enlightenment." "Apart from the Original Mind, outside or inside, there is no deluded mind. The deluded mind is itself the Original Mind."[3] Viewpoints like this look like the real thing, but they aren't.[4]

At the present time, those who practice Zen often produce this sort of view. They seek after these reflections and shadows, and take them to be the Master. Hemp bindings and paper bandages are taken to be the teaching received [when Bodhidharma] came from the West.[5] They raise their fists, point their fingers, raise their eyebrows, and wink their eyes. Some give a shout, and others wipe their sleeves.[6] All of them are living in a demon's cave[7] [of darkness and ignorance]. Their heels are not yet even on the ground. Their trumped-up understanding is not the True Eye [of enlightenment]. On the contrary, they receive a white gourd *inka*[8] and immediately bestow *inka* [on others].[9] They cause [their disciples] to seek after "clarity and spirituality" and to accept this as the teaching of the Patriarchs. In their rushing forward and shrinking back, they create an imitation and make a spectacle [of true Zen].

From the start, scholars do not have the eye of a Zen practitioner. They encounter this sort of demon [teacher] and take them for the real thing. In their whole life they will never be able to see their mistake. Frequently, a person with only superficial understanding will point out their error. The [scholar] dismisses this as false, and is overcome with anger, giving rise to slanderous thoughts and creating unending karma. What suffering! What suffering! How can a person with good intentions not lament this and weep?

Even if you already have morality[10] and know that the Dharma of renouncing the world exists, you do not yet possess true understanding. Therefore, you seek for it beyond seeing, hearing, thinking, and knowing, and take it to be the Master. You accept sayings such as "Birth and death are themselves Nirvana; the afflictions are themselves enlightenment," and treat them as the Buddha's Dharma. If one concludes that "Attaining complete freedom at the precipice of life and death"[11] looks like the same kind of view, then you are like someone blowing on a net and hoping to fill it. It is truly pitiable.

As a result, if you wish to penetrate this matter, then take all these sorts of viewpoints and exhaust them to the bottom and put them down. Without raising even a hair, just diligently penetrate to the heart of the matter. After long days and months, a day will come when you spontaneously enjoy contentment in everyday life. If you give rise to simplistic views and do not cast off your previous way of life, then you will once again receive an erroneous *inka*. If you take this to be the teachings received [from the Patriarchs], then you will destroy the grain and burn the sprouts, and you will never become a true seedling.[12]

I send my good wishes.

A Letter to Acting Head Monk Hōshū

Tetsugen wrote this letter to Hōshū, his leading disciple, while he was away from Zuiryūji. At those times, he generally left Hōshū in charge of the temple, giving him the title *Kanshu,* or "acting head monk." Although the letter is undated, we know from internal evidence that it was written late in Tetsugen's life, perhaps shortly after the New Year in 1681. At that time Tetsugen was in Edo, waiting to present the scriptures to the shōgun. At this stage of Tetsugen's life, the assembly of his disciples in residence at Zuiryūji had grown to approximately one hundred monks.

Tetsugen worries in this text that he will be unable to find a worthy Dharma heir to carry on his work. Although he highly praises Hōshū and his understanding of the Dharma, he was, nevertheless, not yet ready to certify him as an heir. In fact, Tetsugen died without ever bestowing *inka* on Hōshū or on any other of his disciples. Hōshū later became the Dharma heir of Muan, Tetsugen's own Dharma master. The original letter was composed in Chinese. The following translation is based on the version found in the *Yuiroku, The Preserved Writings of Tetsugen.*[1]

A Letter Sent to
Acting Head Monk Hōshū

I received the letter that [you], the acting head monk at Zuiryūji, sent at New Year's. I know that you are well and that your efforts will be untiring. Nothing could please me more. Although the winter lingers now, I am the same as ever, so do not worry about me while I am away.

My only concern is that my Dharma will decline like a temple in late autumn. If only I could find one person or even half a person who possesses the eye of Zen practice. Those who seek only their own enlightenment[2] and fall into the demon's cave[3] [of ignorance and attachment] are as common as flax and millet. They are truly pitiful.

You have a nature determined by your previous existences. Although your wealth and honor may be meager, you have moral principles. You are not in the slightest interested in worldliness. You who now sit as guardian [of my disciples at Zuiryūji] are truly a rarity in these latter days.

You have already given rise to a determined and intense intention [to attain enlightenment]. You have faced the silver mountain and the iron wall,[4] let go your hand while hanging from a precipice,[5] taken a step off the top of [a hundred foot] pole,[6] and met with the Great Death.[7] If you come back to life in this unprecedented way, then you will spontaneously harmonize [with ultimate reality]. If you wallow in even a small amount of intellectual understanding, so-called profound language will stagnate in your mind, and you will revert to the state of ordinary conscious thought. If reality resides before your eyes, then you will revert to the condition of intellectual conceptualization.

It says in the scriptures, "If there is self and others, sentient beings and long life, then one is not a bodhisattva."[8] If you retain any belief in the [false] self, then even if we come to the year of the donkey,[9] how could there ever be a day when you harmonize [with ultimate reality]? You must realize that you yourself Hōshū are the first and most recalcitrant delusion.

When Hōshū is at the barrier, then the barrier becomes his prison. When Hōshū attains enlightenment, then enlightenment becomes a net of mistaken views. When Hōshū perfects the Way, then the Way becomes demonic and heretical. When Hōshū gives rise to understanding, then understanding becomes a shock wave [that disturbs the mind]. When Hōshū gives rise to compassion, then compassion becomes a love of spittle [that is, attachment to the self]. It would be better to slay this Hōshū, and be unfettered and at ease.

When such a time comes, you will already know that the whole earth does not have an inch of land,[10] and that the ten directions cut off all obstacles. Each dharma abides in thusness, and each object of perception gives rise to *samadhi*. Between the demon world and the Buddha world you will freely come and go.

If your thoughts are not yet devoid of even the smallest notion of right and wrong, gain and loss, praise and blame, then basic ignorance will become firmly ensconced. Hidden within the storehouse consciousness, it will move freely through all sensory perceptions, and present manifestations[11] will leave an influence[12] that will not be cut off for long kalpas. The so-call three coats of karmic cause, fetters [that last for] ten thousand kalpas, oh what a falsehood! In this way, even if your wisdom exceeded Śāriputra's[13] and your eloquence were comparable to Pūrna's,[14] I swear that you would not see it even in your dreams.

Although I have not yet attained the land of the ancients, still I have not deteriorated into the rut of today's [masters]. My only regret is that the responsibility for carving [the woodblocks for] the scriptures was heavy and producing the volumes complex. So I have been pulled by karmic connections and have not attained freedom. Now I am old, and for the first time realize my mistake a little bit.

Please take care of your bodily health and do not allow yourself to fall ill. Follow the Way day and night. Leisure and speed have their place. Think about the World Honored One's instructions for playing the lute.[15] One morning you attain [the skill to play] in your mind and respond with you fingers. Then even if you wanted the wondrous music to stop spreading, you couldn't do it.

Part II

Texts Related to the
Buddhist Scripture Project

An Opportunity for Instruction

Tetsugen wrote the *Keen no sō* to promote his plan to improve the availability of the Buddhist scriptures in Japan. In 1663, when he composed it, his intention was to raise enough funds to import an edition of the scriptures from China. He only later decided that it would be better to produce a woodblock edition in Japan. Tetsugen seems to have intended this text for somewhat popular consumption as a promotional device to raise awareness of his undertaking. First, he composed it in Japanese rather than Chinese, which would have allowed for a broader audience. In addition, he employed both positive and negative incentives for readers to donate to the cause, much like the inducements used in popular preaching. It is not known how the document was distributed or to whom. The present translation is based on a modern edition of Tetsugen's writings.[1]

Comments on an
Opportunity for Instruction

In the scriptures, the Buddha is compared to a great physician, the Dharma to a wondrously curative elixir, the monks to nurses, and ordinary people to those suffering from a grave illness. One would say that, in this life, a gravely ill person would find it difficult to recover without [the care of] a physician, even if he had a nurse. Or, if he did have a physician, but lacked medicine, then the physician couldn't treat him. Therefore, the physician, the medicine, and the nurse are all three necessary for recovery. By the same token, in Japan, we have always had the Buddha and the sangha, but we have never had sufficient supplies of the curative Dharma. How, then, can the people's illness be healed? What a deplorable situation!

Therefore, if the Buddha will bestow his blessings on us and the time is ripe, if the emperor comes to our aid, if the lords will participate, and the ministers respond with loyalty, if the people willingly accept [this opportunity to gain merit], and the sangha has accumulated sufficient merit, and if heaven is so moved, then at this time we will try to acquire the medicinal Dharma.

From the middle of last autumn, I gave a lecture series on the *Lotus Sutra* here at Kōtokusan Ryūchōin[2] in the castle town of Kumamoto. The audience gathered like banks of clouds, and participants lined up like so many stars. High-ranking monks from various temples, and Zen monks from the four directions strengthened their resolve to seek the scriptures from China, and so rain down that sweet nectar on this nation Japan. For that purpose, old and young alike emptied their bags and turned out their sleeves [donating all they had]. Unfortunately, we couldn't even fill one person's begging bowl with what we collected. We'll never be able to attain our goal unless we ask people everywhere in the ten directions for help. For this reason, I will not shy away from the exalted, or overlook the lowly. I will not regard one hundred thousand *kan*[3] of rice as too much, or one grain of rice as too little. Whatever people can offer, I will accept. I will take it as it is given, and go on begging.

If a poor woman offers even a single *sen*, although it may seem a meager sum, with that fine thread she will tie a lasting bond with the Dharma. If an orphan without savings amounting to a scrap of toilet paper should give a single grain of millet, he will have planted the great seed of enlightenment. Whether male or female, old or young, whether they are foolish because of foolishness, or wise because of wisdom. The wealthy realize their present wealth came from generosity in previous lives, and so they give all the more. The poor know that their present poverty came from not making sacrifices in the past, and so they are that much more willing to sacrifice now. Each one responds appropriately.

One can even give a clod of earth. [In a previous life] King Aśoka put sand into the Buddha's begging bowl, and one hundred years after the Buddha's death, he attained the rank of universal monarch.[4] It was a pitiful [offering], but not an act of defiance. One can also offer water. You have heard in the chapter on Expedient Means [in the *Lotus Sutra*] that the person who added a drop of water to the inkstone pond escaped from the tortures of King Emma's staff.[5] In the Dharma realm of equality, why make distinctions between the exalted and the lowly? The Eight Schools[6] have no differences. Then why make distinctions between self and other? Why limit it to just the living, when it is particularly appropriate [to make donations] for the sake of the deceased. Rather than just helping oneself alone, at the same time one can help one's parents. Don't exclusively limit this to yourself, but encourage others as well. Sharing the shade of a single tree forms a kind of bond. When streams join to form a river, there is a deep pledge. All the more will you awaken to the enlightenment of the one Buddha who resides in the Pure Land because you entered into a bond with the wondrous Dharma.

Nevertheless, when you observe the world closely, [you see that time rushes past like] water in a swiftly flowing stream or the flash of a galloping horse glimpsed through the crack of a door. Truly, the dew on the morning glories disappears without waiting for the rays of sunlight, and no one knows if the fishes swimming in small streams will live to see tomorrow. Transience cuts short what lies before us, and hell awaits us below our feet. When you are suddenly beset by disease and you think that you are facing death, your arms and legs flail about like a crab thrust into boiling water or a bird struck by an arrow.

You cannot take with you even the rarest jewel from China or Japan [saved up in this life]. The affection and kindness of one's wife and children are now useless. All alone one must take the dark journey to Hades. Struggling is futile, one plunges to the bottom of the land of the dead. King Emma's accusing voice roars like thunder, and the image reflected in the crystal mirror is clear before one's eyes. The sins committed in this corrupt world, even those as fleeting as the dew, cannot be hidden. The good deeds of one's previous life seem less than dust. The tongues of fire in Perpetual and Gateless Hell,[7] measuring five hundred *yojana*[8] in length, terrify you. For one hundred million years, you are tortured with copper rods and iron posts that burn your liver. At this stage, even if they regretted [your plight], who could save you? What good would repentance do you?

For this reason, apprehensive about one's next life in the distant future and to save oneself from horrible suffering in the immediate future, one strives to do what is good right now. If you thereby attain bliss in the distant future, this eternal blessing will give you joy throughout your life. Unfortunately, people in this life are drunk with the wine of fame and fortune, and until the very end they pay no heed to Right Mindfulness.[9] They tie themselves up in the cords of affluence and lose their freedom throughout their lives, just like flies that crave the taste [of sugar] or silkworms bound in their cocoons. Although their life span is limited, their desires are without end. Although their years are already declining, the passions continue to grow. They readily squander large sums of gold and silver on the fruitless amusements of the floating world[10] as if spewing out spittle, but when it comes to the truly worthwhile endeavors that promote enlightenment, giving even a trifling sum is like pulling teeth.

Alas, if people donated only one billionth of what they throw away on trivial amusements, it could be an offering for the enlightenment of their parents in a future rebirth. If they understood the dreadful suffering of endless *kalpas,* they could relieve the grief of their wife and children, which is hard to bear. Just because they cannot see that far [into the future], doesn't mean they won't have to face it. Just because they don't understand the darkness, doesn't mean they won't suffer.

Bestowing blessings on all those [trapped] in the Six Paths[11] goes beyond transforming the human realm alone. At the same time, one has an effect on the afterlife as well, which truly surpasses just alleviating [the suffering] in one's present life.

If one thinks about it in this way, then the merit [from donating money for the scriptures] is a merit among merits. The present root of goodness is the root of goodness for the root of goodness. Therefore it can be regarded as a prayer for the entire country and an offering to the *kami* (deities) of heaven and earth. It repays the debt of gratitude to your lord and your father, and compensates the people for their efforts. That being the case, the so-called exalted ones give for the sake of the lowly and the lowly give for the sake of the exalted. I save others and they save me. Together, we save one another. Along with this, we taste the sweet nectar of the wondrous medicine [of the Dharma] and inherit the light of wisdom of the Dharma realm. Keep on striving! Keep on striving!

[Written on] the fifth day of the tenth month
in the third year of Kambun [1663].

A Brief Account of the History of
Carving the Buddhist Scriptures

Tetsugen composed the *Daizō o kizamu engi sō* in 1669, when he had decided to produce a woodblock edition of the Buddhist scriptures. By this time, the project had already begun, funded by the generosity of a Buddhist nun from Osaka, named Myōu. The History of Carving the Scriptures appears to be a promotional text in the same general spirit as An Opportunity for Instruction. However, in this case, Tetsugen wrote in Chinese. It is possible that this text was intended for an upper-class audience as well as other monks and nuns. The translation is based on a modern edition of Tetsugen's writing.[1]

Brief Account of the History of Carving the Buddhist Scriptures

As you probably have heard, when Kāśyapa Mātanga[2] went to Han China, for the first time the golden words of five sutras[3] reached [China]. When Xuanzang[4] returned to Tang China, the Three Baskets[5] of the sutras thus appeared there. These [scriptures] make known the brilliant wisdom [of the Buddha] to the whole world and open up the path of enlightenment to all living things. Therefore, one after another, monks, men of great virtue, came and exerted themselves in seeking the [correct] words to translate [the scriptures]. Due to the influence of these honorable men and great scholars, the breeze of wisdom blew widely at that time, and the Dharma rain fell everywhere throughout the country.

Indeed, the spread of the Great Dharma has never prospered so much as in China from the Six dynasties through the Tang, Song, Yuan, and Ming dynasties. Throughout the country, there were no fewer than twenty editions of the scriptures.[6] These were strewn here and there like *go* stones, scattered like stars, some kept at court and others preserved at famous monasteries.

Since ancient times, our country [Japan] has been called a Buddha Land. Since the teachings were first received in the East during the reign of Emperor Kimmei,[7] successive emperors have received them, while taking special care to reverence the *kami* (indigenous deities of Japan). [The Buddhist teachings] have come to be revered and followed by the whole nation, counselors, retainers, and all classes of people. Moreover, when we reflect on this, [Japan] is not inferior to places such as India and China, except that from the beginning, there has never been a printed edition of the scriptures published here, making texts quite scarce. Whenever talented men from the various temples and monasteries discuss this, they can only regret it.

Although I was born at the end of the Semblence Age of the Dharma,[8] I was fortunate to become associated with the sangha and gratefully received blessings from the Buddha. [I venture to say that] the circulation of the scriptures is always crucial. It has been perhaps a year since the idea sprouted in my heart. If the time is not ripe, then my prayers will be in vain and I will be unable to make the effort.

This summer, I went to Kyoto and had an audience with Master [Yinyuan] of Ōbakusan.[9] I brought up this matter with him. The master consented and praised [the idea]. I was likewise overjoyed. I consulted with a gentleman who for some time has been donating the cost of my robes and begging bowls and has done two or three other acts of kindness. First, we selected a few of the more important sutras from the scriptures and printed them. Just as by piling up earth one makes a mountain, or by collecting water one makes a river, I pray that someday we will see that [this project] is much the same. If things go well, I may complete the entire [collection of] scriptures. I still cannot tell.

Once, during the reign of Emperor Shenzong[10] of the great Ming dynasty, Master Zibo[11] realized that the volumes of the scriptures were so numerous that in distant regions and poor villages there where those who had not even heard of the most famous titles from the scriptures. Consequently, [his idea] was to transform Buddhist texts into woodblocks, so that it would be possible to transmit them. Everywhere they were seen and heard they would create the seeds of Buddhahood. Eventually, they would introduce a [karmic] connection [to Buddhism] throughout the nation. At the behest of Er Shenzi, Daokai[12] supervised this work. The five great ministers Lord Lu, Si Chengmeng, Lord Feng of Zhen, Fang Boyen, and Lord Wu of Xian heard about this and praised it highly. All of them helped by contributing an annual stipend, each as he saw fit, and in no time the work was completed. Even now, when [an edition of the scriptures] is imported [to Japan] by ship, it is these very books.

These five ministers may perhaps be called the pillars and cornerstones of the Confucian academy. To present oneself at the ministry office and contemplate the Dharma is profound. Alone, [such a person] is daring, determined, and strong. How much more do our nation's lords, retainers, and all classes of people revere the Three Treasures.[13] Mausoleums throughout the land are already all Buddhist temples.[14] Doesn't the sincerity with which [the Japanese] are pleased to do good and esteem the Dharma match all the wisdom of China? It is just that, until now, no one took up the [project] and introduced it. Why not likewise create a similar [karmic] connection? I now humbly serve as the advance guard.[15]

I bow down and pray that the counselors, officials, wealthy folk, good men, and virtuous women in all ten directions would each give rise to the thought of how difficult it is to meet [a Buddha], and to manifest a broad mind to help with [the project]. Fund three to five sutras, or even just a single word or half a verse. Doing so would tie a bond with wisdom and complete this important work, and so turn the wheel of the Dharma and eternally bless our country. As a consequence, I would repay the debt of gratitude to the Buddha lifetime after lifetime and earn some small reward.

A Report on Progress Made on the
New Edition of the Buddhist Scriptures

Tetsugen addressed this report to the Retired Emperor Gomizunoo along with the first copy of the scriptures and an index of the contents. The document is dated the seventh day of the seventh month of the year Empō 6 (1678). Presenting a copy of the scriptures to the retired emperor was more than a courtesy. Gomizunoo was a practitioner of Zen, with a long relationship with many of the early Chinese and Japanese Ōbaku masters. Indeed, he became the Dharma heir of the Ōbaku master Ryōkei Shōsen and is himself regarded as the founder of an important Ōbaku sublineage.[1] Tetsugen's original report is composed in highly formal Chinese, using honorific language appropriate for its intended recipient. The translation is based on the version found in the *Yuiroku, The Preserved Writings of Tetsugen.*[2]

A Report on Progress Made on the
New Edition of the Buddhist Scriptures

Respectfully submitted with true sincerity and reverence, by the loyal monk [Tetsugen] Dōkō, thirty-fourth generation[3] in the transmission of the True Rinzai Sect,[4] of Hōzō Zen'in,[5] Ōbakusan, in the district of Uji, Yamashiro province, in the Kyoto district.

I have heard that while the clear rendering of the Truth was actually done by the Buddha's disciples, that the transmission of the Great Dharma was actually done by the king. When we consider India and China, and think about the Buddhist and Confucian records, they convey to us the past and the present, shining like the sun and the stars. Even though [I,] your servant, am unworthy, I humbly entered into the Gate of Emptiness.[6] The earthen begging bowl and patched robe have long been used by the Buddhas. The morning bell and evening gong have likewise long been dedicated to the Dharma.

When one considers repaying the Four Great Debts of Gratitude,[7] would it be better to spare one's efforts? Therefore, without considering my own uselessness, I generally hold lectures and invite monks and laypeople from all over. Each day I comment on the golden words [of the Buddha]. I try to cause each person to be perfumed with the fragrance of wisdom, and to enable each one to sow the seed of enlightenment. I try to have them melt away their old [misguided] customs and to manifest the True Source.[8] Since the Way has already been spread, it is suitable that I strive [in this way].

Our country is still commonly called a Buddha Land. The emperor [of China] reveres the Dharma. [Japan] does not rank second to China. How much more does our majesty the reigning emperor [rank above the Chinese emperors]? His majesty the retired emperor himself is an ancient sage who is reincarnated, a corresponding manifestation of the Buddha in the present.[9] The flower of his wisdom is brilliantly adorned. The sea of his blessings is vast and deep. He supports the teachings of our sect; his knowledge is boundless.

He confers honors on our monks. His graciousness is not singular. Moreover, the blue roofs [of noble families] and Buddhist monasteries are spread out here and there. Far and wide golden images of the Buddha gleam brightly. The only thing lacking is an edition of the Buddhist Scriptures. In counting editions of the scriptures, there are some twenty in China, but our country does not yet possess even one. Not that our country lacks for texts.

I have heard it said that jade from Chuiji,[10] Chuchan's[11] chariot, the swords of Fengcheng, and pearls from the Chishui river were all exceedingly precious. However, among the treasures of the people, the treasure of the Dharma is foremost. Can one ever forget this? Wherever the treasure of the Dharma exists, there are all the pleasures of heaven. All the spirits protect it. It is the lucky omen among lucky omens, the most laudable thing among laudable things. Therefore, [I] your servant am anxious from morning to night, without a moment to relax. Although I intended to carry out [the project] I am tediously feeble. I am not as strong as a mosquito carrying [the weight of the world] on its shoulders. Whenever I enter here, I pray to the dragon kings and *devas*,[12] and whenever I go out, I tell my patrons. From something insignificant, [the scripture project] has become remarkable. Shallow connections have become profound. Thanks to the power of the Dharma, if I am not mistaken in my thinking, I now inform you that [the new edition] is almost complete. As a matter of course, it has progressed.

By means of this praiseworthy cause, I pray for a boundless reckoning. May the Imperial family prosper forever. May the jeweled leaf long thrive and the realm be peaceful. May rain and sunshine be in accordance with the season. I humbly pray that his majesty, the measure of heaven and earth, will condescend to look on his loyal monk's humble effort. When you are at leisure from your myriad responsibilities, if you were to open [the scriptures] and read them, it would be the greatest happiness for the sect and the greatest happiness for your loyal monk. If you reflect on them, your majesty will become brilliantly enlightened, like the sun and the moon. In benevolence and virtue, how would you differ from Yao and Shun?[13] If you were not an ancient sage reborn as a corresponding manifestation of the Buddha for the world today, then how could I have done this? The reason I have been diligent and not dared to stop is that I hope to repay the great blessing of the Buddha and the patriarchs, as well as to secretly aid your majesty's rule.

I have offended your authority, and so my feelings cannot bear the extreme turmoil and agitation. I respectfully offer the sutras along with an index, and present them to you.

An Account of Completing
the Buddhist Scriptures

Tetsugen composed this formal report for the Shōgun Tokugawa Tsunayoshi in the year Tenna 1 (1681). He intended to submit it along with a copy of the scriptures and an index as a part of his petition for official government permission to begin publication. Such permission was technically required for all publications at the time. Tetsugen never completed his mission, however, because he returned to Osaka to help his disciples cope with the famine in early Tenna 2. He then died before he had another opportunity to travel to Edo. His leading disciple Hōshū completed Tetsugen's task in 1690; he included a copy of Tetsugen's report. The original text is composed in highly formal Chinese. The translation is based on the version found in the *Yuiroku, The Preserved Writings of Tetsugen.*[1]

An Account of Completing
the Buddhist Scriptures

Respectfully submitted with awe and reverence by the monk Tetsugen, founder of Jiunzan Zuiryūji, in Settsu province, the Kyoto region, the great nation of Japan. I would venture to say that, although the Buddha nature is completely pure, we constantly allow shock waves of worldly knowledge to upset the mind. Righteous heaven is limitless, yet it is only the sun of wisdom that shines from above. The basis is great and its marks are everywhere. The time had come and the opportunity necessarily ripened. Therefore, the Golden Immortal, the Lord of Enlightenment[2] [the Buddha] came down from heaven to Kapilavastu[3] and spread the teachings in the lands south of Mount Sumeru.[4] He surpassed the best of the multitude of sages, and he alone is called Heavenly Being among Heavenly Beings.[5] He penetrated to the origin of all dharmas. Truly his wondrous understanding is miraculous. In the twenty worlds of the Lotus repository,[6] his efficacy is without limit. In the one hundred million mountains and rivers of Indra's Net,[7] he appears and disappears freely. His jeweled hair[8] illuminates the world like the autumn moon suspended in the blue sky. His golden countenance when meeting the people is like a jewel mountain rising from the green sea.

At his first sermon in the Deer Park, [the Buddha] distinguished the divisions of large and small. In his last words at the Ajiravatī River,[9] he divided the teachings into the partial and the perfect. For this reason, even Pāpīyas[10] and the heretics broke down and lowered their flags. The Hindu king Indra constantly revered the blessings received [from the Buddha]. What else could he do?

There came a time when [the Buddha] gave up teaching and abandoned [his role as] the refuge for the four kinds of sentient beings.[11] When he had withdrawn his brilliance for a long time, [sentient beings] became lost in the darkness of the Three Worlds.[12] Therefore, a bell was sounded on the peak of Mount Sumeru, and [the sangha] collected the writings in the cave of Pippala-guha.[13]

The [teachings] were gathered in India. After more than a thousand years has passed, they were transmitted east to China, and brought benefits to a multitude of souls. [The teachings] reached Japan, coming in contact with the splendid sacred lineage [of our imperial family] for the first time when Kudara wished to offer tribute to the imperial court.[14] They held high the sun of the Buddha, and [allowed] the waves of his benevolence to flow widely. This enabled orphans in their blindness to open wide the eye of wisdom, and caused those who were departing to suddenly receive a jeweled robe.[15] Therefore, emperors and retainers revered and loved [the Buddha's teachings] no less than those throughout the five regions of India,[16] and all classes of people took refuge in them surpassing all other nations. The only thing missing from that time for more than one thousand years was that a woodblock edition of the scriptures had not been published. In just the same way, a sliver of moon is not perfect light. It is similar to [the time] when sweet rain has not yet fallen [after a long drought].

If I reflect respectfully, the reigning *shōgun* represents a good omen as one who protects the emperor. From his jeweled palace, he sends down respect [for the Buddhist teachings], and heavenly wisdom fills his breast. Taking advantage of every opportunity, his vast compassion aids the people, bestows blessings on high and low according to their station. The lords of broad heaven shout for joy, like a kettle boiling. Wise people on the face of the earth have good intentions like waves welling up. Even the sun and the moon shine more brightly because of him, and the mountains and rivers change their hue for his sake.

[I], the monk Tetsugen, was fortunate to have been born during a peaceful and prosperous reign. The Dharma ocean unites all its tributaries. Although I have never [heard] the sound of the reclusive *kalavinka* [bird],[17] I once experienced the pleasure of a blind turtle encountering a log.[18] I collected donations from believers everywhere, and making an effort, carved all of the texts. If the Four Phrases[19] have already destroyed hell, how can the scriptures not assist the pure teachings? Therefore, for a time, the carving and printing exhausted my meager abilities. The transmission [of the scriptures] for the next one thousand years will depend on your virtue and influence.

The work is now complete. Fortunately, nothing major remains after this. I dare to avail myself of prosperous times, and have especially brought [the scriptures] to offer up to you first. I respectfully hope that the nation will be tranquil and the years prosperous. May your rule be perfect like a golden goblet.[20] May it always be well regulated like the harmony of the changing seasons. I hope that you are preserved for ten thousand years of shining prosperity and that you receive one thousand years of wealth and happiness. May the military and literary arts be like the sun and the stars moving above those in high office. May the people be well fed and provided for.

Perceiving your peaceful and noble governance, I write this letter with unceasing awe and reverence.

Part III

Poetry

Tetsugen wrote poetry throughout his career as an Ōbaku monk. Japanese Buddhist monks and nuns traditionally used poetry to serve a variety of purposes. In many cases, an exchange of poetry with a lay disciple or visiting dignitary served as a form of social exchange. In other cases, they composed verses to commemorate special occasions, to mark the passing of a friend or colleague, or to honor important religious figures from the past, especially former teachers and sectarian founders. Within the Zen world, monks and nuns often composed poetry to express their understanding of the Dharma, and sometimes they presented these verses to a teacher as a part of their practice. It was also customary for them to compose a verse on their deathbed.

The poems presented here are a selection of thirty-six verses preserved in the *Yuiroku, The Preserved Writings of Tetsugen*,[1] They represent approximately one-third of the total number of verses found there. All of the verses were composed in classical Chinese. The majority of the verses were written in lines of seven characters each; only the last three included here (numbers 68, 69, and 70) were composed in lines of five characters. Selections were made to illustrate the wide variety of purposes and occasions for which Tetsugen wrote poetry. All of the verses have an introductory line that provides the date of composition, the individual for whom it was composed, or some indication of the occasion that inspired it. The numbering was added, and corresponds to the order of the verses as they appear in the *Yuiroku*.

Poetry

---

1. RESTORING THE ANCIENT FOUNDATIONS OF HŌSENJI (TREASURE SOURCE TEMPLE)[2]

The land is dense with old pines, thousands of years old.
My crooked staff turned sideways, I search for the Treasure's Source.
The well is gone dry, I regret that the well rope is too short.
The mountain deities always protect the change of the seasons.
I taste the sweet dew and instantly I am consoled this day.
Filling and enriching my withered heart, I thank the ancient worthies.
Overflowing, when will the mysterious source run dry?
Happily, I see its benefits pouring over human beings and *devas*.[3]

2. ADMONISHING THE AGE

Human beings do not yet understand Nanke's dream.[4]
Through one hundred years of conflict, they pursue love and hate.
The decayed rope is not a snake; pointless fear.
Flowers [appear] in the sky without cause, just the result of staring.
Going in circles without rest, like an ant going around on a plate.
Ceaseless movement that never stops, like a fly seeking the stench.
For the sake of recompense, a person covets the nectar inside the well.
Momentarily surprised; a pair of mice nibble at the withered wisteria.

4. THREE POEMS FOR THE NEW YEAR OF 1677

The present goes and the past retreats without any variation.
Heavenly fortune, the season returning shows signs of one hundred
    blossoms.
The smoke is warm; through the window the plum tree is about to spew
    forth buds.
The snow melts; in the garden, the grass tries to push up shoots.
The limitless aspect is not another thing.
Brilliance that dazzles the eyes of everyone in my home.
Not serving spiced saké, three cups of saké.
Just bending down to visit, I boil one cup of tea.

Hoping to spread the sea of the scriptures, I make anchor west and east.
How many times will I greet the Spring and see the purple [blossoms]?
The world does not understand the endless merit [of the scriptures].
Since morning, repeatedly congratulating [one another], "Ten thousand
    years of life!"
One thousand gold coins spent in vain, seeking to be apart from the world.
Has it ever happened even a tiny bit? I give alms within the Dharma.
Hair and beard suffer bitterness, like the whiteness of the snow.
The sacred texts, when will they be complete?

On my crooked staff, I rest for a moment in the purple cloud room.
A plum tree revealed through the south window emits a subtle perfume.
Carrying the Dharma in my old age, I am ashamed of my scant strength.
In accordance with karma, I entrust myself to be tossed by the waves on the
    sea of the scriptures.
Valleys and mountains [extend] for ten thousand miles. How far off is the
    Spring?
Wind, moon, and the whole sky, the person is not fortunate.
Devoted to the source, I am unconcerned with the present and the past.
An awesome sound [reverberates] for a long time, outside I enjoy the wind
    and the light.

5. SENT TO A FRIEND IN ZEN PRACTICE

For the sake of the Dharma, always seek out excellent people.
How can you bear intimacy with someone you already dislike?
One morning coming together without any division.
Many years of coming and going, truly there is a karmic cause.
The monk now forgets to exert his strength.
On what day can the monastery return to the Spring?
What they wish for with common mind, like the efficacy of warm
    friendship,
Is that after a long time, they will take a difficult bay and make it an
    essential port.

8. GIVEN TO THE ATTENDANT MONK HŌSHŪ

Eighteen years of service without neglect.
The karmic connection was designed over many lifetimes.
Zen mind like a straight pine [standing] on the peaceful blue mountain side.
The essence of the precepts like a full moon in a clear blue sky.
Secret words are explained, and you realize the meaning of the Buddha.
True words give rise a warning, and you surpass human nature.
Do not say that from the beginning I defeat you.
My gall bladder and intestines are upset every day for your sake.

11. AN EMOTIONAL RESPONSE TO HEARING OF A DEATH

To the west at anchor, to the east adrift on the shores of the river and sea,
My white head dreads hearing the incessant announcements of death.
On this day, I wipe away tears shed for your sake.
You taught me when to enjoy this body.
It is difficult to understand the thousand kinds of sentiments which human
    beings have.
It is easy to pass through the finest of Springs in the back garden.
The issue of one hundred years, I make dreams within dreams.
How many people attain clear understanding?

14. TEN MISCELLANEOUS POEMS
ON THE SEA OF THE SCRIPTURES

The steep roof of my thatched hut leans toward the riverbank.
Tender greens and sweet spring water nurture my sick body.
The land is so narrow that it is difficult for passengers to pass by on horse
    carts.
The writings are numerous, and I am happy to come face to face with people
    of sacred wisdom.
Idle, I am unconcerned about matters of wealth and fame.
Just ordinary days are fine; the mind and eyes become new.
Trusting to fate, I stroll in the broad daylight.
Without my realizing it, this transient world changes from winter to spring.

On the ocean of the scriptures, seven thousand volumes of wondrous text,
Year after year, reprinting them and hoping to bring them to completion.
The truth is distant from words and images; the self is brightly shining.
The tongue raises up waves, but who makes the pronouncement?
One necessarily discriminates based on talent, separating the sharp from the
    dull.
Do not despise the teachings of the sect; they include the one-sided view
    and the perfect.
How can I endure the bitter suffering? My merit is just about finished.
I leave behind my past wisdom and see righteous heaven.

Why do people of the Way live in the blue layer?
Forget the mind even within the world of dust, and approach the steep
    mountains.
One morning breathing easily, you lose your head in a thousand feelings.
At home, it is hard to seek after what one has already surpassed; a pair of
    dreams,
In a state where one opposes returning and accords with illusion,
Some love and others hate the work.
It is like a person instantly achieving skill some day.
In the same way, a small insect becomes a giant phoenix.

Floating on the Western sea or toward the East,
The forest comes down to the water's edge, this old village.
Green bamboo surrounds the eaves and keeps out the oppressive summer
    heat.
Balmy breezes come in while I sit, bringing a little coolness.
Blue waves flow at the front gate, reflecting the moon.
The lotus [rises] above the pond, its color reflected on the temple.
Now happily, the great wisdom [of the scriptures] brings many volunteers.
For the sake of promoting the printing of the scriptures, they build a golden
    castle with a boiling moat.[5]

In a three-mat thatched hut inside a bamboo forest,
I preserve for a little while the illusory self, and long for the old style.
The ocean gathers up one hundred rivers; I uncover a pure mirror.
The bridge crossed two countries, bending [like] a long rainbow.
Wealth and fame easily taint us; a temple on the city wall.
Meditation and wisdom are difficult to perfect; the old man withdrawn
    from the world.
Since ancient times, how many people have been hindered by the five
    desires?[6]
It is not like stepping backward with both eyes empty.

When hungry, then take a meal; when weary, sleep.
Why seek for wizards in foreign places?
If one becomes confused in the mind, then worldliness will give rise to
    mental anguish.
My hut is far removed from the market in the neighboring city.
The pagoda of one thousand fathoms towers over the short grass.
Numerous fishing boats paddle along the deep river.
Riding pleasantly along the river bank, they take their leisure.
On the horizon, the moon rises, a round jewel mirror.

Frost on the leaves that rustle and scatter, winter once more.
In the garden, the best loved bamboo mingles with the pines.
The waves roar as they crash on the shore.
The snow shining white fills the peak of Mt. Fuji.
The old mirror illuminates the mind, the writings of India.
A resounding noise startles me from my dream, the dawn bell.
The Dharma declines and the Way deteriorates, and an evil wind burns.
I do not know at what time to raise the victory flag.

The whole world wrangles, I exist in a peaceful place.
Who knows that the temple exists on a narrow point?
Human beings suffer in mind and body for one hundred years.
In my three-mat hut, heaven and earth are spacious.
A shining jewel on one's forehead, it would be better to understand oneself.
The two eyes of one born of a mother are blinded, deceived by others.
Cooking fresh foods, today I wet my tongue.[7]
For ten thousand *kalpas,* I never refuse to swallow iron balls.

Morality is truly waned and grown dull.
All through life, contented with my lot, I nurture foolishness.
At sunset, leaning on my staff, I stand by the river bank.
Tourists row their boats and raise cups of saké.
In the Buddha world, who understands the body and the earth?
Human beings find it difficult to comprehend the suffering caused by
    wealth.
Neglectful, I am able to recognize the nature of river gazing.
Who will take care of my hair, [grown long] like the weeds?

The grass hut is tranquil like a mountain forest.
Guests are few at my gate; the moss in the garden grows thick.
Great gentlemen and elder statesmen are rare acquaintances.
Each spring blossom and autumn moon is a dear friend.
In front of the window, the flowing stream burbles like a lute [lit. winter
    jewel].
On an upper branch, cicada voices harmonize with the unadorned lute.
In a single thought, I forget my mental function without a single inch of
    land.
The empty sky and the great earth use up the yellow gold.

20. PRESENTED TO THE BUDDHIST LAYMAN TENZAN
WHEN HE TOOK THE TONSURE AND DONNED THE ROBE

The body appears as the district magistrate and enters the busy streets.
The patched robe[8] transmits the Dharma; it has many rice paddies.
Starting off or stopping, advancing or retreating, the spirit of a gentleman,
Reversed or in order, length or breadth, the Zen of a living Patriarch.
Contact with things, and in the end twirling the white staff.
Deceiving people, straightforward face, stretching out an empty fist,
The new opportunity is exceptional; worldly peace is fathomed.
In accordance with the stream, the fragrance extends ten thousand years.

28. GIVEN TO THE HIGH SEAT HŌSHŪ

After many *kalpas,* the karma is now ripe.
For the sake of your teacher, for the sake of your younger brother, you
    ponder calmly.
Your mind on me, a fish roams in the water.
My teachings given for you, the moon enters the stream.
Each one of us strips one shoulder and carries the great Dharma.[9]
Together promulgating the Dharma, benefiting all regions.
In order to wait for that day, we ride a mysterious crane.[10]
Ten thousand strings of cash wrapped around Hōshū's waist.

29. A FUNERAL POEM FOR THE BUDDHIST LAYMAN ZEN'AN

While transmigrating through the Three Worlds, one knows not.
Dreams are familiar; through the north window, the autumn evening is long.
The five desires agitate the mind; the pleasures of heaven above.
For ten thousand years one's bones are boiled in a cauldron of boiling
    water.[11]
One's eyes suddenly open upto the sun.
This place is deep, the place of nirvana [lit. tranquillity and extinction].
Not this life and not this death,
Pine, wind, river, and moon, one enters one's birthplace.

40. GIVEN TO A MONK READING THE *ŚURAMGAMA* [SUTRA]

Seeking for the mind in the seven places, and crushing mistaken thoughts,
Eight returns, discerning sight and exposing the true spirit.[12]
You are able to recognize the master's face,[13]
If a traveler approaches the inn.

41. MEETING AN OLD FRIEND

Separated east and west for twenty years.
You exclusively chant the Buddha's [name], while I practice meditation.
We meet together, why argue over high and low.
The wind and the moon originate in the same heaven.

43. GIVEN TO A LAY BELIEVER HŌKŌ NINSHŌ[14]

Depending on one's nature, you ramble across the heavens; unfathomable.
In accordance with karma, you are set free far and wide; what does the
Buddha know?
The cold weather goes and the hot weather passes, for ten thousand *kalpas*.
Throughout the whole day, when you are weary, lie down, when you are
hungry eat.

44. GIVEN TO THE FAITHFUL BELIEVER JŌNYŪ, WHO CHANTS THE BUDDHA'S NAME

The body is healthy, the years pour out; your ears and eyes are [still] clear.
Contented and unselfish, you reject personal glory.
Reflected light, in a single moment you penetrate the self.
For the first time you realize that practitioner and Dharma[15] are complete in
one body.

52. GIVEN TO A ZEN PRACTITIONER FROM A DIFFERENT FAMILY, WHO WAS REFLECTING BACK ON HIS MOTHER

Once, you knew yourself; a deity entrusted to your mother's womb.
How long will you experience hardship and perfect your talent?
Filial devotion in scraps and pieces, all is reality.
Wind in the trees, you run out of time and never return.

53. IMPROMPTU

A narrow track passes through a forest of brambles.
Without regard, I walk across the wide empty sky.
Suddenly, I pass beyond the shining moon and the pure breeze.
I live at ease within a cauldron of boiling water and a furnace of hot coals.

54. WHILE POLING IN THE MOONLIGHT, FLOATING WITH THE CURRENT

The long river is drenched in moonlight, flowing up to touch the heavens.
Riding pleasantly in my spare time,[16] I pole a small boat.
The drunken man does not understand the music of the universe.[17]
With the voices of wind and string instruments in the background, I roam
aimlessly.

57. GIVEN TO A DEAF PERSON WHO ASKED THE MEANING OF THE ŚURAMGAMA [SUTRA]

What rule misses the light, but can see form?
A difficult slope; without ears, but hearing voices.
One wishes to know the secret seal, like the coming storehouse.
In the distance, one escapes the senses and their objects, and enters the
    Unborn.

58. WHEN VISITING THE COTTAGE OF MR. MUKAI

The shining moon is reflected on the flowing water in front of the gate.
The old pines on the mountain peaks harmonize with the unadorned flute.
No one realizes the pleasures of being in the midst of this.
Mountain flowers and wild birds are my dear friends.

61. GIVEN TO THE ZEN PRACTITIONER ETSUDŌ, WHEN STAYING AT HŌSENJI

One thousand ancient pines, where cranes ought to nest.
In a grass hut of three mats, I enjoy nourishing my body.
Not traveling east or west on the road of fame and fortune,
Naturally the Mind Ground exhausts the fine dust.

62. GIVEN TO NORITOMI TESSEN, FOLLOWING THE SAME PROSODY

The Way cuts off clinging to objects and transcends past and present.
Seeing the river as I endure my grief, I mistakenly become engrossed.
I walk and turn around, although I arrive at a profound and quiet place.
In just the same way one's mind seizes onto one's mind.

63. EULOGY FOR THE NUN MYŌU OF KANNONJI[18]

Overturning the pathway of life and death, coming and going,
You collect and unite the ten directions into a single home.
Just comprehending moment by moment the cultivation of merit and
    wisdom,
With clear understanding, you spread more flowers on top of brocade.

64. GIVEN TO A DISCIPLE

Not yet knowing the diamond precepts of the true self,
One turns outward, seeking and missing one's eyes.
Just like a blind man lives under the sun,
But always scans the whole sky searching for the light.

68. WITH EMOTION

One hundred years of a human life,
My age surpasses half of that.
White hair on my head, like frost on the grass.
Growing thin in appearance, at the edge of the pond.
When I look at writings, my eyes are grown dim.
When I chant the sutras, my voice echoes weakly.
Alas, it is all up with me! What more can I lose?
I retain only the peace of the Mind Ground.

69. CELEBRATING JITSUDEN OSHO'S FIFTIETH BIRTHDAY

Your dignity is from the beginning distinguished.
On New Years' Day, you empty the past and the present.
Long life equal to the beauty of South Peak (Mt. Heng),
Merit exceeding the depth of the Northern Sea.
You see widely with the third eye of insight.
You vow to surpass the Mind of the old Buddha.
Born of a mother, truly the Original Self.
One million [pieces of] red and yellow gold.

70. WHEN VISITING REISEKI (SPIRIT STONE) HERMITAGE

Bound to the hut for two or three years,
I live peacefully at the edge of a waterside village.
Passing through snow, the pine stands like strong armor.
Waiting for the season, the dragon hibernates in the abyss.
One mind, long extinguished and at peace.
The myriad things depend on cause and effect.
Wisdom goes, the place of two circles.
Enduring for the sake of acting as a field of merit[19] for the world.

Part IV

Other Letters and
Historical Documents

An Affadavit Concerning
the Dharma Debate in Mori

Tetsugen wrote this statement explaining events that occurred in the city of Mori from his perspective for Lord Kurushima Michikyo, the *daimyō* (provincial governor) of Bungo province. Tetsugen composed it after he had left the area, either late in 1674 or early in 1675; it describes an incident from the eleventh lunar month of 1674. Members of the True Pure Land sect of Buddhism objected to Tetsugen's teachings and requested a debate. They believed that Tetsugen, a former True Pure Land priest, was preaching against their sect's practice of married clergy and meat eating.[1] No Dharma debate, which were in any case illegal in Tokugawa Japan, ever actually occurred. The leaders of the True Pure Land group were arrested, and in a separate letter Tetsugen requested that Kurushima pardon them. (See the next selection.)

Tetsugen's affadavit represents one of the only sources for Tetsugen's lecture style, since he never allowed his disciples to record his lectures. It appears that when lecturing on the *Śūramgama Sutra*, he paraphrased the original text quite closely, translating it into clear Japanese. The original affadavit was written in Japanese. This translation is based on a modern edition of Tetsugen's writings.[2]

An Affidavit Concerning
the Dharma Debate in Mori

On the occasion [in question, I], Tetusugen, was invited by Lord Kurushima Shinano[3] of Kusu in Higo province and visited with him there from the end of the tenth month [of 1674]. Starting on the second day of the eleventh month, I lectured on the *Śūramgama Sutra*[4] at [Lord Kurushima's] family temple Anrakuji.[5] When I had been visiting there for two or three days, but before I began my lectures, a large group of priests from the Ikkō sect[6] from the areas of Kusu and Hita [in Higo], and Nakatsu and Usa in Buzen province met together. They made their opinion known to Lord Shinano's Administrator of Temples and Shrines, Obayashi Bei. They said, "At this time, Tetsugen is invited to lecture on the *Śūramgama Sutra*. This Tetsugen along with a person named Kegan [Zen'etsu][7] from Usuki are evil monks who slander the Ikkō sect. No doubt, [Tetsugen] will slander us this time as well. If that is the case, a large group of us intend to visit him and have a Dharma debate. Please grant us your permission." The Administrator of Temples and Shrines responded, "Tetsugen will certainly lecture on the *Śūramgama Sutra,* but there is no reason to believe this will cause the sort of difficulties you suggest."

I lectured first of all about the good and evil of the False Dharma and the True Dharma in the Final Age,[8] which are referred to as the Three Absolutes[9] in the *Śūramgama Sutra*. Those who practice without keeping the precepts set out by the Buddha all represent the False Dharma. The reason for this [is as follows:] Although practices such as chanting the *nembutsu,* seated meditation, and reciting the sutras are each practiced differently depending on the abilities of the believer, the precepts against taking life, stealing, sexual misconduct, lying, and the like are absolute, regardless of the sect. Not to keep them is unacceptable. Therefore these precepts are called "absolutes."

In the first place, if one does not keep the [precept against] sexual misconduct, then the ongoing cycle of birth and death never ends. If one does not keep the precept against sexual misconduct, then even if one practices and seems to attain [higher] meditative states and wisdom, one will certainly fall into the realm of demons. The best will become demon kings, the average will become demon men and the worst will become demon women. After my death, during the Final Age of the Dharma, these demon families will abound in the world. They will have no fear of human beings. Despite the fact that they openly practice sexual misconduct, they will be called "good teachers." In this way, they will delude all sentient beings and cause them to fall into the pit of passion and wrong views, and so to lose the path of enlightenment. Someone who practices without keeping the precept against sexual misconduct is like a person who steams sand and then tries to eat it. Even if they practice for a million *kalpas,* it will still be nothing more than "steamed sand." Even if they attain something that seems to be *satori,* because its root of sexual misconduct is still sexual misconduct, they will transmigrate through the three [hateful] realms [of hell, hungry ghosts, and animals], and not be able to escape. Teachings such as these that I offer are called the Buddha's teachings. Not to teach them would be to teach like Pāpīyas.[10]

In the second place, if one does not keep the precept against taking life, then one cannot escape from the cycle of transmigration. If one does not keep the precept against killing, even if one accumulates merit, engages in meditation, and does all sorts of other practices, one will certainly fall into the realm of the *oni.*[11] The best will become very powerful *oni,* the average will become flying *yakshas,*[12] and the worst will become earth-bound *rakshasas.*[13] After my death, during the Final Age of the Dharma, these monsters will abound in the world. Although they themselves eat meat, they will maintain that they have attained enlightenment. How can it be that after the death of the Thus Come One, we regard monks who eat the flesh of sentient beings as disciples of the Buddha?

As you no doubt realize, those who eat fish and birds, even if they practice and seem to attain *samadhi,* they are merely great *rakshasa.* When this life ends, they will certainly fall into hell. They are not disciples of the Buddha. We call this kind of teaching the teaching of the Buddha. Not to teach it would be to teach like Pāpīyas.

How can this be? Thieves don the robes of the Thus Come One [the Buddha], take on the appearance of a monk or nun, and so turn the Buddha into an object for sale and make him into the source of their livelihood. They create all sorts of [bad] karma, and say that it is all the teachings of the Buddha Dharma. Instead, they malign those monks who keep the precepts as followers of the Lesser Vehicle.[14] They cause countless sentient beings to go astray, and cause them to lapse into the Gateless Hell.[15] One must not take sutras that do not reveal the full meaning of the Dharma as one's own opinion and so cause those with less learning to err. In the same manner, [the Buddha] strictly taught even the third and the fourth precepts against stealing and lying.[16]

When they heard I was reading this sort of material, they believed I was [doing so to] slander the Ikkō sect. On the contrary, I was not disparaging them at all. This is just the way the Buddha transmitted his precepts. Under the circumstances, since [they believed] that I had slandered the Ikkō sect, they spread it about in the nearby provinces that they would come together and crush me. They designated Kōtokuji in Tonotsuru in Kusu as their meeting place, and all gathered. There was, however, one learned monk who had specifically read the *Śūramgama Sutra*. He refused to join the mob, and it is not just the subtemple of Higashi Honganji who says this.

The monks from Nishi Honganji sent word by messenger to the Administrator of Temples and Shrines, saying, "At this time, Tetsugen is slandering the Ikkō sect. We wish to have a Dharma debate with him." The Administrator of Temples and Shrines responded, "Since Dharma debates are prohibited by law, you cannot have one. Furthermore, I myself have had the opportunity to listen to Tetsugen's sermons each day, and to the very end have not heard him disparage any sect at all. Even if you have your doubts about Tetsugen, there does exist in the sutra, as he said, such a thing as the Three Absolutes for all ears to hear. If you would like to question him about the contents of the *Śūramgama Sutra,* then you may go and ask him one by one. This is the etiquette for *mondō*[17] in the Zen sect. If you question him in this manner, then even one thousand of you may ask questions." [The monks] replied, "We do not want to ask him one by one in that manner. We want to go in and question him all together."

Things went on and on in this manner. The Administrator of Temples and Shrines sometimes threatened and sometimes coaxed, but he was not about to consent [to their request]. Once again, a monk said to be from Shōrenji in Hita came as an envoy. He said, "Although we have said various things, all this time you have not given us your consent, nor have we managed to have a religious dialogue or Dharma debate. We intend to rush into the lecture site en masse and take Tetsugen captive." The Administrator said, "If you are unreasonable and rush in and use force, then there are things that we can do. You must not do such a thing." Despite this, [the monk from] Shōrenji said, "Even if each of your retainers were to kill five to eight of our monks, [it would not matter.] The numbers that have flocked to Hita from the Chikugo and Chikuzen region are so boundless, that it costs us more than two *koku*[18] [approximately ten bushels] of food to feed us all each night. In this sense, we already have permission, and tonight a great throng will go uninvited. Since Tetsugen cannot easily reach your protection, he will finally be in our hands."

The retainers consulted about this. They concluded that since Tetsugen is a person with a great vow [to print the scriptures], and what is more, since he is a monk from a different province, it would be shameful if a mob burst in and attacked him. So they decided that it would perhaps be better if the Zen monks who had gathered from all directions should leave Anrakuji. The monks [at Anrakuji] replied, "Whatever [the Ikkō monks] may have said, it surely won't come to [violence]. If they said such a thing, it was probably intended to make us end the lectures. If they truly meant to attack us, they would have acted as secretly as possible and burst in without warning. If they felt that they needed a debate, then they would have written a note and addressed it directly to Tetsu-gen. Going to see the Administrator of Temples and Shrines and saying they were apt to do such a thing is certainly just a threat. If we keep this in mind, we do not need to accept your proposal [that we all disperse]." Although the monks consulted among themselves and decided this, the retainers remained worried about it.

Again and again, there were consultations between Anrakuji and Tetsu-gen. [Anrakuji monks] said, "As things stand, negotiations have broken down. You don't think that it is a good idea, do you?" I replied, "Since they have gone so far as to gather into a mob, they probably won't stop at that. No doubt some harm will come of it. When a large crowd gathers to do something, even under safe conditions, something can happen. If there were to be a disturbance, even a small one, [there are several concerns.] First there is the fear [of a response] from the shogunate. Second, there is the anxiety among the [local] retainers. Third, this is not the way of Buddhist monks. I say this because, generally speaking, monks do not fight with others. The term "monk" is originally an Indian word that is rendered more fully "sangha." In Chinese, the sangha is called *shuwagō,* or "a gathering of people who live together in harmony." "Shu" means a crowd of people. Even if a crowd of one thousand or ten thousand people were to gather together, no matter what happens, they do not set up "self," but live in harmony without fighting. Therefore the gathering is called *shuwagō.*

In as much as they are given the title *shuwagō,* those who live together harmoniously, it is not appropriate for monks to fight. They don the *kesa*[19] of gentleness and patience, they abide in the mind of great compassion, and they do not keep swords or fighting staffs. For example, a person who is cowardly and runs away in an emergency is not what we mean by the word "samurai," even if he is wearing the strong armor of a warrior and carries a spear or long sword. He is therefore not a samurai. Perhaps this is what the ancient sage [Confucius] meant when he said, "If a cup is not a cup, why call it a cup?"[20]

What happened was due to my reading the *Śūraṃgama Sutra* (J. Shuryō-gongyō). The term "ryōgon," or "heroic valor," is an Indian word, rendered more fully "shuryōgon."[21] In Chinese, this is called "issaiji kukyō kengo," or "the su-preme strength of all things." This is because it concerns the enlightenment of all Buddhas, *Bodhisattvas* and Patriarchs. If one awakens to this enlightenment, it is like waking up from a dream and [realizing that] all the myriad things are delusions. Within a dream, even though one sees images of cities and country-side, mountains and rivers, as well as terrifying things and pleasant things, plea-sure and suffering, none of them exists at all. After one awakens, one realizes that from the start they were all a dream. Calling the *Śūraṃgama Sutra* "issaiji kukyō kengo," the supreme strength of all things, means that in the same way, "all things" are but appearances in a dream. *Kukyō* means supreme, and supreme strength means the stage of ultimate reality when one has awakened in which nothing ceases or changes.

Since thoughts within dreams are all false delusions that pass away, none of them are ultimate. This is what it means in the *Diamond Sutra* when it says, "Phenomenal things are dreams, delusions, foam and reflections."[22] The state after awakening is strong, and so it is called "diamond wisdom." In the *Śūramgama Sutra* it teaches, "Illusions are the Diamond King."[23] When you realize this diamond in itself, and the light of wisdom appears, the beginningless cycle of birth and death, the vicissitudes of human life, the delusions of greed and anger, and the battles over right and wrong, true and false all disappear at once, just like waking up from a dream. There is nothing one can argue about. Even if one tried to be deluded, there is nothing to be deluded about. Self and other are not two. The mind and its objects [of perception] are one. The Emptiness of the ten directions surpasses the Three Worlds, just as the moon illuminates all the myriad things or a bird soars through the empty sky. There is nothing to grasp or to cast off. Nothing to hate or to love. The original mind is eternally abiding and unceasing, and the Dharma realm has the one aspect of equality.

In the *Lotus Sutra*, this is taught as the Buddha's enlightened view.[24] In the *Nirvana Sutra,* it is called the pleasure of extinction.[25] This is precisely the Great Emptiness of the Śūramgama in which the Buddhas and the Patriarchs abide. The mind which the Buddhas and the Patriarchs transmitted, known as the Zen lineage, is also this [same thing]. It is called *bodhi*, nirvana, *Dharma-kāya*, and original enlightenment. Although all these names are distinguished, in essence they are all the One Mind. All sentient beings are deluded about the essence of the One Mind. They therefore conceal [from themselves] the principle of the *Dharmakāya*'s Original Enlightenment, and therefore cannot attain the enlightenment of nirvana, *bodhi*. They think that the physical body [made from a temporary] configuration of the four great elements is the self, and they believe that the delusionary objects of the six senses are the mind.

[This delusion] can be compared to the following: When the light of the sun illuminates the whole world, one can focus the sunlight with a crystal and light an incense stick. Someone asks, "Where is the fire?" The incense stick replies, "The fire is within me." The person asks again, "Do you mean that outside of this incense stick there is no fire?" The incense stick replies, "If you look throughout the world, outside of me there is no other fire at all." The incense stick thinks to itself that it is glad that it was lighted. When the incense stick burns itself out and the flame extinguishes, it laments, "Oh, the fire has extinguished." It would be like one incense stick fighting with another. This one hates that one. If on one occasion the sun grew so bright it filled the whole world more and more, the incense stick would not be gladdened by being lighted in the first place, or saddened when it goes out. There would be no fight between this stick and that. When one realizes that the substance of sunlight and the substance of the incense stick are just one substance, then issues over this and that, birth and death, right and wrong, true and false never existed at all.

People's original mind is also like this. The *Dharmakāya* of the ten directions is equal and illuminates [everything] like the sun. This is called Great Sun Thus Come One[26] and also the Light of All Buddhas.[27] We call Amida Buddha "the Buddha of Immeasurable Light," and Mahāvairocana Buddha "the Light that Shines Everywhere." In the *Lotus Sutra,* it explains it as "the light of white hair,[28] and the *Perfect Enlightenment Sutra* calls it "the Storehouse of Light."[29] All of these [terms] refer to the light of the Original Mind.

All living beings fail to realize this mind, and become attached to the Four Great Elements. They take this [temporary configuration] to be the "self" and take deluded thoughts to be their mind. They argue over self and other, birth and death, just as if they had completely forgotten the great light of the sun, and think that the flame on the incense stick is the self. This is referred to as the inversion of ordinary people. One place in the *Śūramgama Sutra* calls it the first level of delusion. Although forgetting the light of the sun is one level of delusion, thinking that the flame of the incense stick is light in its entirety and wondering if there is no other light is another level of delusion, isn't it? When one can cast off these silly delusions and return to the *Śūramgama* which is like the sunlight, it is just as if one had awakened from a dream and so had not thought to compare right and wrong, in contrast to the flame of the incense stick.

Now, if I were to firmly set up a distinction between self and other and strongly argue over right and wrong even though I was lecturing on the *Śūramgama Sutra*, it would be like striking my mother's face with the *Book of Filial Piety*.[30] I would never awaken from the dream of all things, or realize the mind of supreme strength. Although I am not yet enlightened, wouldn't I have acquired some small inkling of its mind-set? If I did not swiftly withdraw, but set up self-conceit and fought back, then it would have been like confronting a dream with a dream, or fighting bubbles with bubbles. The Śūramgama is like the great ocean and delusions are like bubbles. If one knows the great ocean of the Original Mind of the Śūramgama, then would one need to fight with traces of delusions of the attachment to the self?

It says in the *Śūramgama Sutra,* "You do not understand at all the wondrous true mind within things, starting from form and mind, and extending outside to mountains, rivers, sky and earth. It is like casting off the one hundred thousand pure oceans, leaving only one bubble, and then saying you have penetrated to the depths of the great ocean. You are people who abide in delusion."[31]

While reading this sort of sutra, why would I sharpen the spearhead of self-pride and fight? Even if they pierced me with a sword or ran me through with a spear, why would I hate them? It says in the *Śūramgama Sutra,* "It is like wind blowing light or a sword cutting water."[32] Someone of old said, "Raising one's head to face a drawn sword is like cutting the spring wind." Perhaps, since I am so unskilled, I was not able to cut the wind or to pierce the water. Nonetheless, why would I try to make bitter enemies, or bear a grudge, and so bring harm to many sentient beings? Wouldn't that be the same as trying to kill myself? Would I know such hatred?

The Buddha said, "If you do not accept the poison of vilification nor try to drink it down like sweet dew, then you will not be called or perceived to be an influential person."[33] Even if one does not try to drink the sweet dew, one must not open up a slanderous mouth and spew out venomous words, and thereby bind oneself with the cause for falling into hell. This it what it means to take on the name of a monk and put on the robe of forebearance.

I said, "Since I came here [to promote this kind of teaching], fighting would be absolutely foolish. I would prefer to leave here promptly. If I do so, things will probably quiet down by themselves, the way a fire goes out when it lacks kindling." The retainers said, "Whatever you suggest will be fine. Let's do as Tetsugen suggests." And so, in the early dawn of the twenty-seventh day of the eleventh month, when I was about to depart from this region, I received the consideration of the chief retainer. I was escorted by two monks from Anrakuji and ten samurai as far as Kashiranashi, a harbor in Bungo. From there, I was escorted by boat as far as Tsuruzaki by the two monks and two samurai.

Letter to Lord Kurushima

Requesting that He Spare Lives

Tetsugen wrote this letter to Lord Kurushima to request a pardon for the True Pure Land priests arrested after the incident in Mori (described in the previous selection). The relationship between this text and the affadavit is unknown, as is their relative timing. The letter is dated the sixth day of the first lunar month of Empo 3 (1675). Given the discrepancy between the old Chinese calendar and the modern calendar, that would have actually been late in 1674 in modern reckoning. The letter was composed in Japanese. The translation is based on a modern edition of Tetsugen's writings.[1]

Letter to Lord Kurushima
Requesting that He Spare Lives

I appreciated receiving your letter, [sent by] messenger. It causes me great delight that your province grows ever more tranquil, as you indicated in your last letter. The circumstances of your humble monk remain unchanged.

Last winter when you invited me to visit, some Ikkō sect monks said various things, and so I returned home to my province. Afterward, you thought it appropriate to summon and confine the head priests from Senkōji and Kōrinji,[2] because they had truly been unreasonable. However, since what occurred at that time concerned the Dharma, it is distinct from worldly matters. I would be still more grateful to you if you would pardon their offenses and restore them to their previous positions.

The reason that the Buddha, the Thus Come One, appeared in this world and taught the Dharma was to reverse the delusions of sentient beings and allow them to climb up to the fortress of enlightenment. Thereby, when a person accepts the teachings and practices the Way, falsehood returns to correctness, delusion enters into enlightenment, self-pride becomes no-self, and fighting and argumentation become harmony. This is precisely the mark of becoming a disciple of the Thus Come One and of keeping his Way. If one does not accept his teachings, however, but sets up the self and engages in fighting, then this is not the Way of the Thus Come One's teachings.

As an example, Shen Nong[3] tasted the one hundred [medicinal] herbs and taught the world the way of medicine. Even if an unskilled doctor intends to treat people's diseases and to save them from the suffering of illness, he may exacerbate the illness and increase the suffering because he does not understand the nature of the disease nor the principles of medicine. Nevertheless, this doctor does not [cause harm] intentionally. It is simply because his mind is foolish and his actions clumsy. It can't be helped.

All Buddhas make no-self foremost and so negate the dual attachments to the concept of an abiding self and to the concept that all dharmas have an abiding nature. They reject the two desires for wealth and greed. They attain the two fruits of *bodhi* and nirvana. They practice both benefiting the self and benefiting others. They cast off delusion for themselves and stop just short of entering ultimate enlightenment. In this way they cause all sentient beings to attain the way of ease and emancipation. This is the way taught by the Buddha, and shared by all [Buddhist] sects.

To violate the way of [the Buddha's] teachings is the same as turning sweet dew into poison or harming oneself with the holy sword. It is the ultimate foolishness. It is equally foolish to try to distinguish between this and that rather than to accept foolishness as foolishness.

The reason those monks caused such a stir was that they did not know that I was quoting directly from the admonitions of the Thus Come One. The golden words of admonition were therefore inverted in their ears, and what should have been medicine, in the end tasted bitter in their mouths. They spread rumors here and there like ordinary people or children. In much the same way when one dog howls to the sky, ten thousand dogs pass it along as true. Without investigating the root cause, they assembled a mob. Although nothing happened and no crime was committed, after the event took place, it seemed as if a crime had occurred. If a fight breaks out over the rule to cease fighting, it is the same as medicine exacerbating the illness. It never went beyond scheming.

I pray that in your great wisdom you will realize that this error was without root, and restore the two temples to peace. Then we will awaken from this series of dreams and be able to return to the tranquillity and calm of former times. Giving rise to even one thought, one deluded idea, is like giving rise to a dream. If the thought goes too far, and one commits a crime, then one adds dream upon dream, piles suffering upon suffering, and so passes from darkness into still more darkness. If one can realize it is a crime and reject the thought, then it amounts to neither good nor bad. As always, the willow is green and the flower crimson.

My sermon was likewise a dream of deluded thoughts that tried to banish one illusion with another. The monks' various rumors [arose] because they had many dreams when I showed up, and so they wanted to fight. There was the dream that I would give up and go home, and the dream that they would capture me and condemn me. One morning, when we become wide awake, this will all seem a perfect joke.

If it were to reach me that for this sort of reason you pardoned the crimes of these two temples and acted as if nothing had happened, then I would have read the *Śūramgama Sutra* and you would have heard the true teachings of the ephemeral Diamond King.[4] This would be an indication that you had entered into the wondrous practice of the Śūramgama. If you do not act in this way, then it will be difficult for you to attain the meaning of the *Śūramgama Sutra*.

Please, please, pardon these temples. If there are other men who have commit-ted crimes, then please grant them all amnesty as well.

Waves that arise from the water all return to the water. If a matter arises from the Dharma, then we must without exception return it to the Dharma. Does the Dharma have a wave of right and wrong? Does the Dharma have argu-ments over self and others? Certainly not. Since all things are like the Dharma, all things ultimately are tranquil and extinguished. Each dharma abides in its own place. "Heaven and earth reign, and nurture the myriad things." The world will of itself become peaceful and the nation will be tranquil forever.

Dated the 6th day of the first month.
Sincerely yours, Tetsugen
Addressed to: Lord Kurushima Sakon
Tamai Saburobee
Kurose Yosaemon
Futagami Denbee

Letter to Yamazaki Hanzaemon
Regarding the Famine

Tetsugen sent this letter to a lay disciple and supporter, the townsman Yamazaki Hanzaemon who lived in the Aoyama residential district. Yamazaki is listed as one of the contributors to the Scripture project. The letter was written approximately one month before Tetsugen's death, and only a week before he became ill. Tetsugen had just recently departed Edo to return to Osaka to direct his temple's famine relief efforts. Before he left Edo, he borrowed one thousand *ryō* of gold from a sympathetic *daimyō* (provincial governor), probably Lord Hosokawa of Higo. Apparently, those funds were already dwindling, and his normal fund-raising efforts at public lectures were insufficient. Tetsugen includes graphic detail of the suffering he witnessed as a means to motivate Yamazaki's generosity. He is also unusually blunt, making a direct request for a specific amount of money. The original text is written in Japanese. The translation is based on a modern edition of Tetsugen's writings.[1]

Letter to Yamazaki Hanzaemon[2]
Regarding the Famine

I shall write just a few lines. [I hope that] you are still in good health and have been taking good care of yourself. As I said in my last letter, I reached the Kyoto/Osaka area without any problems along the way. I began distributing alms on the thirteenth day of this month, and since the twenty-first, I have been lecturing on the *Awakening of Faith*.[3] I am glad to say that all the arrangements have gone smoothly.

With almsgiving almost at a standstill throughout the region, the beggars are facing hard times. Since we have been distributing alms, we have been able to save many people. On the thirteenth, about two thousand, on the fourteenth, six thousand, and since the fifteenth about ten thousand people. To date, we have been able to reach more than twenty thousand people. I do not have enough at hand to meet these tremendous expenses. However, if I stop giving alms, they will all die of starvation. So I must not stop, even if I have to sell the temple or chop off my fingers to offer to them.

People with the intention [of helping the poor] are scarce, but we do not lack for scarcity. One day during this period, we took a break from almsgiving because it rained, and many people seemed greatly distressed. There are people who steal even the dregs of shōchū[4] to eat. Rice bran flour is naturally regarded as a highly prized food. Other people take barley, grind it into flour, and eat that. Those who cannot manage even this sort [of desperate measure] are the ones who will starve to death.

I have heard that tenants cry that they are starving all day long and throughout the night, so even the landlord class face trouble. Since I started distributing alms, people have not ceased their weeping, and even their landlords are convinced [that they must cut the rent]. I am pleased that this level of charity is helping many people.

With such large crowds, even if I were just ladling water from the Yodogawa [river] to distribute, I couldn't continue. While the number of people in distress now approaches twenty thousand, I can see that more than half would starve to death, so neither can I stop. Somehow or other, I would like to continue for another thirty to fifty days. Therefore, beginning yesterday I am doing my best to offer my usual [fund-raising] talk to teach the Dharma. I have not had much success.

Last year, we were cooking rice gruel and distributing a few sen, whatever was appropriate for each person. The days passed by, and with the divine protection of the dragon king,[5] somehow one-half to one-third of the people could contribute alms. In this way we saved a great many people. Now I am asking to borrow a little money from you. If I were to receive two hundred *ryō*[6] from you, then I could not only reach Osaka as I have described, but even be able to reach a little ways into the Kyoto area.

These are recent developments. I barely started yesterday [preaching to fund-raise], so I cannot easily extend my reach toward Kyoto. If I can make something of my work here [in Osaka], I would like to be able to go to Kyoto and help people there. If it we somehow possible for you to send me the same amount of money that you donated toward the scripture project, I can tell you it would be a tremendous benefit. Even if I have to borrow money, I know I won't let Osaka slip, even with just what I have now. But with just this amount, I can't extend my reach to Kyoto. If I tried to distribute alms in Kyoto, I would exhaust my resources in five to seven days.

Since this sort of situation is rare in one lifetime, or even in two lifetimes, I ask you to give rise to a great belief in your own Buddha nature and to send me funds in the amount of two hundred *ryō* as mentioned above. I would like to immediately borrow one hundred *ryō* from Konomu Saemon[7] here in Osaka. I ask that you directly reimburse him later. Although I imagine that raising the funds will be difficult even for you, the situation here is beyond endurance, and so I ask this of you.

Only one in one hundred of those who gather here [to receive alms] is a [professional] beggar. [The rest] are all townsmen or farmers from the countryside. Since we started giving out rice gruel last year, there were three or four thousand people [coming], or at the very most five or six thousand. Despite our efforts, it is said that as many as ten or fifteen dead bodies turn up every day.

Regarding the distribution of alms, giving out a little money has proved successful, and much more convenient than rice gruel. So much so, that people who did not participate in the past, do so now. Up until yesterday, the twenty-first, we had enough each day to give to everyone. However, we can't continue in this way. Starting today, they will each receive one *go*[8] of rice. For lack of a better distribution method, we distributed [the rice] wrapped in heavy tissue paper. Starting yesterday, the monks from the temple gathered, and without stopping, wrapped through the night up to this morning. They wrapped some thirty bales of rice. As a result, everyone got blisters on their fingertips, and laughed that it would make it difficult to do anything else. The thirty bales of rice were not nearly enough, and we couldn't wrap any more. So we gave the rest five *sen*[9] each and sent them off. Even though it was just paper money, it was a vast amount. I have asked [the people] to bring along containers [for receiving rice], starting tomorrow.

As the situation deteriorates, and I see it before my very eyes, I feel that I must continue doing this at all costs. Even if it means chopping off my fingers and breaking my bones to give them as alms. It is difficult to describe the situation in words. Some of the people are nearly 70 or 80 years old, leaning on staffs, but they find it difficult to relinquish their lives. Others are children of five or three years, dragged along by the hand by their mothers. Some wear a begging bowl. Some wear straw matting. Some of the sick or blind have not washed their hands even once in a year's time. Their hands look as if they had seven or eight coats of lacquer on them. There are some who haven't eaten anything in ten days, and so [their stomachs] have become swollen and distended. Others have gotten so thin that they are nothing but skin and bones. Truly, the path of hungry ghosts[10] [appears] before my eyes and [I see] human beings living in hell.

The sight of them clutching what they receive reminds me of Maudgalyā-yana's mother.[11] She too dwelt in the path of hungry ghosts, and grasped the bowl of rice [her son] brought to her. Heaven and earth reverberate with the sound of them crying out as they are pushed about by the large crowds. Their shouts of "Give me some! Give me some!" shake the mountains and rivers. Traffic on the road is more numerous than ants visiting Kumano [Shrine],[12] as the saying goes. They have more lice on their bodies that there are sesame seeds in an oil shop. If we thrust into the crowd even slightly to keep them from pushing, the lice move onto our robes, and [hang there] like so many suspended sesame seeds. When I tried to distribute [alms] personally, fifty of those "lacquered' hands grabbed at me and pulled on my hands. I cannot describe how foul their stench was upon my nostrils.

At first, we used two entrances [for distribution]. They rushed them so badly, that we [started] using four. Distribution went so fast, that it looked like a *tengu*'s nest.[13] Even with four doors, it was still too narrow and they rushed them. So starting tomorrow, we will distribute from six doors. Originally, we had a fence made from bamboo poles and stakes, measuring about five or six inches across. On the morning of the fifteenth, they pushed it over with one shove. We still don't have this fence firmly [repaired], so the monk named Hōshū[14] thought we should put out the *heikan*,[15] and he told some younger monks to do so. On the morning of the sixteenth, while I was away, [the crowd] pushed it down, crushing fourteen or fifteen people nearly to death. Some of them somehow recuperated. They were made to drink a stimulant and sprinkled with water. When they started breathing a little, they were fed some rice gruel. Almost ten people were revived, but another six people died. It was a pitiful occurrence. Just when we thought we had enough money [to save lives], suddenly a million people were trampling each other to death. How could things deteriorate further?

When I returned, I was shocked [by what had happened], but nothing could be done. After that, the number of people continued to increase, but we took various steps. We built fences in several places. We put up fence posts as big as logs and lashed on sideways large bamboo about one foot in diameter, like water barriers or horse guards. We made it as narrow as possible, to [force them to go] single file. We used unlimited ingenuity and common sense to keep people from pushing one another to death.

We considered adding on three hundred to five hundred foot soldiers to prevent further problems. Otherwise the fifty or sixty young monks might end up trampled to death by beggars as they hold back the rising tide of people who come from morning to night to eat. It is a time to roll up our sleeve. Although we continue bravely, we soon will not have the means to go on.

You could accumulate one thousand or even ten thousand gold coins in your storehouse, and keep them idling useless in your coffers. But if you give alms at a time like this, you will build merit for countless *kalpas* in the future and this will become the basis for becoming a Buddha. This world is a shameful place, where even giving alms to others is jealously slandered by hard hearts that are closed up and idle. It is precisely such people who will be born as beggars or fall into the path of hungry ghosts!

I ask that, if at all possible, you use your skill to raise the money requested above. I cannot write more, but have only expressed one part in one hundred of my thoughts.

Yours sincerely,
Tetsugen
Dated the 22nd day of the 2nd month [1682]
Addressed to Yamazaki Saemon and company

I ask that you extend my regards to your wife, to Konomu Saemon, and the townspeople. In haste.

Appendix

Biographies

The Deeds of Master Tetsugen, Founder of Zuiryūji Temple

Tetsugen's leading disciple Hōshū wrote this traditional biography of his first master. He dated the text the first day of the third lunar month of the year Shōtoku 4 (1714), so he probably composed it in honor of the thirty-third anniversary of Tetsugen's death. For most individuals, that anniversary marks the final memorial service in a long series of services commemorating their death. It was commonplace for Zen disciples to author such biographies and to prepare posthumous publications of their master's writings. Hōshū was likewise responsible for preparing the *Yuiroku, The Preserved Writings of Tetsugen.*

Little is known about Tetsugen's childhood, and the biography begins with a fairly vague account of an exceptionally bright and devout child. The story does not truly begin until Tetsugen meets Yinyuan, the founder of Ōbaku Zen, and becomes a Zen monk. No overt mention is made of his earlier affiliation as a Jōdo Shinshū (True Pure Land) priest. The biography includes such standard Zen features as accounts of Tetsugen's exchanges with Ōbaku masters, the account of him receiving Muan's certification and Tetsugen's death poem. It also recounts a number of miraculous stories related to Tetsugen in life and in death. This translation is based on a modern edition of Tetsugen's writings.[1]

The Deeds of Master Tetsugen, Founder of Zuiryūji Temple

[The Master's] precept name was Dōkō and his common name was Tetsugen. He was born on the first day of the first lunar month of Kan'ei 7 (1630), in the Mashiki region of Higo province to the Saeki family. His father's name was Jōshin, and he fervently prized [the teachings of] Mahayana Buddhism. In his later years he joined the Lotus Society.[2] His mother, whose name is unknown, was a virtuous woman.

From very early childhood, Tetsugen was clever and surpassed other children. His parents loved him dearly. When he was seven years old, his father first taught him the Kanmuryōjukyō (The Meditation on the Buddha of Infinite Light Sutra).[3] He immediately memorized it thoroughly. At thirteen, he cut his hair, donned monk's robes, and joined Dharma Teacher Kaiun[4] of the same region.

[When Tetsugen was] seventeen, it happened that Dharma Teacher Eishō [Saigin][5] was lecturing in Buzen on the *Awakening of Faith*,[6] and Tetsugen heard his lecture. [Saigin's] voice penetrated [Tetsugen's] heart and moved him, and he gave rise to a deep and wise understanding. On one occasion, one of the senior monks [attending the lectures] praised [Tetsugen's] talent.

One day, Tetsugen received word of his mother's death. He returned to his home village to perform the memorial services for her. In the Spring of Keian 3 (1650), he departed for an education, going to Kyoto with a number of companions with the same intention. He enjoyed attending lectures wherever he could. He was constantly honing his understanding of the Indian and Chinese Buddhist texts. For this reason, his fame spread throughout the four directions.

In the autumn of the first year of Meireki (1655), the Ōbaku Master Yinyuan came to Japan and was staying for a time at Tōmyōzan [Kōfukuji in Nagasaki].[7] Wishing to pay his respects, Tetsugen waited for a boat in Osaka. It happened that he traveled on the same boat as the lay believer Lord Kurokawa,[8] the shogunate's administrator of Nagasaki. [When he arrived in Nagasaki,] he changed his robes[9] and entered Tōmyōzan [Kōfukuji]. He explained that he was eager to seek the teachings.

Master [Yinyuan] knew at a glance that Tetsugen was a vessel of the Dharma. He allowed him to follow the other monks and enter the monks' hall to begin practicing *zazen*. Tetsugen immediately cast aside what he had previously learned, and took up the matter of his Original Nature untiringly noon and night. Before very long, Master [Yinyuan] accepted an invitation from Fumonji[10] in Settsu [and departed].

At that time, Master Muan was presiding [as abbot] at Bunshizan [Fukusaiji in Nagasaki].[11] Tetsugen went right over and knocked at his gate. One day, Tetsugen entered [the master's] room and sharply stated his points, without trying to strike a mutual understanding. The master struck [Tetsugen] and dismissed him. Tetsugen presented a verse and withdrew. He roamed about like a wild crane or a wisp of cloud, stopping here and there, without staying in any place for long. Eventually, he entered Fumonji and paid his respects to Master [Yinyuan]. Then he returned once more to Bunshizan [Fukusaiji] and was permitted reentry into [Muan's] room.

In the autumn of Kanbun 1 (1661), Tetsugen went to Bungo because he heard that [the abbot of] Tafukuji[12] would be lecturing on the *Śūraṃgama Sutra*. Tetsugen's robes were torn and shabby, and he didn't look like an ordinary monk.[13] The other monks held him in great disdain, until the abbot had him review the lecture. Then those who had despised him regretted it and apologized.

In the Spring of Kambun 3 (1663), Tetsugen accepted an invitation to lecture on the *Śūraṃgama Sutra* at Zenjōji in his home village. He analyzed the subtle points, and never hesitated over its words and verses. He analyzed it as readily as one can cut bamboo at the joints with a sharp knife. Those who heard him all said that he explained the hidden meanings that even Changshui[14] and Gushan[15] had missed. At that time, Hōshitsu the abbot of Daijiji[16] invited Tetsugen to stay in [the subtemple] Juyōken, which he had just restored.

The following year, Tetsugen lectured on the *Lotus Sutra* at Myōkōji in Chikuzen, because he was earnestly requested to do so. In Chikuzen, there is a mountain in Uminonaka, called Shika no shima.[17] [The mountain] is lush [with foliage] and quite beautiful, uniting heaven with earth. For generations it has been passed down that this land represents the daughter of the dragon king Sāgara.[18] The main shrine is grand, and its overall effect quite impressive. In a separate building is enshrined an image of Mañjuśrī.[19] When Tetsugen was not lecturing, he visited there, and said that it is a sacred place which represents the meaning of the Devadatta Chapter [of the *Lotus Sutra*].[20] Therefore he lectured [on that chapter] beside the shrine. The local people were able to hear things they had never before heard.

The following year [1665], Master Zhifei[21] reopened Kōjuzan [Fukujuji],[22] and held the dedication ceremony for the sake of the nation. Tetsugen quickly made his way there and entrusted himself [to the master's guidance]. The master gave him a position superior to [the other monks], and expected him to advance to high rank. One day, Master [Zhifei] instructed the monks, asking, "How does one remove something like oil absorbed by noodles?" He had the monks express their own understanding. Testugen replied, "Stop mixing noodles!" The master praised him highly.

When the summer [retreat] was completed, Tetsugen returned to Juyōken. At that time, a drought was becoming oppressive. Tetsugen decided to pray for rain for the sake of the local people. He set a time period of seven days, and led the monks in reciting the *dharani* from the *Śūraṃgama Sutra.*[23] On the last day, black clouds arose in all four [directions], and a great deal of sweet rain poured down. Far and wide, everything was saturated. The people of the region were exceedingly pleased.

Tetsugen once lamented, "Since ancient times, our country has been called the land of the Buddha. Since the Dharma first arrived in the East, we have never lagged behind China in establishing monasteries or creating [Buddhist] images. Generation after generation, famous monks and men of virtue have never been scarce. From the beginning, the only thing we have lacked is our own edition of the Scriptures. Throughout the country, there must be a shortage of scriptures. It says in the sutras, 'Among the 10,000 practices of a Bodhisattva, spreading the treasure of the Dharma is foremost.' Fortunately, I was born in a well-governed age, and was thankfully able to join the sangha. I must make an exhaustive effort to do just that. I will bind people from all over this country to the powerful karma of the eternal *prajña.*" Therefore, he traveled to Osaka, accompanied by two or three disciples, and developed his plans to print the entire scriptures.

In the Spring of Kanbun 8 (1668), Soken Zennō[24] and several believers invited Tetsugen to lecture on the *Awakening of Faith* at Gekkō Shōja. At that time, a person named Myōu Dōnin[25] from Kannonji came and attended the lectures. When she heard the plan to print the scriptures, she had an awakening of mind and joyfully donated one thousand *ryō* of platinum. Tetsugen was overjoyed. He said, "I have heard that even a tower one thousand feet tall must begin as just a foundation. I now already have my foundation. Surely I will print the entire scriptures." He quickly made his way to Ōbakusan [Mampukuji] to tell Master Yinyuan.

The master said joyfully, "I came to Japan for the sake of the Dharma. The *shōgun* gave me land and I have made progress in building this monastery. Spreading the Dharma has flourished and all has gone as I intended. The only thing missing was an edition of the scriptures. Without realizing it, my withered body has remained alive so that I might hear this glorious news. This old monk's wishes are now fulfilled." He composed a verse praising [Tetsugen's plan]. He then gave to Tetsugen the Chinese edition of the scriptures he had been keeping. He separated out a parcel of his land and let [Tetsugen] use it for a storehouse for the scriptures.

Tetsugen leapt for joy. He built Hōzōin (Treasure Storehouse Temple)[26] on this land, and opened the Inbō[27] [Print shop] in Kyōto. First he studied the list of contents, and then selected ten volumes to be printed. The wood block carvers swarmed like bees, and the donors gathered like a herd of deer. It almost equaled the time of Master Zibo.[28] Eventually, Tetsugen gave positions to all of his disciples.

Tetsugen traveled to Edo expressly to make connections and to lecture on the *Śūramgama Sutra* at Kaiunji in Asakusa. At that time, from high-ranking honored monks of various temples and famous *daimyō* of the day down to brave samurai, fierce henchmen, street children and housewives, [a crowd] camped out waiting for the scheduled time because they were afraid there would not be enough seats. In no time at all, Tetsugen collected sufficient funds. The event was very successful, like no other.

When the lectures were over, Tetsugen went to Ōbakusan [Mampukuji] to visit Master Muan. Muan asked him, "I heard that you lectured on the *Śūramgama Sutra*. It says in the sutra, 'When you look at looking, this looking is not looking. It cannot attain the looking that is apart from looking.'[29] What does this mean?" Tetsugen answered, "This seeing and hearing are not seeing and hearing. It cannot come to you through external voices and forms." The master said, "This is still the dualistic seeing of a dualistic mind." Tetsugen replied [with a verse]:

The wind blows in the blue sky
The floating clouds have disappeared
The moon rises over the blue mountains
A single round jewel.

The master approved of this.

In the Spring of Kambun 10 (1670), some faithful from Naniwa restored Yakushiji,[30] and invited Tetsugen to become the founder of the restored [temple]. The temple was located at the site where Jinja Myōō first appeared bearing the *Large Sutra of Perfect Wisdom*.[31] Tetsugen felt that he had a karmic connection [to the place] and made up his mind to go there. He changed the name and called it Jiunzan Zuiryūzenji (Cloud of Compassion Mountain, Lucky Dragon Temple). Disciples from far and near came under his influence and bustled about like water settling at the bottom [of a ravine] or clouds collecting in a valley.

In Kanbun 11 (1671), Master Muan received orders [from the *bakufu*] and established Shiunzan [Zuishōji][32] in Edo. He invited Tetsugen to accompany him; he gave him [the title] Zōyaku (Key to the Storehouse), and made him an administrator.

In the autumn, when Tetsugen returned to Zuiryūji, he passed through far off Hamamatsu along the way. The monks at Zuiunji invited him to hold a lecture. Before this, the wife of a Mr. Kaba died in a neighboring village. One day her spirit took possession of a family member and said, "I had a jealous nature in ordinary life, and so after death I am being tortured in the nether world. The suffering is unspeakable. A few days hence, a living bodhisattva will visit Zuiunji. I would be tremendously grateful if you would seek his mercy and have him say a memorial service on my behalf." Although the family was doubtful about this, just then Tetsugen arrived. Mr Kaba went and saw him, and told him about the above mentioned events. Tetsugen recited a verse and said a memorial service.

The spirit [of the deceased woman] once again took possession. She said, "Thankfully I have received the bodhisattva's Dharma power, and will now quickly escape from the suffering of transmigration. I beg you to thank him for me." When she finished speaking, [the possessed relative] collapsed to the ground. She slept through the night and awoke. She remembered nothing, and asked what had happened.

In the spring of the following year (1672), Tetsugen lectured on the *Śūramgama Sutra* at Zuiryūji. In the Autumn, he again headed for Edo. The wife of Mr. Ii from Sōun'in founded Kaizōan, and allowed Tetsugen to stay there. (In Shōtoku 3 [1713], she received official government permission and converted the hermitage into a temple.) During a night of meditation, Tetsugen composed a verse, which said:

A narrow track runs through a forest of thorns
Unawares, I step off into the wide open sky
Suddenly I transcend the shining moon and pure breeze
And live at peace within the cauldron of boiling water in a
furnace of burning embers.

In the Spring of Empō 1 (1673), Tetsugen accepted an invitation from Lord Yamaguchi [Daimyō of Hitachi], and visited his region of Hitachi. At that time Master Yinyuan took ill. Remembering one's master is tantamount. When Tetsugen heard that [Yinyuan's] condition was poor, he took to the road, traveling both day and night. When he arrived [at Mampukuji], the master had already died. Tetsugen prayed the memorial service along with the all the monks. It is said that they offered up prayers without ceasing to pay homage [to the master].

Earlier, Master Damei[33] had settled in the eastern portion of Ōbakusan, establishing Tōrin'in. His land was remote, and thus safe from the dangers of fire. Master [Damei] wished to protect the wood blocks of the scriptures. Personally writing out the testament, he traded his land with Tetsugen's, and converted [Tōrin'in] into Hōzōin. Tetsugen was deeply moved and pleased. He built a large storehouse [on the new site], and there stored the wood blocks for the scriptures.

In the Spring of Empō 2 (1674), Tetsugen heard that his father was ill, so he returned home. He administered medicinal infusions and undertook Pure Land practices.[34] After his father died, Tetsugen converted the house he had inhabited into Sanbōzenji (Three Treasures Zen Temple),[35] and offered up incense to his deceased parents.

Lord Hosokawa Minamoto, governor [of Higo] again invited Tetsugen to come to the castle, and he applauded the purity of Tetsugen's words and deeds. "No one in the province does not know what sort of monk you are. Truly you are a treasure of the province." [Lord Hosokawa] emptied his heart and inquired about the Dharma, paying deep homage to Tetsugen. From that time on, [Lord Hosokawa] aided in the printing of the scriptures by donating one thousand gold coins.

In the autumn, Hōzan Saichō[36] invited Tetsugen to visit Satsuma province. [Tetsugen] bestowed the name Fukushōji (Good Fortune and Prosperity Temple) on the large temple there. When asked, he lectured on the *Śūramgama Sutra*. At that time, some princes from Ryūkyū visited Tetsugen at Fukushōji, and asked him many questions about the essentials of the Dharma.

Lord Kuroshima,[37] the governor of Bungo, was Tetsugen's friend [in the Dharma] from the beginning. He invited Tetsugen to lecture on the sutras at Anrakuji. Tetsugen exalted the Buddha's commandments with all his might. There were some villainous fellows in that area who deeply despised Tetsugen. They gathered a great many followers from near and far, and tried to inflict harm on him. They even tried to defy the governor. Tetsugen had a lenient heart, so he acted as if he had heard nothing of this. The governor sent officials to escort him [safely] out of the area. He then rounded up the three ringleaders and put them in jail. When Tetsugen heard this, he sent a monk to beg for their release. The governor was moved and said, "If it is my teacher's wish to repay his enemies with benevolence. . . ." In the end, he pardoned them.

In the Spring of Empō 4 (1676), Tetsugen visited Master Muan. During their *mondō* (question and answer session), their understanding of the kōan was in agreement, and Tetsugen received *inka*. In the fourth month, the anniversary of his father's death was coming up, and so he lectured on the *Lotus Sutra* at Zuiryūji. In the autumn, he again went to Edo. Lord Inaba,[38] a councilor to the *shōgun* heard that Tetsugen had arrived. He sent an offering and asked about the Way. Their conversation came around to the matter of printing the scriptures, and Tetsugen explained the state of affairs. Lord Inaba could not stop praising him.

In the autumn of Empō 6 (1678), Tetsugen was just about to finish up the work of carving the woodblocks [for the scriptures]. Tetsugen then wrote his report to the emperor. He attached it to the sutras and presented it to the Retired Emperor Gomizunoo. The emperor was exceedingly pleased and praised it, saying to his retainers, "The volumes of the scriptures are so numerous, and yet he printed them well. One must call his resolve firm and genuine. Truly, [Tetsugen] is a meritorious servant of the Buddhist teachings and will receive good fortune in his next life as well. Such distinguished service to the court is unprecedented."

At one time, the land for Zuiryūji was crowded by private homes, and it was not good for practicing the Way. Tetsugen was given land by the government and moved [the temple] there. He built the Daiyūden (main worship hall) and celebrated its completion by lecturing on the *Śuraṃgama Sutra*. In no time at all, he built the Senbutsujō (monks' hall) and the Enbōdo (lecture hall). The grandeur of this temple was the crowning glory of the Zen temples south of the [Yodogawa] river.

It happened that a city dweller out of spite falsely accused a fellow servant of poisoning their master; he eagerly informed the government. Tetsugen was saddened that, although free from guilt, the fellow had been sent to death row. He quickly made an appeal for the man's pardon. He said, "He is truly without guilt. If there is any clear evidence, then I will submit to the guilt in his stead." As a consequence, tens of people had death sentences commuted. There was no one who was not moved when they heard about this.

Afterward, Tetsugen attached the "Account of Completing the Scriptures" to the scriptures, and again went to Edo hoping to present it to the *Shōgun*. In the first month of Tenna 2 (1682), he suddenly told some people, "I will face the great matter [that is, death] at the end of this spring. Therefore, I cannot stay here." Then accompanied by several disciples, he returned to Zuiryūji. Monks and laypeople from Edo climbed on the shaft [of his cart] and begged him to stay.

That spring there was a terrible famine in the Kyoto/Osaka region, and numerous homeless people were out on the streets. Tetsugen was sick at heart over this, and spend a lot of money and grain to save the starving poor. The people he saved from starving to death each day numbered more than ten thousand. A month passed. At the time, people started calling him "the bodhisattva who saves the world."

On the twenty-ninth day of the second month, Tetsugen suddenly took ill. He did not alter his usual practice of preaching on behalf of the community. As his illness grew worse and worse, he gradually took less food and drink. Various doctors urged medicines on him, but he calmly withdrew from them, knowing he would never recover.

On the seventh day of the third month, Tetsugen gathered all of his disciples to settle his affairs for after his death. Afterward he said, "My work is finished. Fortunately, you will prosper through the years. Be careful not to become embroiled in worldly desires. Just continue on the Way, and moment by moment investigate the Great Matter. Such a one is my Dharma heir. Printing the scriptures spreads the wise commands of all the Buddhas. For that purpose, I endured great suffering, and now the [task] is complete. If you pass the scriptures on forever, then there is no need to say anything about my teachings."

Master Muan sent a messenger monk with a letter to Tetsugen asking about his illness. Tetsugen thanked him for his kindness via the messenger. The next day, [Tetsugen] wrote a letter thanking everyone for all they had done to protect the Dharma. During these several days, people came constantly to ask about his illness. They filled the street.

On the twenty-second day, Tetsugen looked for a piece of paper and wrote down a verse. It said:

Fifty-three years of falling down seven times and being thrown down eight.
Mistakenly discussing *prajna,*
My sins stretch up to the heavens.
Peacefully floating on a sea of lotuses,
I tread through the water across heaven.

When he had finished writing, he passed away peacefully. It was just ten o'clock in the morning. This exactly fit his comment, "I will face the Great Matter at the end of Spring." Those who knew of this thought it wondrous.

Tetsugen had reached the worldly age of fifty-three, and had worn monk's robes for 40 springs and autumns. When it came time to change his undergarments, his arms and legs were as flexible as normal. For the three days that he was lying in state, Tetsugen's countenance was as if he were still living. On the day of his cremation, more than one hundred thousand people came to bid him farewell. Each of them brought flowers or incense. As they walked [around the coffin], they made offerings of them. The sound of their wailing shook the forests. People from distant and remote villages, even those who had never actually met the master, could not help but sigh when they heard he had departed this world.

Master Muan and other high-ranking monks from all over wrote verses to express their grief. They lamented that the teachings would probably decline [because of Tetsugen's death]. Eventually, [his disciples] buried Tetsugen's remains and built a pagoda in the western corner of Hōzōin. This expressed their feeling that, although dead, the master would never forget the scriptures.

Master Gaochuan[39] from Bukkokuji once wrote of Master [Tetsugen], "This master's virtue is difficult to fathom. He was a phoenix among monks and a dragon in the Dharma. He was blessed with much talent and much wisdom. He understood the teachings and followed them. He never shirked his responsibilities, and his merit can encompass a whole generation. He brilliantly instructed thousands of people, explaining the subtle meanings [of the scriptures]. He published the holy teachings of the Tripitaka without regard for his own sacrifices or his own merit. The Way has been advanced throughout the whole nation, and his fame has permeated the Court. If he was not the reincarnation of Tzu-po, then he must have been the more ancient Sheng-kung.[40] How can one describe his lofty accomplishments? By using the constellations as the letters and the vault of heaven as his tombstone." People praised this as an accurate account.

Tetsugen's bearing was impressive. His intentions and behavior were correct, and he was humble about himself. He never corrected others or put on airs. He was affectionate [with his juniors] and harmonious [with superiors]. He never put up barriers, but had a serene disposition, like the shape of a mountain or the calm of the sea. His learning penetrated all three parts of the Scriptures, and his wisdom was far reaching. He must have been an ancient sage born many times who had exhausted his residual karma, or why would he have been like this?

From the time he became a monk at an early age until the day of his death, for forty years Tetsugen worked without a moment's pause. His intentions to help the [Ōbaku Zen] sect and to promote the teachings never waned over the days and months. Although he earnestly promoted the one Great Matter for the sake of his disciples, he never sanctioned harsh criticism or heated scoldings. He responded to the illness [of ignorance] and offered the medicine [of the Dharma]. He skillfully used expedient means at great length, but he feared that not even one [disciple] attained to his level. For this reason, when anyone became intoxicated by some frivolity, all they had to do was take one glance at the master's face. That sobered them up and they understood his meaning.

Tetsugen distributed food and clothing to the poor and satisfied each one's need. He provided medicine for the sick, without them [needing to] leave their own homes. When he saw an abandoned child on the road, he would entrust it to someone and have them feed and raise the child. When he encountered prisoners on the road, he would petition the authorities for their pardon. This broad compassion to benefit others was simply the product of his nature, and not something he consciously cultivated through effort.

Regarding the printing of the scriptures, Tetsugen was not concerned with [how much effort it took], even if it killed him. He lectured on the sutras and commentaries tens of times. The number of people who heard him [lecture] likely reached tens of thousands. He used all the alms he received to fund the printing of the scriptures, so that on his death, there was almost no money remaining.

Tetsugen founded some eight temples. They are by name: Zuiryūji, Hōzōin, Konzenji (Golden Meditation Temple),[41] Kaizōji (Ocean Storehouse Temple),[42] Shomatsuji (Small Pine Temple),[43] Hōsenji (Treasure Source Temple),[44] and Emmeiji (Long Life Temple).[45] A number of people entered [the monastery] to become his disciples. Those who received the precepts from him or requested a Dharma name are too numerous to count.

Someone once said to Tetsugen, "Our sect values illuminating the mind and seeing one's nature, but you are always preaching the sutras and commentaries. Isn't that at variance with the teaching of "direct pointing"[46]? Tetsugen laughed and said, "Isn't what you say a little simplistic? Zen is the water and the teachings are the waves. When you seize onto Zen and throw out the teachings, it's like rejecting the waves and seeking just the water. The teachings are the vessel and Zen is the gold. When you seize onto the teachings and throw out Zen, it is like casting off the gold and looking for just the vessel. The waves and the water are not separate. The vessel is itself the gold. How could Zen and the teachings be two things? If you are in close accord with your nature, then even if you teach until Maitreya[47] is born in this world, you will never have opened your mouth. Don't you remember, the Great Enlightened World Honored One [the Buddha] said, "From the beginning at the Deer Park until the end at the River Hiranyavati, I never taught a single word."

There was also once a person who wrote a letter to Dahui Zonggao,[48] asking him for a kōan. Dahui replied, saying, "I hear that you are always reading the *Perfect Enlightenment Sutra*.[49] The kōans that I give are all in that sutra. Therefore, if you completely understand that [sutra], why bother reading others?" The person withdrew unable to answer.

Tetsugen rarely wrote poetry and verse. But when someone came looking for him, he would teach them freely just as the words came to him. He did not need to deliberate, yet his logic was pure and correct, and he penetrated all the subtleties of the Way. He never allowed [his lectures] to be put down in manuscript form. Hence his *Yuiroku*[50] is a mere two fascicles. It is now circulating throughout the world as a part of [the Ōbaku edition of] the scriptures.

꙰꙰꙰

I, Hōshū Dōsō, gratefully served Tetsugen the longest, and so am well informed about the details [of his life]. When I think about my debt of gratitude for his instructions, it seems no different from heaven sheltering us from above and the earth cradling us from below.

The years have passed peacefully, and already thirty years are gone. Few among the young or the old know the story of Tetsugen's life. Now that thirty years have passed, most of the people who knew him have died. For this reason, without reflecting on my own incompetence, I have written this short summary in order to state it clearly for later generations.

In the third year of Genroku (1690), I received official government permission to publish the scriptures. I attached [Master Tetsugens' memorial] the "An Account of Completing the Buddhist Scriptures," and presented it [to the *shōgun*]. I received funds and finally completed [Tetsugen's] unfulfilled goal. Shōun,[51] one of Tetsugen's other disciples, received permission from Tetsugen and himself carved the images of 500 *arhats*.[52] In Genroku 8 (1695), he received land and built a temple. He enshrined the images there, and for that reason it is called Ten'onzan Rakanji (Arhat temple).[53] He dedicated the temple to Tetsugen and designated him as the founder. It is impossible to fully express the life and deeds of Tetsugen with just brush and ink.

Dated this fourth year of Shōtoku (1714), the first day of the third month.
Respectfully written by the humble monk Dōsō.

The Monk Tetsugen From *Biographies of Unusual People of the Early Modern Period*

A brief biographical sketch of Tetsugen appeared in an eighteenth-century collection of biographies of unusual individuals, the *Kinsei kijin den,* written by Ban Kōkei (1733–1806).[1] The volume included people from all walks of life in Tokugawa society, including samurai, government officials, merchants, scholars, monks, farmers, and townsmen. The volume was intended for a popular audience; it was written in straightforward Japanese, with illustrations by Mikuma Katen. This represents the earliest published source of the popular story that Tetsugen collected funds for printing the scriptures three times before completing the project. It also includes an amusing account of Tetsugen's wife following him to Uji. No Ōbaku sources from the period mention that Tetsugen had been married before he joined the Ōbaku sect.

The Monk Tetsugen From *Biographies of Unusual People of the Early Modern Period*

The monk Tetsugen Dōkō was born in the province of Higo in a branch temple of Honganji. Although he was already married, he was dissatisfied that in the [True Pure Land] sect, people without talent or merit held high rank in the temple hierarchy. Therefore, he went up to Mount Ōbaku and followed [the instruction] of Muan.

His wife came to [Mount Ōbaku Mampukuji] to find him, but he did not wish to meet her. So she camped outside the temple gate and watched for him to emerge. Finally, one day when he had no choice but to go out, she asked him to accompany her to their home province and return to their village. He escaped up the street and returned to the temple.

After he had inherited [Muan's] Dharma, he founded Zuiryūji in the Namba area of Settsu province. Even today, people refer to that temple by his name [Tetsugenji].

Since he had set his mind on printing a woodblock edition of the Buddhist scriptures, he collected funds. At that time, there was terrible starvation throughout the country. Tetsugen was troubled by this and distributed so much in alms that he had less than half of the money [he had collected] left. Just as before, he solicited funds and after several years once again had collected [enough money]. For a second time, many people were dying of hunger because the grain crops had failed. This time as well he gave away all his money. However, due to his great virtue, the third time that he raised the money he completed the edition of the Buddhist scriptures. Even now, in the same manner, the funds from distributing these scriptures are allocated from the main temple to the various branch temples. (In much the same way, this sect also sells a medicine called *kintaien,* and the money is distributed to the sect by the pharmacy Kangakuryō.)[2]

Tetsugen's Buddhist learning was profound, and he skillfully taught the Dharma and taught many of the common people. However, it is said that within his own group of disciples he was not forceful enough and so never designated a Dharma heir. He left his temples to his disciple Hōshū. There were difficulties with some of the others. Hōshū also had extensive Buddhist learning and did virtuous deeds.

Lesson 28: Tetsugen's Edition of the Complete Buddhist Scriptures (From the *Elementary School Japanese Language Reader*[1])

A lesson concerning Tetsugen and his production of the complete Buddhist scriptures appeared in an elementary school lesson book for many years in the early twentieth century. The lesson was originally written by Fukuda Gyōkai (1806–1888), a Jōdo-shū (Pure Land sect) Buddhist monk. The Monbushō (Ministry of Education) produced textbooks to be used in schools throughout the country. These textbooks reflected the the Monbushō's policy that moral values should pervade the entire curriculum. The Tetsugen lesson, which promotes perseverance and dedication the good of the broader society, appeared in the reading textbook. It appeared in two editions, in print from 1918 through 1938. The lesson was cut from the 1941 edition.

Lesson 28: Tetsugen's Edition of the Complete Buddhist Scriptures (From the *Elementary School Japanese Language Reader*)

The Complete Buddhist Scriptures are a large library of collected books concerning the Buddhist teachings. As such, they are revered as an unparalleled treasure by those who are committed to the teachings. Nevertheless, publishing them has never been a simple undertaking. Therefore, in the past, only a few [copies] existed [in Japan], imported from China. Scholars found it very hard to get a hold of them.

Some 210 years ago, there was a monk named Tetsugen at Ōbakusan Mampukuji in [the city of] Uji in Yamashiro [province]. He decided to try to publish the Buddhist scriptures as his life's work. No matter how many trials he had to endure, he pledged that he would complete his task. For many years, he traveled widely to various regions collecting funds. Finally he had raised it all. Tetsugen was overjoyed and was just about to start publishing, when there happened to be a flood in Osaka. There were many killed and injured. Homes were washed away, property lost, and countless numbers of people were [wandering] lost by the roadside. Tetsugen saw these conditions and felt disconsolate. Without hesitation, he decided, "When I determined to publish the Buddhist scriptures, it was in order to spread Buddhism. Spreading Buddhism is done for the sake of saving people in desperate straits. The money that I have received as donations will serve the same purpose whether I use it to finance the Buddhist scriptures or to save the hungry. Although it is necessary to spread the Buddhist scriptures throughout the world, saving people from death is even more urgent." Therefore, he told the people who had donated the money of his intention and received their blessing. He spent all the funds on relief efforts.

Not a penny remained of the funds Tetsugen had collected at such great pains for publishing [the Buddhist scriptures]. However, Tetsugen did not flinch at all. Once again he began to solicit funds and strove at this task for many years. His efforts were not in vain, and once again his long-cherished desire neared completion.

However, this time a great famine occurred in the Kyoto/Osaka region, and people's suffering exceeded even that from the flood. Even though the *bakufu* (military government) set up small relief offices and used its power [to further] the relief efforts, the people's suffering just kept increasing day by day. Once again, Tetsugen made a decision. He explained to the people who had donated the money and halted the publication project. He saved as many people as was within his power.

Twice he had collected funds and twice he had spent it all. As energetic as ever, Tetsugen began to raise funds for a third time. Tetsugen's deep compassion and his determination not to waver from his original decision made a strong impression on people. The number that made donations was unexpectedly high. This time, carving the plates and printing them progressed steadily. Thus, seventeen years after Tetsugen decided to undertake this great project, the publication of the 6,956 volumes of the Buddhist scriptures was finally completed in 1681. It is known throughout the world as the "Tetsugen edition." Truly, it is only from that time that the complete Buddhist scriptures have spread widely in our country. The woodblocks even now are preserved at Mampukuji and fill up a storehouse that has three ridgepoles and covers 150 *tsubo* (about 5,400 square feet).

Fukuda Gyōkai once said in praise of Tetsugen's endeavor, "Tetsugen published the complete Buddhist scriptures three times in one lifetime."

Notes

INTRODUCTION

1. Nosco, "Keeping the Faith," especially pp. 152–155.

2. Duncan Williams discusses the temple registration system in greater detail in *The Other Side of Zen; A Social History of Sōtō Zen Buddhism in Tokugawa Japan*, p. 19ff.

3. For a disscussion of popular Buddhist preaching in Tokugawa Japan, see Elizabeth G. Harrison, "Encountering Amida: Jōdō Shinshū Sermons in Eighteenth-Century Japan." Unpublished Ph.D. dissertation, University of Chicago, 1992.

4. See Winston King, *Death Was His Kōan,* Peter Haskell, *Bankei Zen,* and Norman Wadell, *The Unborn.*

5. Williams 2000, p. 3.

6. Much more information is available regarding monastic training in the later half of the Tokugawa period and the modern period. For example, for discussions of kōan practice in the Rinzai tradition, see Michel Mohr, "Emerging from Nonduality: Kōan Practice in the Rinzai Tradition since Hakuin" and G. Victor Sōgen Hori, "Kōan and *Kenshō* in the Rinzai Zen Curriculum," in *The Kōan: Texts and Contexts in Zen Buddhism,* Steven Heine and Dale S. Wright, eds. (Oxford 2000).

7. For a bibliography of recent works in Western languages on Tokugawa religion and thought, see Janine Sawada, 2002. For works in both Japanese and English, see Williams 2004.

8. Michel Mohr, JJRS 24 April 1994.

9. For a more complete discussion of Ōbaku Zen, see Baroni 2000.

10. For a discussion of the Chinese founders and the first generation of Japanese converts, see Baroni 2000, pp. 55–84.

11. Baroni 2000, p. 106ff.

CHAPTER ONE

1. Before Buddhism and Shinto were officially separated by the Japanese government during the Meiji period, the distinctions between shrines and temples and Shinto

priests and Buddhist monks were far less definitive than they are today. In addition to large Buddhist-Shinto complexes, smaller shrines commonly contained a small Buddhist hall and, conversely, Buddhist temples incorporated small Shinto shrines on their grounds. Buddhist monks sometimes held positions at the larger shrines, and provided Buddhist services there. In other cases, the same individual served as both Shinto priest and Buddhist monk. Monks who provided Buddhist services at Shinto shrines are referred to as shrine monks, *shasō,* to distinguish them from other Shinto priests.

2. In most cases, source materials from the Tokugawa period refer to the True Pure Land sect as Ikkōshū or Ikkō sect, known today as Jōdo Shinshū in Japanese. The term "Ikkō" literally means "singleminded," and is used because of the sect's singleminded reliance on Amida and their exclusive practice of the *nembutsu.* The term is closely associated with Rennyo (1415–1499), the eighth patriarch, regarded by some as a second founder, who popularized the term in his writings. I have chosen to use the English name True Pure Land throughout the book.

3. Akamatsu, *Tetsugen zenji,* p. 8.

4. *Kinsei kijin den,* written by Ban Kōkei (1733–1806) and illustrated by Mikuma Katen, is an eighteenth-century collection of biographies of unusual individuals. The volume includes people from all walks of life in Tokugawa society, including samurai, government officials, merchants, scholars, monks, farmers, and townsmen.

5. Akamatsu, *Tetsugen,* pp. 177–186.

6. T 12, no. 365. The *Kanmuryōjukyō* is traditionally said to have been translated into Chinese by Kālayasas (383?–442?); no Sanskrit original is extant, and scholars now believe that it was originally composed in Chinese. The sutra tells the story of Queen Vaidehī who, while imprisoned by her wicked son, was instructed by Śākyamuni Buddha in sixteen forms of meditation centered on Amida Buddha and his Pure Land (*jūrokkan*).

7. Shimoda p. 86.

8. Sessō was a Pure Land believer in his youth, but converted to Rinzai Zen and practiced at Tafukuji in Bungo province where he subsequently became the second abbot. In 1646 he received the purple robe and became abbot at Myōshinji. Several of the day's leading Rinzai monks practiced under him, including Gudō and Daigū. His Dharma heirs include Kengan Zen'etsu (1618–1690), who likewise served as abbot at Tafukuji and later played an influential role in Tetsugen's life.

9. Tōfukuji has been one of the leading Rinzai Zen temples in Japan since its founding in the mid-thirteenth century, and was later ranked as one of the Gozan temples. The regent Fujiwara Michiie (1193–1252) funded the building and Enni Ben'en (1202–1280) served as founder and first abbot.

10. T. 32, no. 1666 and no. 1667. *Dacheng Chixin lun* (J. *Daijō kishin ron*), a short discourse on Mahayana thought that provides a summary of Mahayana Buddhism's basic teachings. The text is traditionally attributed to Aśvaghosa, and the two versions Chinese translations are attributed to Paramārtha (499–569) and Śikṣānanda (d. 710). However, there is no evidence that a Sanskrit version ever existed, and scholars now believe that it was probably originally composed in Chinese. The text was one of the basic scriptures for Huayan thought, and was an influential text for the Zen school as well. See Yoshito S. Hakeda, *The Awakening of Faith.*

11. Shimoda, *Meisō Tetsugen,* p. 34.

12. Akamatsu, *Tetsugen*, p. 49.

13. The *Kōmori bōdanki*, attributed to Tetsugen includes a very interesting autobiographical preface that purports to describe the early experiences that lead to Tetsugen's conversion to Zen. As discussed at length in chapter 3, the biographical material is spurious.

14. *Sentetsu zō den, Kinsei kijin den, Hyakka kikō den,* p. 199, and *Kinsei kijin den,* p. 59.

15. As quoted in Minamoto, p. 41.

16. The term *hōki* indicates a person of great promise in a Buddhist sense, especially one with the potential to become a Dharma heir.

17. The entries for Kurokawa's audience recorded in Yinyuan's *nempu* are included under the sixth month of 1655; they indicate that he became a lay disciple at that time. *Ingen zenshū,* vol. 11, pp. 5211 and 5217.

18. Yinyuan was allowed to bring a limited number of Chinese disciples with him to Fumonji as his personal attendants. However, during the initial period of house arrest, Japanese disciples were not permitted to join his assembly. For a description of the restrictions placed on Yinyuan at Fumonji, see Baroni, *Ōbaku Zen,* pp. 44–52.

19. Yoshinaga Utarō, *Tetsugen zenji,* pp. 8–10. Yoshinaga based this conclusion on a quotation from the *Jimoku tekkō,* a text of 15 fascicles written by Tetsugyū, which briefly describes Tetsugen's early encounters with Ōbaku Zen. The *Jimoku tekkō,* also known as the *Tetsugyū zenji jimoku tekkō,* was first published in Genroku 13 (1700), the year of Tetsugyū's death.

20. The wide variety of chronologies include: Shimoda, pp. 2–8, Minamoto, *Tetsugen,* p. 385, and Nakamura Hidemitsu, *Tetsugenji kiroku,* p. 6. Shimoda's is the earliest attempt at a chronology in the modern scholarship; it is based on the Hōzō line's chronology, *Hōzō hage nempyō,* which I have not found elsewhere. According to Shimoda, Tetsugen practiced with Yinyuan at Fumonji in Settsu in 1655 and returned to Nagasaki to practice under Muan in 1657. He then returned to Fumonji where he published the *Gukai hōgi* in 1658. While Minamoto includes entries for the years 1657 through 1659, he does not introduce this information in the main body of the text. His chronology agrees with Shimoda's for the years 1655 and 1657. For 1658, it says that Tetsugen returned to Fumonji and then went on to Kyoto. Tetsugen attended lectures in Kyoto until sometime in 1659, when he returned to Nagasaki to practice under Muan. He left Muan that same year because of internal doubts and returned to his home province, abandoning Zen for a time. Nakamura Hidemitsu adds some interesting details about Tetsugen's life in his chronology of the temple Zuiryūji. He explains that Tetsugen went to Kyoto in 1658 specifically to do research in the scriptures. As a result of his research into the combined practice of Zen and Pure Land, he experienced serious doubts and left Ōbaku for a time. He published the *Gukai hōgi* during a period of restored faith, but left Fumonji in 1659 when those doubts redoubled.

21. *Tetsugen yuiroku,* p. 1b.

22. Shimoda, p. 179.

23. The most common pattern of practice within the Rinzai (and Ōbaku) sect involves an extended period of practice under one master until a reasonable degree of progress has been attained, generally until the disciple has had an initial enlightenment

experience. Once a disciple is somewhat advanced, he commences a period of practice on his own, making occasional visits to his master until such a time that he receives *inka* and becomes a master in his own right. During this period, it is customary to visit other Zen masters and practice under them for short periods of time.

24. Kengan was in the Myōshinji line of Rinzai Zen. He was designated as Sessō's Dharma heir at a young age, and later succeeded him as abbot at Tafukuji at the age of thirty-six, in 1653. The following year, in 1654, he made a trip to Nagasaki to practice with the Chinese master Daozhe at Sōfukuji. He had numerous contacts over the years with Ōbaku monks, including visits with Yinyuan and Muan in Nagasaki, and again later at Mampukuji in Uji.

25. The Heroic Valor Sutra, T. 19, no. 945, an apocryphal sutra in ten fascicles, probably originally composed in Chinese. Translation is attributed to Paramiti. The text is a discourse on the workings of the mind, and much favored by the Zen sect in China and Japan. It should be noted that there are two sutras known by the same name; the other (T. 15, no. 642) is the more famous scripture translated by Kumārajīva.

26. Minamoto, p. 159.

27. Zhifei came to Nagasaki in 1657 at Yinyuan's invitation and served for six years as the abbot of the Chinese temple Fukusaiji. Although he wanted to return to China during that period, he had not yet been permitted to leave the city and visit Yinyuan at Ōbaku-san Mampukuji. Finally, he was granted permission to travel freely in 1663 and he made a trip to the Kyoto area. Satisfied that Yinyuan was not being held against his will, Zhifei decided to return home himself. He never fulfilled that intention. After two years as abbot at Fukujuji from 1665 to 1667, he returned to Nagasaki and entered Sōfukuji. He died there in 1671.

28. Zhifei had previously met Lord Ogasawara Tadazane (1596–1667), the *daimyō* of Buzen, while traveling in Kyoto. Tadazane was already a lay patron of Ōbaku Zen, and had a long relationship with both Yinyuan and Muan. On returning to Kyushu, Zhifei went to Ogasawara Tadazane to request his permission to return home to China. Tadazane granted permission, but convinced Zhifei to delay his journey for a few years. According to tradition, Tadazane's wife played a part in Zhifei becoming abbot at Fukujuji. She had a dream of an arhat sitting on a jade lotus, that she claimed looked exactly like Zhifei.

29. I have written about these debates at greater length elsewhere. See Baroni, "Bottled Anger."

30. *San'yo zuihitsu*, as quoted in Yoshinaga, *Tetsugen zenji*, p. 31. This excerpt is from the ninety-second section of the *San'yo zuihitsu*, which is a compendium of two hundred questions related to True Pure Land practice. The text was written in three fascicles by the True Pure Land monk Erin (1715–1789).

31. Yoshinaga gives a short biographical sketch of him, p. 32.

32. Akamatsu says that Tetsugen and Chikū studied under Saigin at the same time and that they were once friends, *Tetsugen*, p. 65. I have found no primary source to support this claim.

33. The Kurushima family temple was a subtemple within the Sōtō temple Daitsūsan Anrakuji. The temple no longer exists; it burned to the ground in 1883 and was never reconstructed.

34. The association of Tetsugen and Kengan is easily understood in this context, since Tetsugen first heard the *Śūramgama sutra* read by Kengan and probably relied heavily on Kengan's interpretation.

35. *Ikkō ikki* uprisings began in the late fifteenth century and continued until Oda Nobunaga successfully asserted his military authority over the True Pure Land sect. There are many studies of these uprisings. See, for example, Kasahara Kazuo, *Ikkō ikki—sono kōdō to shisō* and *Ikkō ikki no kenkyū*, and David L. Davis, "*Ikki* in Late Medieval Japan." McMullin discusses Oda Nobunaga's campaign against True Pure Land opponents, *Buddhism and the State*, pp. 99–161.

36. Akamatsu, *Tetsugen*, p. 97.

37. The text of Kurushima's letter is given in Yoshinaga, *Tetsugen zenji*, pp. 72–73.

38. Washio takes the strongest position in maintaining that Tetsugen intentionally attacked True Pure Land, seeming to accept the True Pure Land accounts of events uncritically; "Tetsugen zenji no shinshū kōgeki," pp. 426–429, in *Nihon zenshūshi no kenkyū*. Akamatsu argues that Tetsugen taught out of compassion, not intending to attack True Pure Land, and that he did not seek controversy; *Tetsugen*, pp. 67–68, 82 and 92. Minamoto takes an intermediate position, suggesting that Tetsugen had demonstrated an eagerness to fight in the Edo encounter, but that he had matured by 1674 and had taken a more appropriate attitude of restraint and compassion at the time of the later incident in Mori; p. 143.

39. Minamoto, p. 129.

40. T. 19, no. 945, p. 131c, lines 13–14. "The Buddha said, 'Ānanda, you have always heard me teach in the vinaya that practice [consists of] three absolute aspects. That is, the control of mind is the precepts [sila]. The precepts give rise to stillness [dhyāna] and stillness gives rise to wisdom [prajña]. These are called the three pure [literally, without outflow] studies.'"

41. According to Pure Land teachings in Japan, not only had the practice of Buddhist morality from earlier ages become impossible during *Mappō*, but it endangered the believer's salvation by Amida Buddha. This was true because following the precepts implied a reliance on one's own ability rather than absolute reliance on the power of Amida's vow. See discussions of Shinran's teachings related to morality and self-power in Ueda and Hirota, *Shinran: An Introduction to His Thought*, pp. 152–163 and Bloom, *Shinran's Gospel of Pure Grace*, pp. 42–44.

42. *Chizō* is an official title for the monk within a Zen monastery who has been put in charge of the temple's library. Muan gave Tetsugen this position in 1671 when Tetsugen accompanied him to Edo for the official founding of Shiun-zan Zuishōji, the headquarters for Ōbaku in the capital.

43. As quoted in Yoshinaga Utarō, *Tetsugen zenji*, p. 34.

44. T. 19, no. 945, p. 106a, lines 1–2.

45. The image appears in various places in the sutra. See for example T. 19, no. 945, p. 120b, lines 29ff.

46. The term *shin'in* is an abbreviation for *busshin'in*, which indicates Dharma transmission from master to disciple.

47. *Yuiroku*, Gaochuan's introduction, p. 3b.

48. According to the *Deeds of Tetsugen*, starting in the fourth month of 1676, Tetsugen gave lectures on the *Lotus Sutra* at Zuiryūji to commemorate the anniversary of his father's death.

49. Muan is probably referring to the verse (T.9, p. 37a) that immediately precedes the Buddha's lengthy discussion on the so-called "four comfortable conducts" in the fourteenth chapter of the *Lotus Sutra*. Hurvitz translates the verse, "If in the latter evil age a bodhisattva-mahāsattva wishes to preach this scripture, he must dwell securely in four dharmas" (Translation from Hurvitz, *The Lotus sutra*, p. 208). The four comfortable conducts are: (1) to keep away from the wrong people; (2) to understand that all dharmas are empty and exist only as a result of codependent origination; (3) to preach the Dharma consistently; and (4) to preach the *Lotus sutra* only when the time is ripe.

50. *Mokuan goroku*, as quoted by Yoshinaga, *Tetsugen zenji*, p. 80.

51. Nakamura Shusei has collected relevant passages describing Muan bestowing *inka* on all of his disciples, "Mokuan zenji to sono wasō shihōsha."

52. A handwritten copy of the *Zen'aku jamyōron* is preserved in the library at Manpukuji. Unfortunately, the individual who copied out the text wrote in such a poor hand, that I have been unable to decifer the text, even with the help of specialists. I have therefore had to rely upon excerpts of the text published in other sources.

53. *Zen'aku jamyōron*, as quoted in Yoshinaga, *Tetsugen zenji*, p. 133, and Akamatsu, *Tetsugen*, p. 347. Akamatsu gives a more extensive passage in this case.

54. Akamatsu, *Tetsugen*, p. 349.

55. Minamoto, pp. 162–163.

56. Schwaller, p. 55.

57. Minamoto, pp. 162–163.

58. Baroni, *Ōbaku Zen*, p. 147ff.

59. Minamoto, p. 147.

60. It is interesting to note that at one point Akamatsu dated this remark to an earlier period in Tetsugen's life, including it in his discussion of the mondō from late 1669 or early 1670 immediately after Tetsugen's return from Edo; *Testugen zenji*, p. 75. While this may indicate that Akamatsu also found the remark disparaging, he makes no explicit comment about its meaning. In his later, more scholarly text, he dates the remark to 1676 when Tetsugen received *inka; Tetsugen*, p. 47.

61. Minamoto, p. 162; Schwaller, pp. 54–55.

62. *Wakan taihei kōki*, quoted in Yoshinaga, *Tetsugen zenji*, p. 116. The text is otherwise unidentified.

63. Composed by a disciple of Tetsugen, Kyōdō Genzui (1663–1730), in 1723. Kyōdō became the Dharma heir of Hōshū, and succeeded him as head monk at Hōzōin. It was in that capacity that he wrote the brief biography as a tribute to Tetsugen. The complete text is quoted in Shimoda, pp. 17–21.

64. *Eiran gyōjōki*, as quoted in Shimoda, p. 20.

65. *Zen'aku jamyōron*, as quoted in Akamatsu, *Tetsugen*, pp. 339–340.

66. *Zen'aku jamyōron*, as quoted in Akamatsu, *Tetsugen*, p. 347.

67. Akamatsu, *Tetsugen*, p. 348.

68. Tangen, who later wrote disparagingly of Hōshū and to a lesser extent of Tetsugen, did not break with Hōshū at this time, and so he could write about the dispute later. Tangen remained within Hōshū's assembly for several more years, accepting positions of authority at some of Tetsugen's smaller temples. He served for three years as the head monk at Sambōji, the temple Tetsugen established in honor of his parents at his family's residence in Kumamoto. In 1697, Tangen converted to Shingon and changed his Dharma name to Shinryō Rindō. As a consequence of this, Hōshū officially expelled him from the Ōbaku sect the same year. Subsequently, Tangen recorded his version of life under Tetsugen and Hōshū in his *Zen'aku jamyōron*, which appeared in 1701.

CHAPTER TWO

1. A Japanese translation of the Buddhist scriptures was produced only in the modern period, the *Kokuyaku issaikyō*, divided into two parts, Indo senjutsu-bu, 154 vols. (Daitō shuppansha, 1930–1936), and Wakan senjutsu-bu, 101 vols. (Daitō shuppansha, 1936–1944).

2. The first two of these editions, known as the Northern Ming and Southern Ming editions respectively, were the basis of the third, the Wanli edition. The Wanli was produced by comparing and correcting the earlier two.

3. The latter Korean edition, known as the *Koryō de can gyon*, published between 1236 and 1251, is commonly regarded by scholars today as the finest premodern edition of the Chinese Buddhist scriptures. It was known in Japan during the Tokugawa period, but the Japanese seem to have been more familiar with Chinese editions.

4. For a detailed history of the Chinese Buddhist canon, see *Bussho kaisetsu dai-jiten*, vol. 14 (Tokyo: Daitō shuppansha, 1933–1978).

5. Moriya, "Urban Networks and Information Networks," pp. 114–123.

6. Most Buddhist monks learned to read Chinese as a necessary part of their training. During the centuries of conflict prior to the Tokugawa period, Buddhist temples provided the only formal education available outside of the courtier class. Temple schools, called *terakoya*, also taught commoner children who were not studying for a religious vocation to read and write. These schools served an important role during the early part of the Tokugawa period to spread literacy to the nonsamurai populace. See Dore, *Education in Tokugawa Japan*, pp. 252–290.

7. Akamatsu, *Tetsugen*, pp. 282–286.

8. Moriya, pp. 99–100.

9. Moriya, pp. 114–115.

10. Yoshinaga Utarō, *Tetsugen zenji*, p. 24.

11. Myōu Dōnin's name appears in several places in Ōbaku records. She donated 1,200 *ryō* of silver in 1665 to Mampukuji and the funds were used to construct the bathhouse. She is mentioned in Muan's *nempu* and recorded sayings, and from these it is known that she had lost a son and made her donations for the sake of his salvation. Shimoda, pp. 198–201.

12. Perhaps a reference to a passage from the Dao De Jing, number 64. "A nine story tower begins with a mound of earth."

13. *Ingen zenshū*, vol. 11, p. 5251; *Ōbaku Mokuan oshō nempu*, part 2, p. 17a. In the "Brief Account of the History of Carving the Scriptures," Tetsugen reports that he visited with Yinyuan during the summer. According to Yinyuan's biography, however, the meeting took place that autumn.

14. Yoshinaga Utarō gives the text for both verses in their entirety, *Tetsugen zenji*, p. 28.

15. In addition to the Wanli edition, Tetsugen used other texts, including Japanese editions of individual scriptures and portions of the Korean edition, as the basis for parts of the Ōbaku edition. Matsunaga Chikai reviews the existing research on this matter and provides his own findings in great detail in "*Ōbakuban daizōkyō* no saihyōka."

16. *Ōbaku Mokuan oshō nempu*, part 2, p. 17a.

17. The term *inbō* is actually a temple post, referring to the person responsible for engraving seals and other items, mentioned in the *Ōbaku shingi*, T. 82, p. 777b. In this context, it was used as the informal name of the shop in Kyoto.

18. At the time of his death, Tetsugen had approximately one hundred disciples. Temple records were destroyed in a fire in 1749, so more accurate figures are not available.

19. The shop did not remain in the same location throughout its existence. Its role likewise changed several times over the decades. Nevertheless, it was still in operation and under the sect's indirect control until sometime during the Taishō era when it was finally sold.

20. Yoshinaga Utarō, *Tetsugen zenji*, p. 89.

21. For a brief history of the Inbō, see Akamatsu, *Tetsugen*, pp. 126–127.

22. Akamatsu, *Tetsugen*, pp. 225–230; Satō Fumitsugu, pp. 46–54.

23. Akamatsu, *Tetsugen zenji*, p. 144.

24. No one knows which elements, if any, of this story are historically accurate. Akamatsu indicates that there was still a memorial stone for the wife of a man named Takehara at Zuiryūji in 1941, before the temple was destroyed in the fire bombing in 1945; *Tetsugen*, p. 305.

25. *Kan'in* was the financial administrator at larger Zen monasteries. The term is closely related to the term *kansu*.

26. Tetsugyū was Muan's first Dharma heir. At the time of Tetsugen's request for help, Tetsugyū was serving as the first abbot at Chōkōsan Shōtaiji in Edo. He later succeeded Muan as the second abbot at the Ōbaku sect's headquarters in Edo, Zuishōji in 1675. Tetsugyū spent the majority of his career spreading Ōbaku throughout the Kantō region. Baroni, *Ōbaku Zen*, pp. 77–79.

27. As quoted in Akamatsu, *Tetsugen*, p. 296, and Shimoda, p. 207. The biography is otherwise unidentified and I have been unable to identify either the author or the original text.

28. As quoted in Akamatsu, *Tetsugen*, pp. 296–297.

29. The *Deeds of Tetsugen* claims that the crowd was so large that people would come and camp overnight to guarantee a seat. External sources confirm that the crowd was large, numbering around one thousand.

30. Baroni, *Ōbaku Zen*, p. 190.

31. As quoted in Akamatsu, *Tetsugen*, pp. 123–124.

32. Yoshinaga Utarō, *Tetsugen zenji*, pp. 47–48.

33. Shimoda, pp. 236–240.

34. Satō Fumitsugu, p. 29.

35. Kakugen was a native of Kawachi province, born into a deeply religious family named Ueda. In 1648, at the age of ten, Kakugen climbed Mount Kōya and became a Shingon monk. He was known for his scholarship, especially his knowledge of Sanskrit. His writings include over one hundred titles. He had 436 ordained disciples, and bestowed the precepts on over fifteen thousand lay believers. In addition, Kakugen founded several temples, including Emmyōji in his home village in Nishikibe and Ryōunji in Edo. Kakugen met Tetsugen during his stay at Ninnaji in Kyoto in 1674. Kakugen spent a total of three years in Kyoto studying the Buddhist scriptures.

36. As Ryuichi Abe has established in *The Weaving of Mantra*, Kūkai created the classification of esoteric scriptures as a separate classification within the Buddhist canon. The Chinese edition used by Tetsugen would not therefore have designated the esoteric sutras as such.

37. This is based on a passage from the *Ryōun kaizan Kakugen risshi nempu*, for the year Empō 2, when Kakugen was thirty-six years old, as quoted in Yoshinaga, *Tetsugen zenji*, p. 51. According to Yoshinaga's note on p. 52, the index of esoteric sutras can be found in the *Ōbakuban daizōkyō engishū*.

38. According to Matsunaga Chikai, Kakugen supplied texts that appeared in the Korean edition of the Buddhist scriptures, and in this way a small portion of the Ōbaku edition is based on the Korean canon; pp. 155–157.

39. Washio, *Nihon zenshūshi no kenkyū*, p. 429.

40. The entire text of the *Daizōkyō shōkyo sōchō* is reproduced in Akamatsu, *Tetsugen*, pp. 247–271. The first five dedicated volumes are listed separately at the beginning. The listing then proceeds province by province.

CHAPTER THREE

1. See for example *Dharma Lesson in Japanese* Sec. 2, p. XX.

2. Yanagida Seizan, *Shoki zenshū shishō no kenkyū*, p. 153ff.

3. Yampolsky, *The Platform Sutra of the Sixth Patriarch*, p. 145.

4. Baroni, *Ōbaku Zen*, p. 128ff.

5. The staff of Hōzōin produced a completely new edition in 1971, using a plain modern style of characters. In the preface, the editor Suzuki Ryūshu indicates that the original edition is now too difficult for contemporary people to read with ease. In addition, there are two modern critical editions, those by Akamatsu and Minamoto.

6. T. 8, no. 251, p. 848, lines 3–4.

7. T. 8, no, 251, p. 848, line 5.

8. T. 19, no. 945, p. 131, lines 13–15.

9. Daihōkōengaku shutara ryōgi kyō, T. 17, no. 842, p. 913ff. Scholars now regard the *Perfect Enlightenment Sutra* as apocryphal in its entirety. It was, however, very popular among Zen practitioners in premodern times.

10. The debate is discussed at great length by Jaffe, pp. 36–57.

11. T. 15, no. 653, p. 788, lines c14–16.

12. One is preserved at the Hayashi Bunko in the Ōtani University library, the other at the Naikan Bunko of the Tsuzureko Jinja in Akita Prefecture. The latter has been published in Ishikawa (1996). Jaffe, p. 39.

13. See for example, Akamatsu, p. 80.

14. See Jaffe, pp. 36–57 for a description of that debate.

15. See Baroni, 1994.

16. Ishikawa, p. 84.

17. Ishikawa, p. 85.

CHAPTER FOUR

1. Other biographical pieces composed by Tetsugen's disciples include the Eiran gyōjōki written by Kyōdō Genzui (1663–1730). Kyōdō wrote this shorter biography in 1723 to honor Tetsugen as founder and first head monk of Hōzōin, the primary work site for the scripture project within the grounds of Manpukuji. Kyōdō presents Tetsugen as an incarnation of Shōtoku Taishi (572–621), the Japanese imperial regent known for his strong support in establishing Buddhism in Japan.

2. *Ingen zenshū*, vol. 11, pp. 5105–5106.

3. *Ōbaku Mokuan oshō nempu*, pp. 3b and 4b.

4. Historically, the White Lotus Society (*Pai-lien-she*) was a group of monks and laypeople who performed Pure Land practices on Mt. Lu in China; it was founded by the monk Hui-yüan (334–416; J. Eon) in 420 C.E.

5. The name "Tetsugen" comes from the expression *tetsugen dōsei* (iron eyes and copper pupils), from the *Hekigan roku*, case 23; T 48, no. 2003, p. 141a, lines 18–19.

6. Jaffe, p. 117ff.

7. I have been unable to locate the original in Fukuda writings.

8. See Lincicome, 1995.

9. http://www.osakapubliceng.or.jp/rekishi/uekita/p61e.htm.

10. Reps, p. 36.

11. Foster, "How Shall We Save the World? An Anniversary Essay on a Perennial Topic," from the Buddhist Peace Fellowship website, www.bpf.org.

THE DHARMA LESSON IN JAPANESE

1. Hōshū explains in his postscript to the *Dharma Lesson in Japanese* that Tetsugen wrote the sermon for an individual woman. He gives no other information about her identity, and he does not indicate whether she was a nun or a layperson. Minamoto, *Tetsugen*, p. 268.

2. Minamoto Ryōen, *Tetsugen*, pp. 177–272.

3. The original text has no section headings. Those included here are the author's own, based upon the natural breaks in the original.

4. The Sanskrit term *skandha* is often translated as aggregate, and more literally means "pile" or "heap." The five *skandhas* refer to form (J. *shiki*, Sk. rūpa), sensation (J. *ju*, Sk. vedanā), perception (J. *sō*, Sk. samjñā), psychic construction (J. *gyō*, Sk. samskāra), and consciousness (J. *shiki*, Sk. vijñāna). These are the constituent parts of existing things beyond which they have no "self."

5. The *Heart Sutra* (*Hannya shingyō;* Sk. Prajñāpāramitā-hrdaya-sūtra) is under 300 characters long in Chinese, but is regarded as representing the gist of the Buddhist teaching on emptiness. In the context of the original text, the subject of the passage is Avalokiteśvara. T. 8, no. 251, p. 848, lines 3–4.

6. *Hosshin.* Buddhism speaks of three bodies of the Buddha, the Body of Truth (Dharmākaya), the apparition body (Nirmānakāya), and the Body of Recompense (Sambhogakāya).

7. *Sangai.* The three realms or worlds are, the realm of desire (*yokkai*), the realm of form (*shikikai*), and the realm of no form (*mushikikai*). These represent all levels of existence for sentient beings, from the lowest suffering in hell to the highest existence in heaven or meditative states of bliss.

8. T. 19, p. 111c.

9. *Manbō,* sometimes translated as the myriad things, indicates all things.

10. *Akudō* refers to the lower three of the six paths or levels of existence: hell, hungry ghosts, animals, *asuras*, human beings, and divine beings. There are in addition four higher levels, *srāvakas, pratyekabuddhas,* bodhisattvas and Buddhas, which along with the six others are called the ten worlds (*jikkai*).

11. "Thus Come One" (*Nyorai*) is an epithet for a Buddha.

12. *Nijō* refers to the paths of *srāvakas* (*shōmon*) and *pratyekabuddhas* (*engaku*), and are used in Mahayana to describe Theravada practitioners. *Srāvakas,* "those who hear the voice," originally meant direct disciples of the Buddha, but later came to also mean anyone who attains nirvana through Theravada Buddhism. *Pratyekabuddhas* refers to those who attain enlightenment for themselves without hearing a Buddha teach.

13. T. 8, p. 848.

14. T. 19, p. 117.

15. T. 19, pp. 117 and 118.

16. *Shohō jissō.* This expression appears in several sutras, among them the *Lotus Sutra* (T. 9, p. 5c 11). It is interpreted somewhat differently by various sects.

17. *Sōmoku kokuji shikkai jōbutsu.* Found in the *Nirvana Sutra* and explained in others, this line is not unlike others found in the *Lotus Sutra,* such as *somoku jōbutsu.*

18. *Manbō ichinyo* is a verse from the *Xinxinming* (J. *Shinjinmei*) T. 48, p. 376c. This text is a poem of 146 verses attributed to the Third Patriarch of Zen, Sengcang (J. Sōsan; d. 606). Blyth translates the verse "All things are as they really are," in *Zen and Zen Classics,* vol. 1 (Tokyo: Hokuseido Press, 1966), p. 102.

19. T. 19, p. 147b, 10–11. Tetsugen's text is slightly at variance with the Taishō edition. His uses *ichiji* (translated as "temporarily"), where the Taishō uses *shitsu.* There is no significant change in meaning.

20. *Daihōkōengaku shutara ryōgi kyo,* T.17, p. 914c. This sutra is generally regarded as apocryphal in its entirety. It was, however, very popular among Zen practitioners including Tetsugen who used it, along with the *Śūramgama Sutra,* as the basis for the position that the teaching and meditation are one (*kyōzen itchi*).

21. *Ingen zenshū,* vol. 1, p. 409.

22. Tetsugen alludes here to the Pure Land Sutras without actually quoting from them.

23. *Fushō, fumetsu.* Often translated as unborn and undying, this expression is found in several sutras, including the *Heart Sutra,* T. 8, p. 848. It was popularized by Tetsugen's contemporary Bankei Yōtaku (1622–1693).

24. *Muryō jubutsu,* Sk. Amitayus. Another name for the Buddha Amida.

25. *Amidakyō,* Sk. *Sukhāvatīvyūha,* T. 12, pp. 346–348. This sutra was translated by Kumārajīva circa 402, and is one of the three basic texts for Pure Land Buddhism (*Sanbu kyō*). It describes the pleasures of Amida's Pure Land, and depicts various Buddhas praising Amida.

26. Tetsugen paraphrases from the sutra here. The sutra describes the water in the Pure Land, which has eight good qualities. The birds' songs proclaim "the five virtues, the five powers and the seven steps leading towards the highest knowledge"(Cowell, pp. 95–96), which on hearing, causes human beings to recall the Buddha, the Dharma, and the Sangha. Likewise, the sound of the wind in the trees has the same effect. For full English translation, see E. B. Cowell, *Buddhist Mahayana Texts,* pp. 89–103.

27. Again, Tetsugen is paraphrasing; the original has parallel lines for the Buddhas in each direction. *Kōchō no zessō,* the broad tongue, is one of the thirty-two marks of the Buddha, and alludes to the Buddha's eloquence.

28. T. 9, p. 8b. This and all other translations from the *Lotus Sutra* have been adapted from Hurvitz, *Scripture of the Lotus Blossom of the Fine Dharma,* p. 37.

29. T. 9, p. 9b 10. Hurvitz, p. 41.

30. *Rokuji,* the six objects corresponding to the six senses. They are forms, sounds, scents, tastes, textures, and thoughts. Because sentient beings give rise to desires when they encounter these objects, they are called "dusts" to suggest their potential to taint or sully the mind.

31. *Gokon,* the five senses that correspond to the first five of the six dusts. It is a little odd that Tetsugen did not use the term "six roots" (*rokkon*), the natural complement for the six dusts.

32. This saying can be found in the Record of Linji (Ch. *Linji lu*), T. 47, p. 499c. In this passage, Linji is exhorting his followers not to seek for the Buddha and the Patriarchs, because they will then become fetters.

33. Buddhist texts usually mention 136 hot hells, rather than 130 as mentioned here.

34. *Sanbon kurui gaki. Sanbon* refers to upper, middle, and lower grades, and *kurui* to the nine kinds of *gaki. Gaki* (Sk. *preta*) refers to the second lowest of the six paths in which one suffers perpetual hunger that cannot be satisfied.

35. *Asura* are nonhuman beings characterized by their fierceness and constant fighting. They represent the level just above the human in the six paths. Although there can be good *asura* who protect Buddhism, and this is not universally interpreted as one of the so-called hateful paths, in this context Tetsugen is stressing the quality of suffering inherent in it.

36. This is a standard listing of suffering, which roughly corresponds to the examples of human suffering that the young Sakyamuni encountered in the *Buddhacarita*. Examples of its use are too numerous to cite.

37. Tetsugen has paraphrased the *Dao De Jing*, number 64.

38. Stories of people becoming demons and snakes and so forth abound in collections of Buddhist stories like the *Konjaku monogatari* and the *Nihon ryōiki*. See Marian Ury, *Tales of Times Now Past* for a partial translation of the *Konjaku*, and *Miraculous Stories from the Japanese Buddhist Tradition: The Nihon Ryoiki of the Monk Kyokai*, translated by Kyoko Motomochi Nakamura.

39. Unidentified.

40. T. 17, p. 915c.

41. This is a paraphrase of an earlier citation from the *Lotus Sutra*, see note 28 above.

42. T. 12, 450a.

43. Unidentified.

44. T. 12, 450a. This is the second part of the verse identified in note 28.

45. T. 17, p. 913b 24–25.

46. *Yuishikiron*, or more fully *Jōyuishikiron* (Sk. Vijñapti-mātratā-siddhi) T. 31, no. 1585. This is the primary text for the Hossō school. It comprises various commentaries on Vasubandhu's *Trimsika karika*.

47. T. 31, p. 48a. There is a minor variation between Tetsugen's text and the Taishō edition.

48. T. 8, p. 756c.

49. Huike (J. Eka; 487–593) was the disciple and Dharma heir of Bodhidharma who is said to have brought Chan to China. Tradition says that Huike cut off his arm and presented it to Bodhidharma in order to show his determination. See McRae, especially chapter 2, for what little is known of him historically.

50. Huineng (J. E'nō; 638–713) is known as the author of the *Platform Sutra of the Sixth Patriarch*, which begins with a short account of his life. For a discussion of his life

and the sutra, see Philip Yampolsky's introduction to his translation, *The Platform Sutra of the Sixth Patriarch*.

51. T. 8, p. 755c, 25–26. Tetsugen abbreviates the line that reads, "The three worlds cannot be attained because the past mind has passed away, the present mind does not abide for even a moment, and the future mind does not yet exist."

52. T. 9, p. 5c, 11. Hurvitz, op. cit., pp. 22–23.

53. *Isshin*, the ultimate or Buddha-mind, which penetrates all directions to see things as they are.

54. The expression *honrai muichimotsu* means that there is nothing to cling to, since all things are empty. It appears in the *Platform Sutra*, T. 48, p. 349a.

55. *Itchin*, literally "one dust" or "one defilement."

56. *Shin shinnyomon*, from the *Awakening of Faith* (T. 32, p. 576a). Hakeda translates this passage, "The revelation of the true meaning [of the principle of Mahayana can be achieved] by [unfolding the doctrine] that the principle of One Mind has two aspects. One is the aspect of Mind in terms of the Absolute (*tathata;* Suchness), and the other is the aspect of Mind in terms of phenomena (*samsara;* birth and death)." Hakeda, trans., *The Awakening of Faith*, p. 31.

57. *Shinshōmetsumon*. See note 56.

58. *Shisō* are the four marks characterizing all phenomena: arising (*shō*), abiding (*jū*), changing (*i*), and passing away (*metsu*).

59. *Goyoku*, the five desires generally refer to attachments that arise in connection with the five senses. There are alternative lists, such as desire for wealth, sex, food and drink, fame, and sleep.

60. *Jūaku* are killing living things, stealing, sexual misconduct, lying, saying harsh words, saying words that cause disharmony between others, idle talk, greed, anger, and wrong views.

61. *Gogyaku* are killing one's father, killing one's mother, killing an *arhat*, causing the Buddha's body to bleed, and causing disunity among the *sangha*.

62. *Gyōku* is one of the three basic kinds of suffering endured by sentient beings. The other two kinds of suffering are contact with what one hates and separation from what one loves.

63. T. 17, p. 914a.

64. T. 17, p. 915a.

65. *Ryōgakyō* is one of the basic texts for Zen Buddhism. It teaches about the psychological process of enlightenment culminating in the eighth consciousness, the *alaya* consciousness. There are three translations in Chinese, they are all found in T. 16, nos. 670–672.

66. T. 16, p. 505c.

67. *Ikkō danmu* is one of the heretical views about emptiness that advocates complete rejection of the self and the world and denies the process of causality. No definite cognate exists in English, so I have chosen to translate the term *nihilism* in order to convey in a single term the negative qualities of the position.

68. T. 9, p. 5c; Hurvitz, op. cit., pp. 22–23.

69. T. 9, p. 9b; Hurvitz, op. cit., p. 41.

70. T. 9, p. 43c; Hurvitz, op. cit., p. 243.

71. *Mugen jigoku*, "the hell of unending pain," is another term for *avici* hell, the lowest of the Buddhist hells.

72. *Shozenten* is the lowest of the four meditation heavens in the realm of form over which the god Brahma rules.

73. The parable of the Burning House is found in the *Lotus Sutra*, T. 9, p. 12; Hurvitz, p. 58ff.

74. T. 17, p. 915c.

75. *Honrai no menmoku* is used in the *Mumonkan* (T. 48, p. 295a) and other Zen texts as an expression for the true self or original nature.

76. *Honji (honchi) no fūkō* is used in the *Hekigan roku*, case 99 (T. 48, p. 223b) with the same meaning as *honrai no menmoku*.

77. Changshui Zixuan (J. Chosui Shisen; d. 1038) was a disciple of Huijue (see note 79 below). He wrote a commentary on the *Śūramgama Sutra* in Chinese.

78. T. 19, p. 119c.

79. Huijue (J. Ekaku; dates unknown). A prominent Sung Dynasty Linji master, who was a disciple of Fengyang Shanzhao (947–1024). Huijue lived on Mount Langye and he is sometimes referred to as Master Langye.

80. This exchange is recorded in Changshui's biography in the *Zoku dentōroku*, T. 51, p. 511b.

81. Pūrna (J. Furuna) was one of the ten great disciples of the Buddha, renowned for his eloquence. Tetsugen was compared to him because of his talent for lecturing.

82. Guifeng Zongmi (J. Keihō Shūmitsu; 780–841) was the fifth patriarch of the Huayen school, and also regarded as a third generation Zen master in Heze's lineage. He held the position that the teachings and meditation are one, and wrote a commentary on the *Perfect Enlightenment Sutra*.

83. Unidentified.

84. *Shaba* literally means endurance. It refers to this world in which sentient beings endure pain and affliction.

85. *Honbun no denchi* literally means the portion of land designated to an individual at birth, and is used here as a synonym for original face.

86. T. 19, p. 110c.

87. T. 19, p. 130a.

88. *Hachiman shisen no bonnō* is an expression for all afflictions that hinder one's progress toward enlightenment.

89. *Guren daiguren* (Sk. Padma and Mahāpadma) are the seventh and eighth of the eight freezing hells. The names indicate that they are so cold that the sinners' skin turns crimson and is torn into lotus blossom shapes. They are described in the *Daichido ron*, T. 25, p. 176ff.

90. *Gokai* are the five precepts taken by lay Buddhists, not to kill, not to steal, not to commit adultery, not to lie, and not to drink alcohol.

91. *Jūzen* are: not killing, not stealing, not committing adultery, not lying, not saying evil words, not saying words that cause enmity between others, not engaging in idle talk, not being greedy, not being angry, and not having wrong views.

92. *Hakku* are: birth, old age, illness, death, separation from what one loves, contact with what one hates, not getting what one seeks, growth of mind and body (*gounjōku*).

93. *Gosui* are: clothes becoming soiled, flowers in headdress withering, the body emitting a foul odor, perspiring under the arms, and becoming disinclined to take the appropriate seat or position.

94. *Tajō (dajō) ippen, isshikihen, daishitei no hito, Fugen no kyōgai* all appear in the *Hekigan roku* (cases 6, 42, 41, and 5, respectively) as expressions for breakthrough experiences that are not yet the great enlightenment. Fugen is the Bodhisattva Samantabhadra who represents meditation.

95. T. 19, p. 155a.

96. Linji Yixuan (J. Rinzai Gigen; d. 866) was the first master in the lineage that bears his name. Both the Ōbaku and Japanese Rinzai sects are part of this lineage.

97. Deshan Xuanjian (J. Tokusan Senkan; 782–865) was one of the prominent masters of the Tang Dynasty, well known for his use of shouts and the stick on his disciples.

98. *Inka* are seals of recognition used in the Zen school bestowed by a master on a disciple to certify the disciple's attainment of enlightenment.

99. *Katsu* is a shout characteristic of many Rinzai masters. It is often used to jar disciples out of the constraints of discursive thought so that they may attain enlightenment.

100. Kujari (Sk. Makkhali Gosāla) was a philosopher in ancient India and one of the six opponents of the Buddha. We know of his thought from the *Jōagongyō* (Sk. Dīrghāgama) T. 1, no. 1, and the *Daihatsu nehangyō* (Sk. Mahāparinirvanasūtra) T. 1, no. 7. He denied the truth of karmic causality. His teaching is one of the classical examples of wrong views. He is likewise mentioned in the *Śūramgama Sutra*, T. 19, no. 945, p. 121c, line 10.

101. T. 19, p. 111a.

102. *Kenmon kakuchi* refers to all the workings of the six or eight (depending on the school of thought) consciousnesses.

103. T.19, p. 109a.

104. Tetsugen makes reference here to a state of "equilibrium" or "centrality" spoken of in Neo-Confucian texts. The *locus classicus* for all Neo-Confucian discussion of this state is found in the first chapter of *The Mean*. For Juxi's comments on this passage from *The Mean*, see *Reflections of Things at Hand*, translated by Wing-tsit Chan, pp. 129–130.

105. *Daihasshiki* is another term for the *alaya* consciousness, since it is the eighth of the eight consciousness used by Yogācāra (Hossō) thought to describe perception. The first five correspond to the five senses, the sixth to the mind that discriminates objects, the seventh, called *manas* consciousness, is ego awareness, and the eighth is the *alaya* consciousness, which acts as a kind of storehouse for all sensory perceptions and thoughts.

106. *Sangai yuishiki* is the opening line of the *Yuishikinijuron*, T. 31, p. 74b.

107. *Konshin* are the five senses; *shushi* (or *shuji*) are the "seeds" that make perception possible; and *kikai* is the "vessel realm," the physical environment.

108. T. 19, p. 124c.

109. *Kenshō jōbutsu* is a very common expression in Zen texts for enlightenment.

110. *Daigo daitetsu* is another expression for enlightenment used by Yinyuan, see *Ingen zenshū* II, p. 932.

111. *Jakumetsu iraku* is found in the *Nirvana Sutra*, T. 12, p. 451a.

112. T. 19, p. 131a.

113. T. 19, p. 113c.

114. Tetsugen appears to be paraphrasing a line from the Genjō kōan chapter of Dōgen's *Shōbōgenzō*, found in T. 82, p. 25a. Francis Cook translates the verse, "Because the wind is eternal, the wind of Buddhism manifests the yellow gold of the earth and turns the rivers into sweet cream." Cook, *Sounds of Valley Streams*, p. 69.

115. Yunmen Wenyen (J. Unmon Bun'en; 864–949) was a founder of one of the "Five Houses" of Chan during the Tang dynasty. Many chapters from the *Mumonkan* and *Hekigan roku* concern him. See Urs App, *Master Yunmen* (Kodansha International, 1994).

116. *Hekigan roku*, T. 48, p. 239b.

117. Zhaozhou Ts'ung-shen (J. Jōshū Jūshin; 778–897) was a eccentric Tang master who appears often in the kōan collections. See Dumoulin, vol. 1, pp. 167–168.

118. *Hekigan roku*, T. 48, p. 263a. Tetsugen's quotation differs somewhat from the Taishō text.

119. *Hekigan roku*, T. 48, p. 226c.

120. *Mumonkan*, case 46, T. 48, p. 298c.

INSTRUCTING THE COMMUNITY

1. In East Asia, the Buddha's birthday is traditionally observed on the eighth day of the fourth lunar month.

2. The mother of Siddharta Gautama, the historical Buddha.

3. Avalokiteśvara, the bodhisattva of infinite compassion who is able to save all sentient beings, wherever they may be.

4. *Shidai*, earth, water, fire, and wind. According to Buddhist thought, human beings, like all other phenomena, are comprised of a composition of these four elements

5. An intense state of concentration achieved through meditation, in which the distinction between subject and object is transcended.

6. Within the *Śūramgama Sutra*, the Buddha uses an example of cataracts causing an individual to see illusionary flowers in the sky to explain the arising of mistaken views. T. 19, no. 945, p. 120b, line 29ff.

7. In East Asia, the death of the Buddha is traditionally commemorated on the fifteenth day of the second lunar month.

8. Unborn (*mushō*) and Undying (*fushi*) are parallel terms used to describe Buddha nature as beyond birth and death. Although all phenomenal things arise, change, and pass away, they are all characterized by emptiness, and in this sense are not subject to birth and death.

9. An indirect reference to the line "kyakkonka koshisen fudan" (Under the heel, the red silk thread has not been cut), a turning word used by the Chinese Linji master Songyuan Zhongyue (1132–1202). The silk thread refers to sexual relations between men and women.

10. A figure mentioned in the *Śūramgama Sutra*, T. 19, no. 945, p. 121b, line 10ff. Yajñadatta looked at himself in a mirror, and became angry that he could not see his own face. He decided that he was possessed by a ghost and had lost his head. He thus drove himself insane.

11. *Kōgai no haru*, literally the spring ouside of the four kinds of kalpas. The phrase refers to the state of enlightenment.

12. *Ango*, the rainy season retreat held by Buddhist monasteries during the summer months, traditionally from the middle of the fourth lunar month until the middle of the seventh lunar month. Zen monasteries generally hold two three-month retreats, one in summer and the other in winter. During these periods, the monks or nuns in residence intensively practice meditation.

13. *Kyakkonka*, literally "under one's heels." The expression is used in Zen literature, such as case 53 of the Blue Cliff Record, to refer to the original self.

14. See note 11 above.

15. Many meditation halls in Japan have an image of a dragon painted on the ceiling.

16. A means by which all sentient beings can be saved. In the Universal Gate chapter of the *Lotus Sutra*, Kannon saves numerous sentient beings by assuming thirty-thee different forms.

17. Yang Guifei (d. 755) the favorite concubine of the Tang dynasty emperor Xuanzong (r. 712–756). She is regarded as one of the four great beauties from Chinese history. She was blamed for the An Lushan rebellion, and forced to hang herself with a silken cord given her by the emperor.

18. The fabric from Sichuan was regarded as especially elegant, hence the term came to be used for any beautiful fabric.

19. Lingyun Zhijin (n.d.), a Tang dynasty Chan monk who attained enlightenment after seeing peach blossoms.

DHARMA WORDS

1. The translation is based on the version found in the *Tetsugen Zenji Yuiroku*, first fascicle, pp. 3a–4a.

2. Yoshinaga, *Tetsugen zenji*, pp. 101–102.

3. The perfect wisdom of an enlightened being.

4. Good or bad karma from a previous existence that impacts the present life.

5. The eight levels of human consciousness that the Yogācāra school of Buddhism uses to describe the human psyche. The first five consciousnesses correspond to the five senses. The remaining include mind consciousness, ego consciousness, and the store-house (*alaya*) consciousness. According to Yogācāra thought, everything we experience in the phenomenal world is a product of the eight consciousnesses of the mind.

6. *Honbun no denchi,* a Zen term used synonymously with Original Nature.

7. The image of warf and woof comes from weaving. The warp runs the length of the cloth, while the woof is woven into it.

8. Tetsugen is alluding here to a famous verse attributed to the Buddha immediately after his birth. He is said to have exclaimed, "In heaven above and earth below, I alone am worthy of reverence. This is my last birth, I am born for enlightenment." The passage is found in several scriptures, including the Daitōsaiiki, T. 51, no. 2087, p. 902a, line 27.

9. Hoshino Kanzaemon (1642–1696) was a well-known archer of the day, from Owari province. In 1666 he won the tournament and set a record for shooting 6,666 arrows through the hall at Sanjūsangendo. In 1668, he lost to Sonoemon Kasai. In 1669, Hoshino again broke the record, shooting 8,000 arrows over a period of about twenty-four hours. Although he said that he had the strength to continue, he stopped so as not to discourage others from attempting to break his record. He was known as the best archer in Japan for many years.

10. *Konsan,* an abbreviation for *konchin sanran,* literally "sinking into darkness and disturbed by distractions" and could be translated more freely as depressed and distracted.

11. *Jiko menmoku,* a Zen expression for the original state of enlightenment, which we all possess. In this case, it refers to the attainment of enlightenment. The expression is found throughout Zen literature, especially the *Mumonkan,* Case 23, T. 48, no. 2005, p. 296a, lines 1–3.

12. *Sangai,* a Buddhist expression for the worlds inhabited by unenlightened beings, the realms of desire, form and formlessness. In the lowest realm of desire, sentient beings experience various forms of sensual desire. In the realm of form, sentient beings possess a physical form, but do not experience desires. In the highest realm of formlessness, sentient being have no physical form and exist in meditative states.

13. *Nijō* refers to *śrāvakas* (voice hearers) *pratyeka buddhas* generally associated with Hinayana Buddhism. In the Mahayana traditions, they are regarded as inferior to those in the third vehicle, bodhisattvas, because they focus selfishly on their own attainment of enlightenment.

14. The text is corrupt here.

15. The text is corrupt here.

16. Huike (487–593; J. Eka) is regarded as the Second Chinese Patriarch of Chan Buddhism. Tetsugen refers here to Case 41 of the *Mumonkan,* T. 48, no. 2005, p. 298a lines 15–24.

17. Tetsugen alludes here to a passage in the *Śūramgama Sutra* in which the Buddha tells Ananda that his perception of false appearances based on external objects has

confused him to such an extent that he would confuse a thief for his own child. T. 19, no. 945, p. 108c, lines 20–21.

18. *Tetsui*, the outermost of the seven mountain ranges around Mount Sumeru which forms the outer periphery of the world in Buddhist cosmology.

RESPONSE TO LAY BUDDHIST NORITOMI TESSEN

1. *Tetsugen Zenji Yuiroku*, second fascicle, pp. 2a–3a.

2. *Shujinō*, an alternate form of the more common *shujinkō*. The expression literally means master, and is used in Zen literature as another term for one's Original Nature. The term is used in Case no. 12 of the *Mumonkan*, in which Ruiyan calls to himself as master. T. 48, no. 2005, p. 294b, line 19.

3. It is not clear from what source Tetsugen is quoting. From the context, it appears that these expressions may have appeared in Noritomi's original letter to Tetsugen. In any case, they are quite similar to statement found throughout Mahayana literature, including Zen writings. The problem seems to be how the expressions were used, and not necessarily with the ideas expressed.

4. Tetsugen paraphrases a line from Case no. 10 of the *Hekiganroku*. The original reads: Nitaru koto ha sunawachi nitarizenaru koto ha sunawachi imada zenarazu. T. 48, no. 2003, p. 150b, line 13.

5. Bodhidharma coming from the West is a common Zen expression for the teachings or the essence of Zen.

6. Pointing fingers and the other actions mentioned here are all reminiscent of teaching techniques employed by the great Zen masters of earlier periods. Tetsugen suggests that while his contemporaries imitate the external behavior, they lack the internal insight.

7. *Kikutsuri kakkei*, a Zen term describing unenlightened existence, especially when a person is mistakenly attached to the teaching of emptiness, an attitude somewhat akin to nihilism.

8. *Tōga no insu*, a term which implies a false certification of enlightenment, one bestowed on an undeserving disciple, or more likely, bestowed by a false teacher. Used in Case no. 98 of the *Hekiganroku*, T. 48, no. 2003, p. 221c, line 3.

9. *Inchaku*, literally "the seal makes an imprint." The term is rare, but found in *Juanxin fayao* of Huangbo, T. 48, no. 2012, p. 382a.

10. *Reikon*, literally the root of spirituality. The term means either morality or virtue.

11. *Shōji gantō ni oite daijizai o u.* Found in Case no. 1 of the *Mumonkan*, T. 48, no. 2005, p. 293a, line 9.

12. *Shusō*, a term for a Dharma heir or a true disciple who can transmit the teachings of the school.

A LETTER SENT TO ACTING HEAD MONK HŌSHŪ

1. The translation is based on the version found in the *Tetsugen Zenji Yuiroku*, second fascicle, pp. 3a–4b.

2. *Shōshō reirei*, a term used in the *Record of Linji* to mean radiance and brilliance. T. 47, no. 1985, p. 502b, line 12.

3. *Kikutsuri kakkei*, a Zen term describing unenlightened existence, especially when a person is mistakenly attached to the teaching of emptiness, an attitude somewhat akin to nihilism.

4. *Ginzan teppeki*, a Zen expression for enlightenment or ultimate reality, which appears inaccessible to ordinary people.

5. *Kengai sasshu*, an expression for enlightenment found in Case no. 32 of the *Mumonkan*, T. no. 2005, p. 297b, line 2.

6. *Kantō shinpo*, an expression for enlightenment, the title of Case no. 46 of the *Mumonkan*, T. 48, no. 2005, p. 298c, line 11.

7. *Daishi ichiban*, a Zen expression for enlightenment, indicating that one surpasses the old patterns of discriminative thought.

8. Not identified.

9. *Ronen*, a Zen expression indicating that something that will never happen. In the Chinese calendar of twelve-year cycles, there is no year of the donkey.

10. *Daichi ni suntdo nashi*, an expression for enlightenment that transcends the distinctions of large and small. Found in the *Recorded Sayings of Dahui*, T. 47, no. 1998a, p. 853c, lines 18–19.

11. *Gengyō*, a concept from Yogācāra thought. Experiences based on sensory perception cause seeds in the *Alaya* consciousness. Present manifestations are then caused by the seeds. These manifestations appear to be objective, external reality, but are actually the product of the conscious mind.

12. *Kunjū*, perfuming impressions that influence the seeds in the *Alaya* consciousness.

13. Śāriputra was one of the ten outstanding disciples of the historical Buddha, renowned as the foremost in wisdom.

14. Pūrna was one of the ten outstanding disciples of the historical Buddha, renowned as the foremost in wisdom.

15. Unidentified.

AN OPPORTUNITY FOR INSTRUCTION

1. Minamoto Ryōen, *Tetsugen*, pp. 275–283.

2. Sōtō temple, founded in 1600 by Denshi Rinteki. It is located in Kumamoto city, in Kumamoto prefecture.

3. A *kan* is a unit of weight approximately equal to 3.75 kilograms, or 8.27 pounds. One hundred thousand *kan* would weigh 827,000 pounds, and is obviously used here as an impossibly large amount.

4. According to traditional biographies of King Aśoka, in a previous lifetime as a boy named Jaya, Aśoka made an offering of dirt to the Buddha as he passed through the city of Rajagra, vowing to become a king who would honor the Buddha. The Buddha was not insulted by the boy's action, but saw the offering as the seed for his future

existence as king. See John S. Strong, *The Legend of King Aśoka* (Princeton, 1983), pp. 198–201.

5. From Indian mythology, known as Yama in Sanskrit. Emma is the ruler of demons, who confronts the dead with a record of their actions and determines subsequent reward or punishment. According the Chinese Buddhist tradition, Emma is one of ten kings who govern the netherworld. The episode mentioned here has not been identified in the Taishō edition of the *Lotus Sutra*.

6. The Eight Schools of Japanese Buddhism include the six Nara period schools, Kusha, Jōjitsu, Ritsu, Hossō, Sanron, and Kegon, as well as the two Heian period sects of Tendai and Shingon. The expression may imply all forms of Buddhism.

7. *Avici* hell, the worst of the eight Buddhist hells.

8. An ancient Indian unit of distance, based on the how far the royal army could march in one day, approximately fifteen to twenty kilometers.

9. *Shōnen* is one part in the Eightfold Path of Buddhism.

10. *Ukiyo*, the pleasure quarters found in larger Japanese cities during the Tokugawa period. The pleasure quarters included brothels, theaters, tea houses, and public baths.

11. *Rokudo*, the six realms of existence into which sentient beings may be born: hell dwellers, hungry ghosts, animals, human beings, ashura and heaven dwellers.

A BRIEF ACCOUNT OF THE HISTORY OF CARVING THE BUDDHIST SCRIPTURES

1. Minamoto Ryōen, *Tetsugen*, pp. 275–283.

2. Buddhist monk from central India who, according to legend, rendered the first Chinese translation of the *Sutra in Forty-Two Sections* with the assistance of Ju Falan. Legend says that the Emperor Ming Di (r. 57–75 c.e.) had a dream that prompted him to bring translators including Kāśyapa Mātanga to China to work on translating Buddhist scriptures, which would have been the first in Chinese. No translations by Kāśyapa Mātanga are extant.

3. Tradition credits Kāśyapa Mātanga with translating five sutras in addition to *the Sutra in Forty-Two Sections*. None are extant.

4. Xuanzang (596–664), a Chinese Buddhist monk who traveled to Central Asia and India to study Buddhism and collect Buddhist texts. He departed China in 629, and returned in 645 with 657 texts. He then turned his attention to translating some of these texts into Chinese, completing 73 translations.

5. Tripitaka; the collection of Buddhist scriptures. In many contexts, the term refers exclusively to the Theravada scriptures, but in East Asia, the term is often used more broadly for all the Buddhist scriptures, Mahayana and Theravada alike.

6. A Chinese woodblock edition of the Buddhist scriptures was first produced during the Song dynasty, with a government-sponsored edition completed in 983 c.e. Numerous editions were produced over the centuries following that time. Tetsugen based his own edition on a late Ming dynasty edition, known as the Wanli edition.

7. Buddhism was first transmitted to Japan from Korea, when the king of Paekche sent an image of the Buddha and some scriptures to Emperor Kimmei (r. 531–571).

According to the account found in the *Nihongi*, this occurred in the year 552; other sources date the event to 538.

8. The second of three ages of the Dharma after the death of the historical Buddha. The Semblence Dharma follows the age of the True Dharma. According to some Buddhist traditions, during this intermediate stage, the doctrines and the practice of Buddhism remain intact, but the attainment of complete enlightenment was no longer possible. Tetsugen's comment is somewhat strange, since most Japanese assumed that the Semblence Age was long past, and that they were indeed living in the third and final age of the Dharma, known in Japanese as *Mappō*.

9. Yinyuan Longqi (1594–1673) was the founder of the Ōbaku sect in Japan. Born in China, Yinyuan emigrated to Japan in 1654 and founded the main monastery of the sect, Ōbakusan Mampukuji. See Baroni, *Ōbaku Zen*.

10. Shenzong reigned from 1573 until 1634.

11. Daguang Zhenge (1543–1603), Chinese Buddhist monk who served as abbot at Jingliang monastery in Beijing.

12. Micang Daokai (n.d.) began the Jiaxing edition of the Buddhist scriptures in 1587, along with Daguang Zhenge. The edition was completed in 1635.

13. The Buddha, the Dharma and the Sangha, or the Buddha, his teachings and the community of believers. Buddhists revere these three as the basis for their faith.

14. In Japan, families from the nobility and the warrior class built family Buddhist temples (*bodaiji*) for honoring their deceased ancestors. By the Tokugawa period, this was a long-standing custom, and most important families had such a family temple.

15. *Zenbō*. In the Spring and Autumn Annals, this term referred to a reed whip used on frontline troops. During the Ching dynasty, it came to refer to someone seated in the front row at an exam.

A REPORT ON PROGRESS MADE ON THE NEW EDITION OF THE BUDDHIST SCRIPTURES

1. See Baroni, *Ōbaku Zen*, pp. 176–180.

2. The translation is based on the version found in the *Tetsugen Zenji Yuiroku*, second fascicle, pp. 29a–30b.

3. Tetsugen was a Dharma heir of the Ōbaku master Muan. Counting back through the generations of Dharma heirs, he was in the thirty-fourth generation after Linji, the patriarch of the Rinzai sect.

4. Rinzai Shōshū, a term used by Ōbaku monks to refer to the Ōbaku sect in Japan, and to the earlier Chinese Linji lineage from which they counted their descent. The term was first used in China. See Baroni, *Ōbaku Zen*, pp. 22–23.

5. Tetsugen's subtemple at Ōbakusan Mampukuji, which still houses the woodblocks for the Ōbaku edition of the scriptures. The temple was first built in 1669, on a different site, where it was little more than a storehouse. It was soon moved to the present location outside the main precincts of the monastery.

6. *Kūmon*, the term may refer specifically to the Mahayana Buddhist doctrine of emptiness (*sunyata*), but in this case means simply Buddhism.

7. *Shijū no on,* according to East Asian Buddhism, human beings owe debts of gratitude to various benefactors. There are several versions of the list of four great debts. For example, (1) parents, (2) living beings, (3) country and rulers, and (4) the Three Treasures. Alternatives include (1) heaven and earth, (2) teachers, (3) country and rulers, and (4) parents.

8. *Shingen,* emptiness, or one's true nature.

9. Akamatsu's edition of Tetsugen's writings has a different line, which reads, "a corresponding manifestation as of old." See Akamatsu, *Tetsugen Zenji Kana hōgo,* p. 59.

10. A region named in the Spring and Autumn Annals, which was famous for its jade.

11. A region known for its horses.

12. *Ryūten,* in the Buddhist cosmology, these are two kinds of sentient beings that protect the Buddhist Dharma.

13. Two of the ancient legendary Sage Emperors praised by Confucius as ideal rulers, possessed of exceptional wisdom and virtue. Yao is said to have reigned from 2357 to 2256 B.C.E., and Shun, his successor, is said to have reigned from 2255 to 2206 B.C.E.

AN ACCOUNT OF COMPLETING THE BUDDHIST SCRIPTURES

1. The translation is based on the version found in the *Tetsugen Zenji Yuiroku,* second fascicle, pp. 30b–32a.

2. *Kinsen* and *Kakuō* are two epithets for the Buddha.

3. The name of a small kingdom in what is now Nepal and its capital city, the home of the Śakya people. The historical Buddha was born near there, and raised in the city.

4. *Senbu,* one of four continents around Mount Sumeru, located to the south, inhabited by human beings.

5. *Tenchū no ten,* an honorific title given to the historical Buddha.

6. *Kezō nijū no sekai,* the Pure Lands of the Bliss Bodies of various Buddhas.

7. *Taimō,* a metaphor used especially in Huayen Buddhism for the complete interdependence and interpenatration of all things. The Hindu deity Indra's palace is said to be adorned with a wondrous net comprised of mutually reflecting jewels.

8. *Gyokugō,* the tuft of white hair between the Buddha's eyebrows from which he sends forth light to illuminate all worlds. The white tuft of hair is one of the thirty-two marks, or distinguishing physical characteristics, of a Buddha.

9. *Daika,* an abbreviated form of *Arirabatsudaika,* a river near the spot where the historical Buddha died.

10. *Hajun,* an evil king living in one of the heavens, who strives to prevent Buddhists from attaining their goals.

11. *Shishō,* those born from a womb, from an egg, from moisture, and from metamorphosis. Tetsugen alludes here to the death of the Buddha, which is regarded within the tradition as a conscious decision made by a fully enlightened being.

12. *Sangai*, the three realms that encompass all of the six paths in *samsara*, from the heavens down to the hells. The realm of desire encompasses the hells through the lower heavens, where sentient beings experience various forms of desire, including sexuality. The realm of form comprises the middle heavens, where heaven dwellers have material form, but experience no desires. The realm of no form represents the highest heavens, where heaven dwellers have no material form and exist in pleasant meditative states. Although the higher realms are pleasant, sentient beings born in them remain trapped in the cycle of rebirth, and hence are subject to suffering.

13. *Hippakutsu*, the cave near Rajagrha, where the first Buddhist council was held, shorly after the Buddha's death, to preserve his teachings.

14. Kudara is the Japanese name for the Korean kingdom of Paekche. The Korean ruler sent a gilt bronze image of the Buddha along with some Buddhist sutras to Emperor Kimmei of Japan in 538. (The *Nihongi* dates the event to 552.) This represented the first official transmission of Buddhism to Japan.

15. *Eshu*, an allusion to a parable from chapter eight of the *Lotus Sutra* about a young man whose friend sews a priceless pearl into his robe before he sets out on a journey.

16. *Goten*, literally five heavens, the term refers to the north, south, east, west, and central regions of the Indian subcontinent.

17. *Karyō sen'on*, a mythical bird with a sweet song, said to inhabit the Himalaya mountains.

18. *Mōki no ki*, a metaphor for how rare and difficult it is to be born as a human being and encounter the Buddha's teachings. A turtle with an eye only on its stomach, that surfaces only occasionally. In order for it to see the sun, it must cling to a piece of driftwood.

19. *Shiku* may refer to any division into four parts. In Zen Buddhist texts, it usually refers to the four propositions of affirmation, negation, both affirmation and negation, and neither affirmation nor negation.

20. *Kinnō zensei*, a metaphor used for a ruler maintaining the territorial integrity of the nation.

POETRY

1. *Tetsugen Zenji Yuiroku*, first fascicle, pp. 5a–24a.

2. Hōsenji is in Fukai, Sakai city, in Osaka-fu.

3. Heavenly beings who live long, happy lives, but are nevertheless subject to death and rebirth in the cycle of samsara.

4. Nanke is the name of a nonexistent place. A man dreamed that he had become governor of Nanke. Hence, Nanke's dream is a metaphor for an empty or baseless dream.

5. *Kintō*, an abbreviation for *kinjō tōchi*, the image of an impregnable castle is used in Buddhist texts for protectors of the Buddhist Dharma.

6. *Goyoku*, the five desires that arise from the workings of the five senses. In other contexts, it may refer to the desires for wealth, sex, food and drink, fame, and sleep.

7. *Sansun,* literally, "three inches."

8. *Keie,* literally "rice paddy robe." Tetsugen probably refers here to the *rakusu,* a Buddhist robe made from piecing together rectangles and squares of fabric.

9. The image created here is of two people sharing a burden carried on a pole laid across their shoulders. Usually a single individual carries a load in this manner.

10. *Genkaku,* a mythical crane that changes color from white to gray at age one thousand, and again to black at age two thousand.

11. An image of suffering in a Buddhist hell.

12. Appears to be an allusion to lines from the *Śūramgama Sutra,* T. 19, no. 945, p. 106a, lines 1–2.

13. *Shujinō,* an alternate form of the more common *shujinkō.* The expression literally means master, and is used in Zen literature as another term for one's Original Nature. The term is used in Case no. 12 of the *Mumonkan,* in which Ruiyan calls to himself as master. T. 48, no. 2005, p. 294b, line 19.

14. This Buddhist name can be translated Set Free Far and Wide, Entrusted to One's Nature. Tetsugen uses the name within the poem.

15. *Kihō,* can also be translated as "opportunity and Dharma," in Pure Land thought, it means that while sentient beings believe in the Buddha, the Buddha's power saves sentient beings.

16. *Zenyo,* a Zen term referring to time away from the practice of seated meditation.

17. This line can also be translated "The drunken man does not realize the pleasures of the Buddhist teachings."

18. A Buddhist nun who donated one thousand *ryō* of gold to Tetsugen to begin his scripture project.

19. *Fukuden,* Buddhist monks and nuns are compared to fertile fields. When laypeople make donations to the clergy, they accrue merit, just as one harvests crops after planting a field.

AN AFFIDAVIT CONCERNING
THE DHARMA DEBATE IN MORI

1. Baroni, "Bottled Anger: Episodes in Ōbaku Conflict in the Tokugawa Period," in *Journal of Japanese Religious Studies,* vol. 21, nos. 2–3, June–Sept., 1994, pp. 191–210.

2. Minamoto Ryōen, *Tetsugen,* Nihon no Zen goroku, vol. 17, pp. 287–308.

3. Kurushima Michikyo (1629–1700) served as the provincial governor (*daimyō*) of Bungo, on the island of Kyūshū. His family temple was Anrakuji, in the castle town of Mori, where Tetsugen gave the lectures that precipitated the events described in this document.

4. The Heroic Valor Sutra, T. 19, no. 945, an apocryphal sutra in ten fascicles, probably originally composed in Chinese. Translation is attributed to Paramiti. The text is a discourse on the workings of the mind, and much favored by the Zen sect in China and

Japan. It should be noted that there are two sutras known by the same name; the other is the more famous scripture translated by Kumārajīva.

5. Daitsūsan Anrakuji is a Sōtō temple located in the city of Mori, in present day Ōita prefecture.

6. Another name for Jōdo Shinshū, the True Pure Land sect of Japanese Buddhism. The term *ikkō* means "single-minded" and refers to Pure Land believers' exclusive devotion to Amida Buddha and to the sect itself.

7. Kengan Zen'etsu (1618–1696) a Rinzai monk, who served as head monk at Tafukuji in Bungo province. Kengan had very early contact with Ōbaku masters. Tetsugen practiced under his guidance at Tafukuji, and it was Kengan who first introduced him to the *Śūramgama Sutra*. Tetsugen heard Kengan lecture on it during the Autumn of 1661.

8. *Mappō*, according to one Buddhist notion of history, the third and final age of the Buddhist teachings after the death of the Buddha, which will last ten thousand years. *Mappō* is the degenerate age, when the true Dharma has declined to such an extent that no one can attain enlightenment or even adequately practice Buddhism. Eventually, a new age of the Dharma will be ushered in by the birth of the next Buddha, Maitreya. In Japan, it was popularly believed that the age of *Mappō* began during the eleventh century.

9. T. 19, no. 945, p. 131c, lines 13–14.

10. An evil deity who reigns in the highest heaven within the realm of desire. Pāpīyas is an enemy of Buddhism who tries to prevent Buddhist practitioners from attaining enlightenment.

11. *Oni* are demons or ogres from Japanese mythology. They are usually depicted with horns and ferocious faces. They are sometimes associated with the demons that torture sentient beings in hell.

12. *Yakshas* are demons from Indian mythology who harm human beings.

13. *Rakshasas* are demons from Indian mythology with supernatural power to entice human beings, whom they then devour.

14. Hinayana (J. Shōjō), a derogatory name used by Mahayana proponents for the early Buddhist teachings and the surviving Theravada school of Buddhism. Mahayana means Great Vehicle, which is said to enable all human beings to practice Buddhism and attain enlightenment; this is contrasted with the so-called Lesser Vehicle, which is accessible by only a few.

15. *Mugen jigoku*, a Japanese name for *Avici* hell, the worst of the eight great hells described in Buddhist cosmology. The suffering in *Avici* hell is interminable.

16. Throughout the above paragraphs, Tetsugen paraphrases the *Śūramgama Sutra*, T. 19, no. 945, p. 131ff.

17. "Question and answer," discussions between an individual Zen teacher and a student; *mondō* often take place privately during interviews between master and disciple. While the student may challenge the master with a question, the purpose is generally for the student to assert his or her understanding of the Dharma. In other cases, the teacher questions the student to ascertain his or her progress.

18. *Koku* is a unit of volume, used to measure large quantities of rice. One *koku* of rice is approximately 180 liters, or 5 bushels. One *koku* is theoretically enough rice to feed a single individual for one year. Two *koku* would be enough rice to feed approximately 720 people for one day.

19. Buddhist monastic robe.

20. A reference to the *Analects* of Confucius, chapter 6, number 25. "A goblet that is not a goblet. A goblet indeed a goblet indeed." The goblet, *gu* in Chinese, had a standard volume.

21. *Shuryōgon* is actually a transliteration of the Sanskrit term Śūramgama, Heroic Valour. The characters used to render the sound do not carry the same meaning.

22. T. 8, no. 235, p. 752b.

23. T. 19, no. 945, 131a, line 14.

24. T. 9, no. 262, p. 10c, line 4, and p. 13a, line 14.

25. T. 12, no. 374, p. 375a, line 27.

26. *Dainichi Nyorai,* the Japanese name for Mahāvairocana Buddha, the universal Buddha.

27. *Shobutsu no Kōmyō,* a reference to Amida Buddha

28. T. 9, no. 262, p. 2c, line 9, and p. 32c, line 29.

29. T. 17, no. 842. Allusion not found.

30. *Xiao jing,* a Confucian text from the Han dynasty, attributed to Zeng Zi, a disciple of Confucius. The text takes the form of a discussion between Confucius and Zeng Zi.

31. T. 19, no. 945, p. 110c, line 27 to p. 11a, line 1.

32. T. 19, no. 945, pp. 147b, lines 19–20.

33. Unidentified.

LETTER TO LORD KURUSHIMA

1. Minamoto Ryōen, *Tetsugen,* Nihon no Zen goroku, vol. 17, pp. 311–317.

2. Both temples are affiliated with with the Honganji branch of the True Pure Land sect. They are located in Kusu, in Ōita prefecture.

3. "The Divine Husbandman," the second of three legendary Sage Emperors of China, said to have lived and reigned in the twenty-eighth century B.C.E. Shen Nong is said to have compiled a catalog of 365 medicinal plants, which became the basis for traditional Chinese herbal medicine. He is also said to have invented the plough and introduced agriculture to the people.

4. A fully enlightened person; the Buddha. In this case, it refers to the Buddha.

LETTER TO YAMAZAKI HANZAEMON

1. Minamoto Ryōen, *Tetsugen,* Nihon no Zen goroku, vol. 17, pp. 321–333.

2. A townsman from Edo, who lived in the Aoyama residential district. Yamazaki Hanzaemon is listed as one of the contributors to the Scripture project.

3. *Dacheng qixin lun* (J. Daijō kishin ron), a comprehensive summary of Mahayana teachings, traditionally attributed to Aśvaghoṣa. See Yoshito S. Hakeda, trans., *The Awakening of Faith* (Columbia University Press, 1967).

4. An alcoholic beverage, usually distilled from grain or sweet potatoes. Most popular in Kyūshū, where most *shōchū* is produced. The beverage was introduced to Japan from Ryūkyū during the sixteenth century.

5. Dragons, or Naga, are among the eight types of beings said to protect Buddhism.

6. A measure of weight; 200 *ryō* weighs approximately 750 grams, or 26.4 ounces. During the Tokugawa period, the standard gold coin, called a *koban*, weighed one *ryō*. In the modern period, one *ryō* became one yen.

7. Perhaps Ujihara Kisaemon, a merchant from Osaka.

8. A unit of volume, used especially to measure rice. One *go* is approximately 180 ml, or one-third of a pint. It is commonly regarded as a standard serving for one person.

9. In modern currency, one *sen* equals 0.01 yen. In the premodern period, it was not standardized, but is presumably a small amount of money.

10. According to Buddhist cosmology, hungry ghosts are one of the six types of sentient beings that exist, representing one of the three so-called hateful paths in which one suffers great pain. Because their necks are as narrow as a needle, they cannot satisfy their constant hunger, and they are generally pictured with the bloated stomach of a famine victim. Hungry ghosts are said to live just outside of hell or in one of the upper regions of hell. They wander into the human world searching for garbage and excrement to eat.

11. Maudgalyāyana was one of the ten great disciples of the historical Buddha, known for his psychic powers. When his mother died, he used his power to discover her next rebirth. He first searched the upper paths of heaven dwellers and human beings, but finally found her suffering as a hungry ghost. She is said to have eagerly accepted his initial offering of food and water, but they turned to fire in her mouth. Eventually the Buddha explained that the way to feed the hungry ghosts was to make offerings to the sangha at the end of the rainy season retreat. This became the basis for Obon (Sk. Ullambana).

12. Kumano Sansha, three Shintō shrines located in the Kumano district of Wakayama prefecture. These were extremely popular pilgrimage sites during the Tokugawa period.

13. A mythical creature with a long beak, wings, shining eyes, and a human torso with arms and legs. *Tengu* are known as spirits that reside in the mountains, who make their nests in large trees. They are said to kidnap Buddhist monks and tie them to the treetop, implanting in them thoughts of greed and pride to hinder their practice.

14. Hōshū Dōsō (1644–1720) was one of Tetsugen's leading disciples. After Tetsugen's death, he became a disciple of Muan, and received *inka* in the first month of Tenna 4 (1683). He eventually designated some 20 Dharma heirs of his own. In 1714,

he wrote the traditional biography of Tetsugen, the *Tetsugen Osho Kojitsu,* included in the Appendix.

15. A portable wooden structure used to close off the entry gate to a Zen temple.

THE DEEDS OF TETSUGEN

1. Minamoto Ryōen, *Tetsugen,* Nihon no Zen goroku, vol. 17, pp. 367–374.

2. *Rensha,* short for *Hyakurensha,* another name for a Pure Land sect.

3. One of the three Pure Land scriptures, which contains sixteen meditations on Amida Buddha and his Pure Land. Sometimes called the Meditation Sutra. The Chinese translation, T. 12, no. 365, is traditionally attributed to Kālayasas (383?–442?), but no Sanskrit text is extant. Scholars now believe it was probably first composed in Chinese.

4. Kaiun (n.d.) was probably the resident monk at Shōsenbō, a small branch temple of Nishi Honganji in the nearby village of Notsu. Shimoda Kyokusui, *Meisō Tetsugen,* p. 86.

5. Saigin (1605–1663) was the head monk at Eishōji, a large Honganji temple in Buzen province. Saigin later served as headmaster at the True Pure Land educational institute in Kyoto.

6. *Dacheng qixin lun* (J. Daijō kishin ron), a Mahayana treatise attributed to Aśvaghoṣa. T. 32, nos. 1666 and 1667. A summary of the essential teachings of Mahayana Buddhism.

7. Tōmyōzan Kōfukuji was one of three Chinese temples founded by Chinese expatriates in Nagasaki. Kōfukuji was founded in 1623 by merchants from the Yangzi River basin. It was popularly called Nanjing Temple. It later became an Ōbaku branch temple.

8. Kurokawa Masanao (1602–1680) was *bugyo* of Nagasaki at this time. He formed a relationship with Yinyuan from the beginning. He became Yinyuan's disciple in the summer of 1655 when he returned to Nagasaki, a relationship which continued until Yinyuan's death.

9. Japanese monks joining the community at an Ōbaku temple were required to change their robes to Chinese style monastic robes. See Baroni, *Ōbaku Zen,* p. 100.

10. Fumonji is in the town of Tonda, in present day Osaka-fu. It was founded in 1390. In 1655, Ryōkei Shōsen served as its head monk, and it was he who arranged for Yinyuan to reside there. See Baroni, *Ōbaku Zen,* p. 47ff.

11. Bunshizan Fukusaiji was another Chinese temple in Nagasaki, founded in 1628 by merchants from the Zhangzhou region. It was popularly known as Zhangzhou Temple.

12. Kengan Zen'etsu (1618–1696), a Rinzai monk, was abbot at Shōganzan Tafukuji, a Myōshinji line Rinzai temple in Usuki city, in present day Ōita prefecture.

13. This may be a reference to the distinctive Chinese robes and styles of grooming assumed by Japanese Ōbaku monks. See Baroni, *Ōbaku Zen,* pp. 100–101.

14. Changshui Zixuan (d. 1038) was a Sung dynasty Chinese Buddhist monk, originally self-ordained, who studied Huayan thought. He later practiced Chan under

Langye and attained enlightenment. He wrote a commentary on the *Śūraṃgama Sutra.*

15. Gushan (n.d.) was a Chinese Buddhist monk who studied Tientai thought. He wrote a commentary on the *Śūraṃgama Sutra.*

16. Dairyōsan Daijiji was a Sōtō temple in Kumamoto city. Hōshitsu was the seventy-fifth head monk.

17. Shika no shima is an island at the mouth of Hakata Bay in Fukuoka prefecture, at the end of a long peninsula called Uminonakashima.

18. Refers to the dragon princess who attained enlightenment at eight years of age in the Devadatta chapter of the *Lotus Sutra.* Her father Sāgara is the Dragon King of Rain.

19. Cosmic bodhisattva who represents the qualities of knowledge and wisdom.

20. T. 9, no. 262, pp. 34b–35c. The account of the dragon princess attaining enlightenment is found in the Devadatta chapter.

21. Zhifei Ruyi (1616–1671) was one of Yinyuan's leading Dharma heirs, who emigrated to Japan in 1657. See Baroni, *Ōbaku Zen,* pp. 61–63.

22. Kōjuzan Fukujuji is an Ōbaku temple in Kita Kyushu city in Kokura, Fukuoka prefecture. It was founded in 1665 by Zhifei, as the family temple for the Ogasa family. Ogasa Tadazane (1596–1667) was then *daimyō* of Bunzen province and invited Zhifei to serve as founding abbot.

23. T. 19, no. 945, pp. 134a–136c. The *dharani* is a verse with five stanzas, comprised of 439 phrases. *Dharani* are used by Buddhist monks and nuns to ward off calamity, to heal illness and to bring rain, among other things.

24. Soken Zenno (n.d.) was a Sōtō Zen monk.

25. Myōu Dōnin (n.d.) was a Buddhist nun about whom little is known. According to Muan's biography (*nenpu*), Myōu donated one thousand, two hundred *ryō* of gold to Muan for Mampukuji in 1665, and made several other large donation over the next four years. The biography indicates that while she was still a layperson, she lost a son, and that this motivated her generosity.

26. A subtemple of Ōbakusan Mampukuji, now located outside the main precincts of the monastery. The original Hōzōin was little more than a storehouse. The later structure is much larger, and housed the printing operation as well as storage space for the wood blocks.

27. The print shop in Kyoto, where artisans carved the woodblocks was originally located at Nijō and Kiyamachi. It remained in operation in some capacity under the indirect control of the Ōbaku sect until sometime during the Taishō era (1912–1926), when it was sold.

28. Daguang Zhenge (1543–1603), Chinese Buddhist monk who served as abbot at Jingliangsi monastery in Beijing.

29. T. 19, no. 945, p. 113a, lines 17–18.

30. Yakushiji was a dilapidated temple, which Tetsugen initially leased, sometime around 1668. Lay supporters paid to restore the temple in 1670, and Tetsugen renamed it Jiunzan Zuiryūji. The original temple was destroyed in the bombings during World War II. The current temple is a modern cement structure.

31. Daihannyakyō refers to the Mahāprajñā pāramitā sūtra (J. Daihannya hara-mitta kyō) in 600 fascicles, translated by Xuanzang in 659, T. 5–7, no. 220.

32. Shiunzan Zuishōji was the main Ōbaku monastery in Edo, present day Tokyo.

33. Damei Xingshan (1616–1673) was a Chinese Ōbaku monk born in Fujian province. He entered monastic orders in 1632 as Yinyuan's disciple. Damei accompa-nied Yinyuan to Nagasaki, and eventually to Mampukuji. He attained enlightenment in 1663. Damei was seriously ill when he deeded Torin'in to Tetsugen. He died within the month, on the eighteenth day of the tenth month of 1673 at age seventy-three. He originally built Tōrin'in in 1661 for his retirement residence.

34. *Jōgō* is a Buddhist term, which usually refers to chanting the *nembutsu* to assure rebirth in the Pure Land after death.

35. Bonfufusan Sanbōzenji was officially founded in 1680 by Tetsugen. It is lo-cated in the village of Ogawa, Shimo Mashiki region of Kumamoto prefecture.

36. Hōzan Saichō (n.d.) was a disciple of Tetsugen, later known for lecturing on the *Lotus Sutra.*

37. Kurushima Michikyo (1629–1700) was daimyō of Bungo province. See above An Affidavit concerning the Dharma Debate in Mori and Letter to Kurushima.

38. Inaba Masanori (1623–1696) served as counselor to the *shōgun* from 1658 until 1668. He was a strong supporter of the Ōbaku sect, especially Muan and Tetsugyū. He received inka from Tetsugyū in 1688.

39. Gaochuan Xinggong (1633–1695) was one of the prominent Chinese Ōbaku masters; he served as the fifth abbot of Mampukuji. See Baroni, *Ōbaku Zen*, pp. 64–65.

40. Shenggong (n.d.) a Chinese Buddhist monk who is said to have gathered stones as his audience when he lectured on the scriptures, and the stones nodded in agreement.

41. Konzenji is in Toyonaka Osaka-fu.

42. Kaizōji at one time stood in Asakusa, in Tokyo.

43. Shōmatsuji is in Shiga prefecture, Kanzaki city, Gokashō-machi.

44. Hōsenji is in Fukai, Sakai city, in Osaka-fu.

45. Emmeiji is in Okushima-machi, Ōmi Hachiman city, Shiga prefecture.

46. *Jikishi* is an abbreviation of *jikishi ninshin kanshō jōbutsu,* "direct pointing to the mind, seeing one's nature and realizing Buddha." The expression is commonly used to describe the practice of Zen.

47. Miroku is the next Buddha who will appear in the world sometime in the distant future.

48. Dahui Zonggao (1089–1163) was a Chinese Chan master of the Linji (J. Rinzai) lineage who championed the use of kōan as the focus of meditation. He is also famous for destroying the original version of the *Hekiganroku.*

49. Engaku-kyō a scripture in one fascicle; the Chinese translation is attributed to Buddhatara in 693, although it is now believed to have been composed originally in Chinese. T. 17, no. 842.

50. The Preserved Writings of Tetsugen, a collection of Tetsugen's writing compiled by Hōshū.

51. Shōun Genkei (1648–1710), an Ōbaku monk and sculptor who was a disciple of Tetsugen's. Shōun was born in Kyoto, the son of a Buddhist priest. He took the tonsure at age twenty-three when he met Tetsugen. He set out on an extended seven- or eight-year pilgrimage, during which he saw the five hundred arhats at Rakanji in Buzen province, now Ōita prefecture. He vowed to sculpt a set of five hundred arhats, and completed them in 1695. The arhats stand life size, and are accompanied by a sixteen-foot image of the Buddha and two eight-foot attending bodhisattvas.

52. *Rakan*, "one worthy of veneration." *Arhats* are those who have attained nirvana, the highest stage in the Buddhist path. Although not originally regarded with favor in Mahayana Buddhism, images of *arhats* became popular in China and Japan, especially in *Chan* and Zen monasteries. *Arhats* are usually presented in groups of sixteen or five hundred. The group of five hundred is said to derive from the five hundred *arhats* who the Buddha promises will attain enlightenment in the *Lotus Sutra*.

53. Ten'onzan Rakanji, also popularly known as Gohyaku Rakanji (Temple of 500 Arhats), is now located in the Meguro district of the Tokyo metropolitan area. It was originally located in Musashi province.

THE MONK TETSUGEN

1. The first edition of the *Kinsei kijin den* was published in 1790. A later volume, authored by Mikumi Katen with the assistance of Ban Kōkei was published in 1798. The biography of Tetsugen appears in both editions. There are two modern editions: *Sentetsu zō den, Kinsei kijin den, Hyakka kikō den* (Yuhōdo, 1927) and *Kinsei kijin den* (Iwanami shoten, 1940). Both contain identical texts for Tetsugen's biography.

2. *Kintaien* was a "medicine that cures all ailments (*manbyōyaku*) which according to legend was first given to the Ōbaku monk Ryōō in a dream by Gyōtei Zenji, the founder of Hizan Kōfukuji. The pharmacy that Ryōō founded was the Kangakuya, located in the Ueno area of Edo. See Duncan Ryūken Williams, "Temples, Pharmacies, Traveling Salesmen, and Pilgrims: Buddhist Production and Distribution of Medicine in Edo Japan," in the Supplement to the February 1998 issue of the *Japanese Religions Bulletin*, pp. 20–29, and *The Other Side of Zen*, p. 91.

LESSON 28

1. Jinjō shōgaku kokugo tokuhon, in *Nihon kyōkasho taikei, Kindaihen*, vol. 7, pp. 517–519, and vol. 8, pp. 200–202.

Bibliography

Abé, Ryūichi. *The Weaving of Mantra; Kūkai and the Construction of Esoteric Buddhist Discourse.* New York: Columbia University Press, 1999.

Akamatsu Shinmyō, ed. *Tetsugen zenji kana hōgo.* Tokyo: Iwanami shoten, 1989 (Reprint of 1941).

———. *Tetsugen zenji.* Tokyo: Kōbundō shobō, 1942.

———. *Tetsugen.* Tokyo: Yūzankaku, 1943.

———. "Tetsugen to Issaikyōhan." In *Zen bunka,* no. 18 (March, 1960), pp. 56–64.

Akane Shōdō. *Meisō no kotoba.* Tokyo: Chūkei shuppan, 1988.

App, Urs. *Master Yunmen.* New York: Kodansha International, 1994.

Ashikaga Zuigi. *Ryūkoku daigaku sanbyakunen shi.* Kyoto: Ryūkoku daigaku shuppanbu, 1939.

Ban Kōkei. *Kinsei kijinden,* vol. 2. Kyoto: Hishiya Magobe, 1790.

———. *Sentetsu zō den, Kinsei kijin den, Hyakka kikō den.* Tokyo: Yūhōdō bunko, 1927.

———. *Kinsei kijin den.* Tokyo: Iwanami shoten, 1940.

Baroni, Helen J. "Buddhism in Early Tokugawa Japan: The Case of Ōbaku Zen and the Monk Tetsugen Dōkō." Ph.D. diss., Columbia University, 1993.

———. "Bottled Anger: Episodes in Obaku Conflict in the Tokugawa Period." In *JJRS* 21, nos. 2–3, pp. 191–210.

———. *Obaku Zen: The Emergence of the Third Sect of Zen in Tokugawa Japan.* Honolulu: University of Hawaii Press, 2000.

Bloom, Alfred. *Shinran's Gospel of Pure Grace.* Tucson, Arizona: The University of Arizona Press, 1985.

Blythe, R. H. *Zen and Zen Classics,* vol. 1. Tokyo: Hokuseido Press, 1966.

Bussho kaisetsu daijiten, 12 vols. Ono Genmyō, ed. Tokyo: Daitō shuppansha, 1933–1978.

Cook, Francis. *Sounds of Valley Streams.* Albany, New York: State University of New York Press, 1989.

Cowell, E. B. *Buddhist Mahayana Texts.* New York: Dover, 1969.

Dai nihon bukkyō zensho. 100 volumes. Suzuki Gakujutsu, ed. Tokyo: Kodansha hatsubai, 1970–1974

Davis, David L. "*Ikki* in Late Medieval Japan." In *Medieval Japan: Essays in Institutional History,* John W. Hall and Jeffrey P. Mass, eds. Stanford: Stanford University Press, 1974.

Dōkei and Ōuchi Seiran. *Zoku nihon kōsō den.* In *Dai nihonbukkyō zensho,* vol. 64, no. 473, pp. 1–98.

Dore, R. P. *Education in Tokugawa Japan.* London: The Athlone Press, 1984.

Dumoulin, Heinrich. *Zen Buddhism: A History, Volume 2, Japan.* New York: Macmillan Publishing Company, 1990.

Foster, Nelson. "How Shall We Save the World? An Anniversary Essay on a Perennial Topic." From the Buddhist Peace Fellowship website, www.bpf.org (23 July 2003).

Fujishima Tatsurō. *Nihon bukkyō o sasaeta 33 hito.* Kyoto: Hōzōkan, 1991.

Fujiwara Tōen. *Zen no meisō retsuden.* Tokyo: Kōsei shuppansha, 1990.

Furuta Shōkin. *Zenshū kana hōgo.* Tokyo: Daizo shuppan, 1980.

———. "Tetsugen Dōkō o shinobu." In *Daihōrin,* 53/5 (May, 1986), pp. 62–67.

Fushō Kokushi Nenpu. Woodblock edition, 2 fasc. Kyoto: Inbōsho.

Hakeda, Yoshito S., trans. *The Awakening of Faith.* New York: Columbia University Press, 1967.

Haskel, Peter. *Bankei Zen: Translations from the Record of Bankei.* Yoshita Hakeda, ed. New York: Grove Press, 1984.

Heine, Steven and Dale S. Wright. *The Kōan; Texts and Contexts in Zen Buddhism.* Oxford: Oxford University Press, 2000.

Hori, G. Victor Sōgen. "Kōan and *Kenshō* in the Rinzai Zen Curriculum." In *The Kōan; Texts and Contexts in Zen Buddhism,* Steven Heine and Dale S. Wright, eds, pp. 280–315.

Hurvitz, Leon. *Scripture of the Lotus Blossom of Fine Dharma (The Lotus Sūtra).* New York: Columbia University Press, 1982.

Ishida Seisai. Tetsugen to Hōshū. Osaka: Ishida bunkō, 1922.

Ishikawa Rikizan. "Naikan Bunko shozō shiryō no kenkyū (2): *Kōmori bōdanki/Jōkōki* ni tsuite." In *Komazawa Daigaku Bukkyō Gakubu kenkyū kiyō,* No. 54 (Mar 1996), pp. 57–146.

Jaffe, Richard M. *Neither Monk Nor Layman; Clerical Marriage in Modern Japanese Buddhism.* Princeton: Princeton University Press, 2001

Jōetsu Kyōiku Daigaku shozō Ōbaku Tetsugenban Issaikyō Mokuroku. Jōetsu-shi, Japan: Jōetsu kyōiku daigaku fuzoku toshokan, 1988.

Kasahara Kazuo. *Ikkō ikki no kenkyū.* Tokyo: Yamakawa shuppan, 1962.

———. *Ikkō ikki—sono kōdō to shisō.* Nihonjin no kōdō to shisō series, no. 5. Tokyo: Hyōronsha, 1970.

King, Winston L. *Death Was His Koan: The Samurai Zen of Suzuki Shōsan.* Berkeley: Asian Humanities Press, 1986.

Kishimoto Hideo. *Japanese Religion in the Meiji Era.* John F. Howes, trans and ed. Tokyo: Ōbunsha, 1956

Lincicome, Mark E. *Principle, Praxis, and the Politics of Educational Reform in Meiji Japan.* Honolulu: University of Hawaii Press, 1995.

Matsunaga Chikai. "Ōbakuban daizōkyō no saihyōka." In *Bukkyō shigaku kenkyū* 34/2 (October 1991), pp. 132–162.

McMullin, Neil. *Buddhism and the State in Sixteenth-Century Japan.* Princeton: Princeton University Press, 1984.

McRae, John R. *Seeing Through Zen; Encounter, Transformation, and Genealogy in Chinese Chan Buddhism.* Berkeley, CA: University of California Press, 2003.

Minamoto Ryōen. *Tetsugen.* Nihon no zen goroku, vol. 17. Tokyo: Kodansha, 1979.

Mohr, Michel. "Zen Buddhism during the Tokugawa Period: The Challenge to Go beyond Sectarian Consciousness." In JJRS 21/4, 1994, pp. 341–372.

———. "Emerging from Nonduality: Kōan Practice in the Rinzai Tradition since Hakuin." In *The Kōan; Texts and Contexts in Zen Buddhism,* Steven Heine and Dale S. Wright, eds, pp. 244–279.

Moriya Katsuhisa. "Urban Networks and Information Networks." In *Tokugawa Japan: The Social and Economic Antecedents of Modern Japan,* Chie Nakane and Shinzaburō Ōishi, eds, pp. 97–123.

Mujaku Dōchū. *Ōbaku geki.* MS, no date.

Nakajima Shigeo. Nihon meisō 100 hanashi. Tokyo: Rippū shobō, 1980.

Nakamura Hidemitsu. *Tetsugenji kiroku.* Osaka: Zuiryū-ji, 1964.

Nakamura, Kyoko Motomochi. *Miraculous Stories from the Japanese Buddhist Tradition: The Nihon Ryoiki of the Monk Kyokai.* Harvard University Press, 1973.

Nakamura Shū sei. "Mokuan zenji to sono wasō shihōsha." In *Ōbaku bunka,* no. 67 (Jan. 1983), pp. 11–13.

Nakane, Chie and Shinzaburō Ōishi. *Tokugawa Japan: The Social and Economic Antecedents of Modern Japan.* Conrad Totman, ed. Tokyo: University of Tokyo Press, 1990.

Nihon kyōkasho taikei, kindaihen, vols. 7 and 8 kokugo. Kaigo Muneomi, ed. Tokyo: Kodansha, 1963.

Nosco, Peter. "Keeping the faith: *bakuhan* policy towards religions in seventeenth century Japan." In *Religion in Japan; Arrows to heaven and earth,* P. F. Kornicki and I. J. McMullin, eds. (Cambridge University Press, 1996), pp. 135–155.

Ōbaku Mokuan oshō nempu. Woodblock edition, 2 fasc. Kyoto: Inbōsho, 1695.

Reps, Paul. *Zen Flesh, Zen Bones.* New York: Anchor Books, n.d.

Satō Fumitsugu. *Tetsugen zenji monogatari.* Kyoto: Shimeisha, 1927.

Sawada, Janine. "Tokugawa Religious History: Studies in Western Languages." In *Early Modern Japan,* 10/1, pp. 39–64.

Sawada, Janine with James McMullen. "Bibliography Religion and Thought in Early Modern Japan." In *Early Modern Japan,* 10/1, pp. 72–85.

Schwaller, Dieter. *Der japanische Ōbaku-Mönch Tetsugen Dōkō; Leben, Denken, Schriften.* Bern: Peter Lang, 1989.

Shibata Masumi. "Tetsugen zenji kana hōgo no furansugoyaku ni tsuite." In *Zen bunka,* no. 18 (March, 1960), pp. 78–80.

Shimoda Kyokusui, ed. Kokutei kyōkasho ni arawaretaru meisō Tetsugen. Kumamoto: Kumamoto-ken kyōikukai, 1928.

Strong, John S. *The Legend of King Asoka.* Princeton: Princeton University Press, 1983

Suzuki Ryūshu, ed. *Tetsugen zenji kana hōgo.* Uji-shi, Japan: Ōbaku-san Hōzō-in, 1981.

Taishō shinshū daizōkyō. 85 vols. Takakusu Junjirō and Watanabe Kaigyoku, eds. Tokyo: Taishō issaikyō kankō kai, 1924–1932.

Tamamuro Fumio. "Local Society and the Temple-Parishioner Relationship within the Bakufu's Governance Structure." In *JJRS,* no. 28/3–4, 2001, pp. 261–292.

Tetsugen Dōkō. *Tetsugen zenji yuiroku.* Woodblock edition, 2 fasc. Pub. 1691.

Ueda, Yoshifumi and Dennis Hirota. *Shinran: An Introduction to His Thought.* Kyoto: Hongwnaji International Center, 1989.

Ury, Marian. *Tales of Times Now Past.* Berkeley, California: University of California Press, 1979.

Waddell, Norman. *The Unborn: The Life and Teaching of Zen Master Bankei.* San Francisco: North Point Press, 1984.

Washio Junkei. *Nihon zenshūshi no kenkyū.* Tokyo: Kyoden shuppan kakushiki kaisha, 1945.

Williams, Duncan Ryūken. *The Other Side of Zen: A Social History of Sōtō Zen Buddhism in Tokugawa Japan.* Princeton: Princeton University Press, 2005.

———. "Religion in Early Modern Japan." In *Nanzan Guidebook for the Study of Japanese Religions.* Paul Swanson et al. eds. Nanzan: Nanzan Institute for Religion and Culture, 2004.

———. "Representations of Zen: An Institutional and Social History of Sōtō Zen Buddhism in Edo Japan." Ph.D. diss., Harvard University, 2000.

———. "Temples, Pharmacies, Traveling Salesmen, and Pilgrims: Buddhist Production and Distribution of Medicine in Edo Japan." In the Supplement to the February 1998 issue of the *Japanese Religions Bulletin,* pp. 20–29.

Yampolsky, Philip. *The Platform Sutra of the Sixth Patriarch.* New York: Columbia University Press, 1967.

Yanagida Seizan, *Shoki zenshū shisho no kenkyū.* Kyoto: Hōzōkan, 1967

Yinyuan Longqi. *Ingen zenshū.* 12 vols. Hirakubo Akira, ed. Tokyo: Kaimyō shoin, 1979.

Yoshinaga Utarō. *Ōbaku no hanashi 3: Tetsugen oshō no kuchi to ashi.* Uji: Ōbaku shūmon hon'in, 1941.

———. *Tetsugen zenji.* Uji: Ōbakushū monhon'in, 1942.

Index

Affadavit Concerning the Dharma Debate in Mori, 15, 21, 173, 175–181
Akamatsu Shinmyō, 28, 29, 48, 220n32, 221n38, 222n60
alaya consciousness
    confusion about, 57, 64
    in *Lankāvatāra sutra*, 230n65
    and meditation, 71–72, 115, 138
    in Yogacara thought, 126, 232n105, 235n5, 237nn11–12
Amida Buddha, 180, 221n41, 228nn24–25
Amida sutra, 98, 228nn25–26
Ananda, 128, 235–236n17
Asoka, 144, 237–238n4
Awakening of Faith, 12, 13, 33, 43, 191, 199, 201, 218n10, 230n56, 245n3

Baihō Jikushin, 4–5
Bankei Yōtaku, 3, 228n23
Biographies of Unusual People, 11–12, 14, 82–85, 87, 249n1
bodhi, 179, 186
Bodhidharma, 114, 116, 229n49, 236n5
Bodhisattva vows, 3
Book of Filial Piety, 180, 244n30
Buddha(s)
    birth, 121, 233nn1–2, 235n8, 240n11
    contrasted with ordinary beings, 70, 105, 106, 109, 124

death, 122, 233n7, 240n9, 240n11
perspective, 67, 99, 1–8, 124, 185–185
teachings, 57, 72, 73, 75, 107–108, 115, 143, 157, 176, 181
    See also Amida Buddha; Mahavairocana Buddha; Sakyamuni Buddha
Buddhism, Japanese, 1–7, 39, 217nn2–3, 217n7. *See also* Nichiren Buddhism; Pure Land Buddhism; Zen Buddhism
Buddhist scriptures, 4, 20, 39–42, 59, 143, 149–150, 162, 164, 201, 215, 238n5. *See also* Chinese Buddhist Scriptures
Buddhist temples, 2–3, 217–218n1, 223n6, 239n14

Changshui, 111, 200, 231n77, 231n80, 246n14
Chikū, 21–22, 220n32
Chinese Buddhist scriptures, 40, 50, 149, 201, 223nn3–4; in Japan, 1, 3, 20, 40–42, 84, 141, 143, 154, 201, 223n1; Ōbaku edition, 32, 37–38, 39–54, 55–56, 60, 64, 79, 86, 151, 155, 157–159, 206, 207, 216, 224n15, 225n38; Taishō edition, 50; Tenkai edition, 41–42, 50; Wanli edition, 44, 223n2, 238n6

Chōōn Dōkai, 5
Christianity, 2
Confucianism, 1, 4, 71, 114, 150, 153,
        232n104
Confucius, 178, 240n13, 244n20, 244n30
Consciousness, 70–72, 111–117, 126,
        227n4, 235n5

Dahui Zonggao, 208, 248n48
Damei Xingshan, 49, 50–51, 203, 248n33
danka seido, 2
debates, 3, 23, 173, 175, 177
Deeds of Tetsugen, 11, 12, 13, 14, 15, 197,
        199–208
delusion
    dispelling, 116, 124
    mind as, 70, 128–129
    and perception, 99–100, 100–105
    self as, 58, 65–66, 70, 95–97, 99
Deshan, 114, 232n97
Dharma heir, 27, 29, 36–37, 80, 83, 135,
        236n12, 239n3
Dharma lessons (hōgo), 30, 36, 56–57,
        125–129
Dharma Lesson in Japanese, 4, 15, 37, 55–
        56, 57, 59, 62, 64–72, 93–117,
        225n5, 227n1
Diamond sutra, 105, 179
Discourse on Consciousness Only, 105
Dōgen Kigen, 3, 4

Eight consciousnesses. See alaya
        consciousness
Emma, 144, 238n5
emptiness, 65, 97, 109, 112, 114, 115,
        121, 128, 179, 230n67, 237n3
enlightenment
    achievement of, 58, 72, 97–98,
        185–186
    hindrances to, 57, 70
    mistaken, 63, 71, 96–97, 110–111,
        114–116, 133–134, 137–138
    perspective of, 62, 108, 112, 179
famine in Kansai, 32–34, 85, 87, 189,
        191–194, 205, 216
Foster, Nelson, 86
Fukuda Gyōkai, 84–85, 86, 213, 216

Fukusaiji, 16, 17, 200, 246n11
Fumonji, 16, 17, 200, 246n10

Gaochuan, 27, 29, 49, 206, 248n39
Gesshū Sōko, 4
Gomizunoo, Emperor, 53, 151, 204
Great Death, 137
Gudō Tōshoku, 5, 218n8
Guifeng, 111, 231n82
Gukai hōgo, 17, 219n20
Gushan 200, 247n15

Hakuin Ekaku, 4, 5
Heart Sutra, 40, 54, 64, 65, 93, 95, 97,
        227n5
Hōgo. See Dharma lessons
Hoshino Kanzaemon, 57, 125, 127,
        235n9
Hōshū
    and Deeds of Tetsugen, 28, 31, 35, 37,
        80–81, 87, 197, 208
    and Dharma Lesson in Japanese, 64, 93
    foremost disciple, 208, 212
    and Letter to, 36–37, 58
    meeting Tetsugen, 18
    Muan's Dharma heir, 37, 245n14
    poems addressed to, 163, 167
    in Tangen's writings, 223n68
    and scripture project, 37–38, 42, 45,
        46, 53–54, 155, 208
    and Yuiroku, 37
Hosokawa Minamoto, 19, 24, 32, 53,
        189, 204
Hōzōin
    administration, 48, 53, 226n1
    burial site for Tetsugen, 35, 206
    founding, 20, 44, 45–46, 48, , 50, 53
    new location, 50–51, 203, 247n26
Huangboshan Wanfusi, 6
Huijue, 111, 231n77, 231n79
Huike, 105, 128, 229n49, 235n16
Huineng, 61, 105, 229n50

Ikkō ikki, 23, 221n35
Ikkō sect, 175, 176–177, 185, 218n2,
        243n6. See also True Pure Land
        Buddhism

illusion, 68–69, 100–102, 107–108, 110,
        112, 123, 128, 164, 179
Inbō (print shop), 20, 45, 46, 48, 54, 202,
        224n17, 224n21, 247n27
inka
        bestowed by Muan, 27, 28–29, 204,
                222n51, 222n60
        bestowed by Tetsugen, 36
        false *inka*, 63, 71, 114, 133–134
        in Zen practice, 220n23, 232n98

jiin hatto, 3
jishu (instructions for the community),
        57, 119, 121–124
Jōō incident, 14

Kaiun, 12, 75, 199, 246n4
Kakugen Jōgon, 52, 225nn37–38
Kanmuryōjukyō, 199. *See also* Pure Land
        Sutras
Kannon, 121, 234n16
karma, 96, 98, 107, 110, 112–113, 133,
        162, 163, 167, 168, 176, 234n4
Kasyapa Matanga, 149, 238nn2–3
Kengan Ken'etsu, 17–18, 22, 29, 175,
        218n8, 220n24, 221n34, 243n7
kōan, 5, 27, 58, 60, 72, 110, 113, 127, 128,
        204, 248n48
Kōfukuji, 15, 16, 49, 199, 246n7
Kōmori bōdanki, 7, 22, 73–76, 219n13,
        226n12
Kurokawa Masanao, 15, 200, 219n17,
        246n8
Kurushima Michikiyo, 22, 23–24, 173, 175,
        183, 185, 204, 220n33, 242n3
Lankāvatāra Sutra, 109, 230n65
Laozi, 102, 115
Large Sutra of Perfect Wisdom, 202
Linji, 114, 229n32, 232n96, 239n3
Lotus Sutra
        images from, 58, 144, 231n73,
                241n15, 247n18
        in mondō, 27, 222n49
        quoted by Tetsugen, 98, 105, 109,
                179, 180
        and Tetsugen's sermons, 19, 41, 143,
                200, 203

Madyamika teachings, 69
Mahāvairocana Buddha, 180
Maitreya, 207, 248n47
Mampukuji. *See* Ōbakusan Mampukuji
Manzan, 3, 4
Maudgalyāyana, 193, 245n11
meditation
        problems during, 125, 127–129
        relation to precepts, 62, 66, 175–176
        relation to scriptures, 60
        in Tetsugen's teachings, 57–58, 70,
                71, 72, 113–114
        in Zen practice, 4, 63, 234n12
        see also zazen
Menzan, 3, 4, 5
Minamoto Ryōen, 28, 29, 221n38
mind
        and five *skandhas*, 65
        as a hindrance, 70, 127–129, 165,
                169
        relation to enlightenment, 58, 106–
                107, 113–114
        true mind, 96, 101, 104, 114, 126,
                163, 170, 179
        See also Original mind; Mind
                Ground
Mind Ground, 169, 170
mondō, 23, 27, 28–29, 177, 204, 222n60,
        243n17
Mori, incident in, 22–26, 173, 175–181,
        183, 185–186, 221n38
Muan
        bestowing *inka*, 204, 222n51
        and scripture project, 20, 43–44
        and Tetsugen's death, 205, 206
        Tetsugen's practice with, 16, 17,
                26–30, 83, 200, 202, 204
Mujaku Dōchū, 5, 29
Myōu Dōmin, 43, 147, 169, 201, 223n11,
        247n25

nembutsu, 6, 18, 25, 81, 167, 168, 175,
        218n2, 248n34
Nichiren Buddhism, 2
nikujiki saitai (clerical meat-eating and
        marriage), 73–74, 76, 173,
        226n10

nirvana, 100, 108, 109, 112, 116, 122,
    133, 134, 179, 186
Nirvana Sutra, 104, 179
no-mind, 115, 116
no-self, 65, 185, 186
no-thought, 115, 116
Nyōku, 19, 42, 45, 48
Nyōsetsu, 18, 19

Ōbaku geki, 29
Ōbaku sect, 4, 5–7, 61, 79, 81, 82, 197,
    219n23, 239n4, 246n9
Ōbakusan Mampukuji, 6, 17, 20, 43, 44,
    45, 203, 211
Ōbaku shingi, 6
One Mind, 114, 179
original face, 111, 112, 114, 127
original mind, 57, 96, 105, 106, 112, 114,
    115, 126, 133, 179, 180
original nature, 15, 200, 231n75, 235n6,
    236n2, 242n13
original portion, 126
original self, 170, 234n13

Pāpīyas, 157, 176, 243n10
parishioner system, 2
Perfect Enlightenment Sutra, 70, 97, 103,
    104, 108, 110, 180, 208, 226n9
precepts
    and lay practice, 113, 231n90
    and reform movements, 7, 61, 84
    in *Śūraṃgama sutra*, 18, 25, 66,
        175–176, 177
    theme of Tetsugen's teaching, 14–15,
        25, 55, 66, 67, 113
    and True Pure Land Buddhism, 73,
        231n90
psychic construction, 69, 103–111, 227n4
Pure Land Buddhism, 2, 6, 11, 98
Pure Land sutras, 12, 59, 75, 199, 218n6,
    228n22, 228nn25–26, 246n3
pure rules (*shingi*), 61
Purna, 138, 231n81, 237n14

reform movements, 4, 7, 84
Reps, Paul, 86

Rinzai Zen, 4–7, 61, 219n23
Ryōkei Shōsen, 5, 151, 246n10
Ryōō Dōkaku, 49–50, 249n2

Saigin, 12, 13, 14, 18, 21, 199, 220n32,
    246n5
Sakyamuni Buddha, 72, 110, 114, 116,
    229n36
San'yo zuihitsu, 22
Sāriputra, 138, 237n13
Satō Fumitsugu, 52
satori, 176
Schwaller, Dieter, 28, 29
self, 96, 98, 110, 112, 126, 137, 179, 180,
    186, 227n4
Senzaki Nyogen, 86
Sessō, 12, 18, 218n8, 220n24
shingi. See pure rules
Shintō, 1, 4, 11, 217–218n1, 245n12
Shōun Genkei, 208, 249n51
Sōtō Zen, 3, 4–5, 6
storehouse consciousness. *See* alaya
    consciousness
Śūraṃgama sutra
    apochryphal text, 220n25
    commented on in poetry, 167, 169
    dharani, 31, 201
    and incident in Mori, 23–24, 25,
        173, 175–180
    and keeping the precepts, 15, 62, 66
    in Kengan's teachings, 18, 29, 200,
        221n34
    in *Kōmori bōdanki*, 76
    and problems with True Pure Land,
        21, 22, 25
    Tetsugen's use of, 56, 59, 97, 111,
        112, 114, 115, 116, 186, 202,
        203, 204, 205
    and *zenkyō itchi*, 70
Suzuki Shōsan, 3

Takuan Sōhō, 5
Tangen Genshu, 28, 29, 35, 37, 223n68
Tenkai, 41
Tenkai edition, 41–42
Tenkei Senson, 5

Tetsugen Dōkō
  biographies, 7, 11, 13, 37, 74, 79–87, 197–212
  conflict with True Pure Land Buddhists, 20–26, 52, 56, 73
  fundraising, 43–44, 46–48, 49, 83, 85, 143–144, 158, 209, 211
  lack of Dharma heir, 27–28, 36–37, 83, 135
  legends, 1, 79, 83–87, 209–216
  lecturing, 3, 7, 20–21, 29–30, 55, 56, 60–61, 62
  marital status, 11, 82, 83–87, 209, 211
  mondō, 19–20, 27–29, 201, 204, 222n60
  receiving inka, 27–29, 204
  teaching style, 13, 56–59, 64–65
  True Pure Land affiliation, 11–15, 61–62, 74, 81–83
  use of scripture, 59–60, 70, 93
Tetsugenji. See Zuiryūji
Tetsugyū Dōki, 49, 219n19, 224n26
textbook lesson, 1, 7, 84–85, 86, 213, 215–216
three absolutes, 18, 23, 25, 177, 221n40
three places, 45
Tokugawa period, 1–7, 41, 61, 73, 218n3, 223n6
Tokugawa Tsunayoshi, 155
True Pure Land academy, 12–13, 14, 21, 81
True Pure Land Buddhism, 11, 18, 62, 73, 173, 175, 218n2, 220n30, 221n35, 243n6

unborn, 169
unborn, undying, 123, 228n23, 234n8

Xuanzang, 149, 238n4

Yinyuan Longqi
  death, 203
  founder of Ōbaku Zen, 5–6, 239n9
  and scripture project, 20, 30, 43–44, 53, 150, 201
  as Tetsugen's master, 15–17, 75–76, 80–81, 83, 199–200, 219n18
  in Wakan taihei kōki, 32
Yoshinaga Utarō, 16–17, 125, 219n19
Yuiroku, 17, 27, 29, 37, 56, 125, 131, 151, 155, 159, 197, 208
Yunmen 116–117, 233n115

zazen, 15, 58, 113, 114, 200. See also meditation
Zen'aku jamyōron, 28–29, 36, 222nn52–53, 223n68
Zen Buddhism, 3–7, 18, 30, 59, 61–63, 179, 217n6
Zen Flesh Zen Bones, 86
zenkyō itchi, 60, 207, 228n20
Zhaozhou, 116–117, 233n117
Zhifei Ruyi, 17, 19–20, 49, 200–201, 220nn27–28, 247nn21–22
Zuiryūji
  during famine, 32, 85
  founding, 20, 43, 202, 204–205, 211, 247n30
  in local accounts, 85, 224n24
  monastic community, 36, 37, 48, 119, 203, 204–205